CRAFTING AN AFRICAN SECURITY
ARCHITECTURE

The International Political Economy of New Regionalisms Series

The International Political Economy of New Regionalisms series presents innovative analyses of a range of novel regional relations and institutions. Going beyond established, formal, interstate economic organizations, this essential series provides informed interdisciplinary and international research and debate about myriad heterogeneous intermediate level interactions.

Reflective of its cosmopolitan and creative orientation, this series is developed by an international editorial team of established and emerging scholars in both the South and North. It reinforces ongoing networks of analysts in both academia and think-tanks as well as international agencies concerned with micro-, meso- and macro-level regionalisms.

Crafting an African Security Architecture

Addressing Regional Peace and Conflict in the 21st Century

HANY BESADA
The Centre for International Governance Innovation (CIGI),
Canada

ASHGATE

Published by
Ashgate Publishing Limited
Wey Court East
Union Road
Farnham
Surrey, GU9 7PT
England

Ashgate Publishing Company
Suite 420
101 Cherry Street
Burlington
VT 05401-4405
USA

www.ashgate.com

British Library Cataloguing in Publication Data
Crafting an African security architecture : addressing
regional peace and conflict in the 21st century. -- (The
international political economy of new regionalisms series)
1. Peace-building--Africa. 2. Conflict management--
Africa.
I. Series II. Besada, Hany.
327.1'72'096-dc22

Library of Congress Cataloging-in-Publication Data
Crafting an African security architecture : addressing regional peace and conflict in the 21st
century / [edited] by Hany Besada.
    p. cm. -- (The international political economy of new regionalisms series)
Includes bibliographical references and index.
ISBN 978-1-4094-0325-8 (hardback) -- ISBN 978-1-4094-0326-5 (ebook)
1. Security, International--Africa. 2. National security--Africa. 3. Conflict management--
Africa. 4. Peace-building--Africa. 5. Africa--Politics and government--21st century. I. Besada, Hany.
JZ6009.A35C73 2010
355'.03356--dc22

                                                                                2010003695

ISBN 978-1-4094-0325-8 (hbk)
ISBN 978-1-4094-0326-5 (ebk)

Mixed Sources
Product group from well-managed
forests and other controlled sources
www.fsc.org Cert no. SA-COC-1565
© 1996 Forest Stewardship Council

Printed and bound in Great Britain by
MPG Books Group, UK

Contents

List of Figures and Tables

Notes on Contributors

Hany Besada is a senior researcher and program leader at CIGI where he oversees the Health and Social Governance Program. He holds a BA and MA in international relations from Alliant International University in San Diego, where he specialized in peace and security studies. Previously, he was the Business in Africa researcher at the South African Institute of International Affairs (SAIIA) in Johannesburg, South Africa, and research manager at Africa Business Direct, a trade and investment consulting firm in Johannesburg. Mr Besada has worked for Amnesty International, United Nations associations, the Joan Kroc Institute of Peace and Justice and the Office of US Senator Dianne Feinstein. He is the editor of *From Civil Strife to Peace Building: Examining Private Sector Involvement in West African Reconstruction* (WLU Press, 2009) and *Unlocking Africa's Potential: The Role of Corporate South Africa in Strengthening Africa's Private Sector* (SAIIA, 2008).

Dr Jakkie Cilliers has DLitt et Phil from the University of South Africa (UNISA). He co-founded the Institute for Security Studies (ISS) in 1990 that is today one of the largest independent institutes dealing with peace and security issues in Africa with offices in Pretoria, Cape Town, Nairobi and Addis Ababa. Institute activities revolve around arms management, tracking conflict in Africa, peace missions, various issues relating to crime and crime-prevention, corruption and governance, organized crime, money laundering, HIV/AIDS, terrorism, peacekeeping, conflict prevention and defence sector reform. At present most of Dr Cilliers' interests relate to the emerging security architecture in Africa as reflected in the developments under the banner of the Peace and Security Council of the African Union. He is an Extraordinary Professor in the Department of Political Sciences, Faculty Humanities at the University of Pretoria, serves on the International Advisory Board of the Geneva Centre for Security Policy (GCSP) and the Observatoire de l'Afrique, and as independent non-executive director of the South African Banking Risk Information Centre (SABRIC).

Devon Curtis is a University Lecturer in the Department of Politics and International Studies at the University of Cambridge, and a Fellow of Emmanuel College. Her main research interests and publications deal with power-sharing and governance arrangements following conflict, the 'transformation' of rebel movements to political parties in Africa, and critical perspectives on conflict, peacebuilding and development. Her field research has concentrated on the Great Lakes region of Africa, especially Burundi. Previously, Devon Curtis was a Postdoctoral Research Fellow at the Saltzman Institute of War and Peace Studies at Columbia University, and a Pre-doctoral Fellow at the Center for International Security and Cooperation (CISAC) at Stanford University. She has also worked for the Canadian government, the United Nations Staff College, and the Overseas Development Institute. She received her PhD in International Relations from the London School of Economics.

Lieutenant General the Honourable Roméo A. Dallaire (Ret'd), Senator, has had a distinguished career in the Canadian military, achieving the rank of Lieutenant General and becoming Assistant Deputy Minister (Human Resources) in the Department of National Defence in 1998. In 1994, General Dallaire commanded the United Nations Assistance Mission for Rwanda (UNAMIR). His book on his experiences in Rwanda, entitled *Shake Hands with the Devil: The Failure of Humanity in Rwanda*, was awarded the Governor General's Literary Award for Non-Fiction in 2004.

Since his retirement from the military, General Dallaire has been a visiting lecturer at several Canadian and American universities, and has written several articles and chapters in publications on conflict resolution, humanitarian assistance, and human rights. As a Fellow of the Carr Center for Human Rights Policy, Kennedy School of Government at Harvard University, he pursued research on conflict resolution and the use of child soldiers.

General Dallaire became an Officer of the Order of Canada in 2002, and a Grand Officer of the National Order of Quebec in 2005. He has received the Aegis Award for Genocide Prevention from the Aegis Trust (UK) and he serves on the United Nations Advisory Committee on the Prevention of Genocide. In 2005, Canada's Governor General, Her Excellency the Right Honourable Adrienne Clarkson, presented him with the United Nations Association of Canada's Pearson Peace Medal. He is currently researching and writing a book on the subject of child soldiers.

Dr Adedeji Ebo is Chief of the Security Sector Reform Unit in the United Nations Department of Peacekeeping Operations. Prior to joining the UN in August 2008, Adedeji served as a Senior Fellow and Head of the Africa Programme at the Geneva Centre for the Democratic Control of Armed Forces (DCAF), Switzerland from 2003–2008. He was previously Associate Professor and Head of the Department of Political Science and Defence Studies at the Nigerian Defence Academy, Kaduna, and Guest Lecturer at the National War College, Abuja, and Command and Staff College, Jaji, Nigeria. He has been a consultant for various organizations and is a member of the Executive Board of the African Security Sector Network. He is widely published on issues of peace and security, particularly security sector governance and reform.

Dr Benedikt Franke is currently a research fellow at Oxford University's Department for Politics and International Relations while also serving as a policy advisor for the Africa Progress Panel and programme officer for the Kofi

Annan Foundation. He holds a PhD in International Studies from the University of Cambridge and a MA in International Relations from the Johns Hopkins University Paul H. Nitze School of Advanced International Studies. His book *Security Cooperation in Africa: A Reappraisal* was published in summer 2009.

Stefan Gänzle is Associate Professor at the Department of Political Science and Management, University of Agder. Before coming to Norway, he was a senior researcher at the German Development Institute in Bonn from 2008–09. He has been Visiting Assistant Professor at University of British Columbia and a research fellow at the University of Jena, the European University Institute (EUI) as well as a researcher-in-residence at the OSCE. His interests lie in the field of European integration and EU foreign policy broadly conceived. He is the author of *Die Europäische Union als außenpolitischer Akteur: Eine Fallstudie am Beispiel der EU-Politik gegenüber den baltischen Staaten und Russland* [The European Union's Foreign Policy in the Making: The Case of the Baltic States and Russia] (Nomos, 2007) and the editor (with Allen G. Sens) of *The Changing Politics of European Security: Europe Alone?* (Palgrave, 2007). His most recent book is *Adapting to European Integration? The Case of the Russian Exclave of Kaliningrad* (Manchester University Press, 2008), which he co-edited with Guido Müntel/Evgeny Vinokurov. Other peer-reviewed publications have appeared in (among others) *International Journal, Conflict and Cooperation, Défense Nationale, Higher Education* and *Aus Politik und Zeitgeschichte*.

Ariane Goetz is pursuing her PhD in Political Science at Wilfrid Laurier University and is a PhD fellow at the Balsillie School of International Affairs and the Africa Department at CIGI, and at Frankfurt University (Normative Orders). She has a Master's in Public Policy from the Hertie School of Governance. Her research focuses on peace and security, global environmental governance, development cooperation, and accountability ethics. Previously, she worked as a consultant for the German Technical Cooperation (GTZ).

Dr Sven Grimm is Political Scientist and since 2005 has been Research Fellow at the German Development Institute (DIE), where he works on European Development Cooperation and Governance, especially in Sub-Sahara Africa. Before joining the German Development Institute, he was a research fellow at the Overseas Development Institute in London, working on the EU's relations with developing countries. After having studied in Hamburg, Accra/Ghana and Dakar/ Senegal, he completed his PhD thesis on 'The Africa Policy of the European Union – Europe's role in a marginal region' at Hamburg University in 2002. In his current research he particularly focuses on the EU's efforts to promote good governance as well as on the African Peer Review Mechanism (APRM) in Ghana. Also, he presently conducts research on new actors in international development leading an international research group within an EU research project. He has published a number of articles and papers on the European development cooperation, on governance in Sub-Saharan Africa, and on cooperation between both continents as well as papers on new actors in international development.

Michael Hammer is Executive Director of the One World Trust, a UK-based think-tank that conducts research and develops recommendations for reform on issues of accountability and global governance. He leads the Trust's work on international law, peace and security governance, parliamentary oversight of foreign policy and climate change governance. He is also a co-author of the Global Accountability Report. Before joining the One World Trust Michael Hammer worked on human rights, conflict transformation, development and planning issues in Africa and Europe as Programme Director with Amnesty International and Conciliation Resources, and as Projects Manager with sustainability consultants Institut Raum & Energie. Michael has studied in Hamburg and Dakar and holds a Research Masters Degree in Geography, History and Urban Planning.

Thomas Jaye is Senior Research Fellow at the Kofi Annan International Peacekeeping Training Centre (KAIPTC) in Accra, Ghana. Previously he worked as Research Fellow at the Department of Political Science and International Studies (POLSIS) of the University of Birmingham, UK. He writes on regional security issues and in recent times has devoted some time to security sector reform issues. He is author of Issues of Sovereignty, Strategy and Security in the ECOWAS Intervention in the Liberian Civil War (Mellen Press, 2003).

Ayesha Kajee is currently Program Director of the International Human Rights Exchange at Wits University in Johannesburg, Ayesha also lectures part-time in Politics. She formerly ran the programme on Democracy and Political Party Systems at the South African Institute of International Affairs (SAIIA) and also contributed to SAIIA programmes on NEPAD and the Gender Dimensions of Migration. Additional research interests include education, gender, HIV/AIDS and transitional justice. Ayesha has worked extensively on the African Union architecture and the African Peer Review Mechanism. Currently, she focuses on governance in transitional societies.

Ayesha has worked in education in South Africa, the US and Britain; and also managed a national NGO. She has done research consultancies for various entities and has experience as a trainer and facilitator; having designed workshops and seminars for government and civil society.

Ayesha participated in intensive governance studies on Malawi, Mauritius and Ghana between 2004 and 2006. She has also worked in Zimbabwe, Sudan, Rwanda, Liberia, Kenya and Angola. She has presented at events organized by the World Bank, the Royal United Services Institute, and the African Union, among others.

She has served on the boards of Transparency South Africa and the Peace and Development Working Group.

Youssef Mahmoud is currently the Special Representative of the Secretary-General and Head of the United Nations Mission in Central African Republic and Chad (MINURCAT). He previously served for three years in Burundi as Executive Representative of the Secretary-General and Head of the United Nations Integrated Office in that country (BINUB). Prior to these recent assignments, Youssef served as the United Nations Resident Coordinator in Guyana, as Director in the Department of Political Affairs in the UN secretariat in New York, and as senior officer with the United Nations Transitional Authority in Cambodia (UNTAC).

Gilbert Nibigirwe has published numerous articles and is a frequent media commentator on Burundian and Belgian politics. He fled from Burundi in 1993 after the assassination of the first democratically elected President Melchior Ndadaye, and he later served as FRODEBU representative in Europe. He is a specialist on different aspects of microfinance and its role in poverty reduction in Africa, and he previously worked for Fortis Bank for more than ten years in Belgium. Nibigirwe is among the founders of the first Burundian diaspora cooperative, but returned to Burundi in 2009 to work as a lawyer with Mkono & Co. Advocates. He has a Masters of Law (2000) and an Executive Masters in Internal Audit (2008) from the University of Louvain-la-Neuve (Belgium). He is married with two children.

John Mark Pokoo (formerly Opoku) is a Programme Coordinator, Regional Small Arms and Light Weapons Training Programme at the Kofi Annan International Peacekeeping Training Centre (KAIPTC) in Accra, Ghana. This is a capacity building training programme for the 15 National Commissions for Small Arms and Light Weapons in West Africa, delivered on behalf of the ECOWAS Commission. Mr Pokoo previously worked as a journalist with Ghana's *Daily Graphic* for several years and also at the High Commission of Canada in Accra. He has written on civil society contribution to ECOWAS peace and security initiatives and is currently focusing on sustainable SALW programmes in the West Africa sub-region. He holds a Master's degree in Contemporary War and Peace Studies from the University of Sussex and BA in Political Science degree from the University of Ghana – Legon.

Kristiana Powell is a Security Sector Reform (SSR) programme officer with the SSR Unit in the United Nations Department of Peacekeeping Operations. Her main areas of responsibility with DPKO include SSR in Burundi and the Democratic Republic of the Congo, the African Union–United Nations strategic collaboration in SSR and SSR best practices and lessons learned. Before joining the United Nations in November 2007, Kristiana worked for four years as a researcher with the Ottawa-based North-South Institute, focusing on the African Union's peace and security capacities and security sector reform in Burundi. She has produced several publications on these subjects. Kristiana has a Master's in international relations from the University of Toronto.

Siegmar Schmidt is currently Professor for International Relations and Comparative Government at the University of Koblenz-Landau, Campus Landau (Germany). His main areas of research include democracy and development in Sub-Saharan Africa, European and African integration, European and German foreign policy. In 2003–2004 he held the Willy Brand-Chair of the German Academic Exchange Service (DAAD) at the University of the Western Cape (UWC), South Africa. He undertook field research in Eastern and Southern Africa. His recent publications include: The EU Democracy Assistance in Africa: The Cases of South Africa and the Democratic Republic of Congo (DRC), in Knodt and Jünemann (eds), *The EU as an External Democracy Promoter* (Nomos, 2007); The EU Security Policy towards Sub-Saharan Africa (Die EU-Sicherheitspolitik gegenüber Subsahara-Afrika) in Müller-Brandeck-Bocquet (ed.), *The European Union and Africa: New Approaches and Perspectives* [Die Afrikapolitik der Europäischen Union. Neue Ansätze und Perspektiven] (Opladen, 2007) and Germany – the Reluctant Ally. German Domestic Politics and the War against Saddam Hussein, in Bobrow (ed.), *Hegemony Constrained. Evasion, Modification, and Resistance to American Foreign Policy* (Pittsburgh University Press, 2008).

John Siebert became the Executive Director of Project Ploughshares in 2005. Founded in 1976, Project Ploughshares is the ecumenical peace centre of the Canadian Council of Churches. The work of Project Ploughshares includes research and policy development on nuclear disarmament and non-proliferation, the control and reduction of conventional weapons including small arms and light weapons, peacebuilding with partners in the Horn of Africa and the Caribbean, and critical evaluation of Canada's foreign and defense policy from a human security framework. Prior to joining Project Ploughshares, John worked for several NGOs, including the national office of The United Church of Canada (1992–1998) on human rights and indigenous peoples' issues. From 1982–1986 he was a Foreign Service Officer with Canada's Department of External Affairs and International Trade, which included a posting to the Canadian Embassy in Washington, DC. John has an MA from the University of St Michaels College, University of Toronto.

Karolina Werner is a project manager working on the African Initiative at CIGI since 2007. Before returning to Canada, she lived in Austria where she worked at the United Nations Industrial Development Organization and the International Institute for Applied Systems Analysis, among others. Ms. Werner has an MA in conflict resolution from the University of North Carolina, and a BSc (Hons) degree in peace and conflict studies and psychology from the University of Toronto. Ms Werner's research interests include international conflict, with a special focus on Africa, as well as grassroots and indigenous approaches to conflict transformation.

List of Abbreviations

AMIB – African Union Mission to Burundi
AMIS – African Union Mission to Sudan
APF – African Peace Facility
APSA – African Peace and Security Architecture
ASF – African Standby Force
AU – African Union
BINUB – United Nations Integrated Office in Burundi
CPA – Comprehensive Peace Agreement
DDR – Disarmament, Demobilization, and Reintegration
DPKO – UN Department of Peacekeeping Operations
DRC – Democratic Republic of the Congo
EAC – East African Community
EASBRICOM – East African Standby Brigade Coordination Mechanism
EASBRIG – East African Standby Brigade
ECOWAS – Economic Community of Western African States
EU – European Union
ICC – International Criminal Court
IGAD – Intergovernmental Authority on Development
KAIPTC – Kofi Annan International Peacekeeping Centre
NATO – North Atlantic Treaty Organization
NEPAD – New Partnership for Africa's Development
OAU – Organization of African Unity
ONUB – United Nations Mission to Burundi
PLANELM – Planning Element of Brigade
PSC – Peace and Security Council
PSTC – Peace Support Training Centre
R2P – Responsibility to Protect
REC – Regional Economic Community
SADC – Southern African Development Community
SADCBRIG – Southern African Development Community Brigade
SHIRBRIG – Standby High Readiness Brigade for United Nations Operations
SSR – Security Sector Reform
UN – United Nations
UNAMID – UN/AU Hybrid Operation in Darfur

The Centre for International
Governance Innovation
Centre pour l'innovation dans
la gouvernance internationale

The Centre for international Governance innovation is an independent, nonpartisan think-tank that addresses international governance challenges. Led by a group of experienced practitioners and distinguished academics, CIGI supports research, forms networks, advances policy debate, builds capacity, and generates ideas for multilateral governance improvements. Conducting an active agenda of research, events, and publications, CIGI's interdisciplinary work includes collaboration with policy, business and academic communities around the world.

CIGI was founded in 2002 by Jim Balsillie, co-CEO of RIM (Research in Motion) and collaborates with and gratefully acknowledges support from a number of strategic partners, in particular the Government of Canada and the Government of Ontario.

For more information please visit www.CIGIonline.org.

Foreword
Meeting the Demand for Intervention:
The Promise of African Security Architecture

Lt Gen. The Honourable Roméo A. Dallaire, (Ret'd), Senator

Introduction

Insecurity and violent conflict in Africa are met with relative indifference among many international decision-makers, with predictable and terrible results. Despite the adoption of the *Responsibility to Protect (R2P)* doctrine at the United Nations in 2005, and regular pledges to defend human rights more actively, politicians and diplomats around the globe often remain passive observers when faced with massive human rights abuses on the world's poorest continent. The genocide in Rwanda in 1994 and more recently Darfur since 2002 are obvious illustrations of this. For many, the solution lies in enlisting help from those who are not so far removed from human rights abuses and their ripple effects. Practically speaking, this means pursuing 'African solutions to African problems' and supporting leadership initiatives from regional organizations like the African Union (AU).

The collection of thoughts and arguments in this publication provides important follow-up by exploring the roots of conflict in Africa, including abuses of political and military power as well as the struggles to control precious natural resources. Strong, proactive measures are consistently prescribed to prevent conflicts from developing in the first place, but credible African security architecture lies at the heart of an effective, long-term strategy for deterring and responding to conflicts. It allows for an essential shift from external leadership to African leadership, which strengthens and instills a sense of ownership among African policy makers. Discussions around the implementation of an African-led security infrastructure have identified several different approaches for making this transition, including hybrid missions, capacity-building,[1] development of the African Standby Force, and other mechanisms, all with the ultimate goal of developing the capacity within Africa to intervene and protect civilians at risk.

---

1 Capacity building within national and sub-regional security forces, including training establishments such as the Kofi Annan International Peacekeeping Centre in Accra, Ghana.

There are a variety of case studies from Burundi to Sudan to West Africa that highlight different means for entrenching African security architecture, but the guiding principles of all of these avenues are embedded in R2P and in a commitment to capacity-building, two concepts that are closely linked. Without improved capacity in security, governance, or simply resource allocation to sustain any effort in a said sub-region or country, a credible rapid reaction capability will remain elusive, and it will be difficult to move the R2P doctrine from aspiration to reality in Africa.

The Responsibility to Protect and the Demand for African Security Architecture

The R2P doctrine, which was first presented to the international community in 2001 by the International Commission on Intervention and State Sovereignty,[2] grew out of a desire to mitigate preventable tragedies, like those in Bosnia and Rwanda, which shocked the world during the 1990s. The development of the R2P doctrine marks a clear shift away from a state-centric approach to security and a rigid commitment to non-intervention in intra-state crises. With R2P, the international community has begun to formally recognize, and conceptualize, its obligation to intervene in situations where states are unable or unwilling to protect civilians, and prevent or stop massive human rights abuses within their borders.

R2P has provided a basis for discussions about creating an African security architecture. Central to R2P is the need for third parties to have the capacity for timely and effective intervention in crises. The United Nations is identified as having primary responsibility in this regard, but other bodies can, and should, develop the capacity for meaningful diplomatic and military intervention. Chapter VIII of the UN Charter specifically outlines a role for regional arrangements or agencies in maintaining international peace and security. In fact, Article 52 encourages UN Member States belonging to regional organizations to 'make every effort' to peacefully resolve local disputes 'through such regional arrangements or

---

2   In 1999 and 2000, Kofi Annan, Secretary-General of the United Nations, repeatedly challenged the international community to forge a common position on humanitarian intervention in the face of gross human rights violations. In response, the Government of Canada, along with several major foundations, established the International Commission on Intervention and State Sovereignty (ICISS) to evaluate the legal, moral, operational and political aspects of humanitarian intervention, and to produce a report on the subject. The report and the resulting doctrine have come to be known as R2P. International Commission on Intervention and State Sovereignty (2001), *The Responsibility to Protect: the Report of the International Commission on Intervention and State Sovereignty*, (Ottawa: International Development Research Centre), vii–viii.

by such regional agencies *before* referring them the Security Council' [emphasis added].[3]

In particular, it is widely believed that African states must work together through organizations like the African Union to develop the capacity for intervention in the continent's worst conflicts. Many experts consider sustained involvement by African leaders to be an integral part of efforts to improve security over the long term in their region of the world. This rests on the belief that African states are often best suited to intervene when their neighbours cannot or will not protect civilians from massive human rights violations. However, proximity alone will not ensure effective intervention and issues of governance and accountability must be addressed if third party involvement is to alleviate suffering instead of fuelling conflict. Furthermore, efforts to increase acceptance of the legal and moral obligations derived from R2P must not be thwarted by a dearth of resources when political will to take action exists.

In 1995, the Government of Canada produced a report entitled *Towards a Rapid Reaction Capability for the United Nations*, which included a series of recommendations for how to improve the UN's capacity to respond effectively to crises in a timely fashion. Near the top of the list was a recommendation that UN Member States should 'build on the already established practices of convening informal groups of 'friends' to address specific geographic situations',[4] given the importance of engaging those states whose involvement is crucial to the resolution of the dispute or conflict in question. The report also recognizes the utility of delegating authority with its proposal that regionally based operation-level headquarters be established.[5] So far, none of the five HQs have achieved any viable level of operational capability due to a lack of resource commitment from all nations concerned. Constraints like the size of national forces for self-protection, and the inability to standardize equipment acquisition, sustainment or logistics, remain substantial obstacles to achieving a modicum of effectiveness. Lastly, the strategic lift capability required to move and sustain these forces in any sub-region is non-existent. This drastically hampers timely initial deployments, along with the continued support essential to keep forces in the field.

The promotion of African security infrastructure comes with several advantages that will boost the likelihood of 'in house' implementation of R2P. First, there are concrete logistical reasons for promoting the growth of African security architecture. African states often possess knowledge of local terrain and political dynamics that is lacking when intervention originates, and is planned, from outside the continent. Moreover, in geographical terms, proximity to conflict zones can

3   United Nations, 'Charter of the United Nations – Chapter VIII: Regional Arrangements', http://www.un.org/en/documents/charter/chapter8.shtml, accessed 23 February 2009.

4   Government of Canada (1995), *Towards a Rapid Reaction Capability for the United Nations* (Ottawa: Minister of Foreign Affairs and Minister of National Defence), 67.

5   *Ibid.*, 70.

reduce response times and allow for the timely deployment and sustainment of troops, a critical capability in emergencies where saving time means saving lives.

However, there are also more abstract incentives for helping African states and the African Union to develop the means for effective intervention in humanitarian crises unfolding within the continent. The international community has repeatedly demonstrated its unreliability when it comes to mounting timely and sustained responses to crises. The United Nations Security Council's decisions often reflect political tug-of-wars among its members more than the interests or concerns of those on the ground in conflict situations. The inept response from the five permanent members during the Rwanda crisis is an ideal example. The subsequent deployment of French forces in Operation Turquoise reinforced the fact that a permanent member would, and could, have given support before the slaughter if it had wanted to do so at the time. The refusal of the US to get engaged at all reflects the fact that its decision making was based on self-interest and thus prevented the leadership required to support African nations coming into the fray.

Furthermore, critics of R2P allege that it simply provides Western governments with a pretext for self-interested interference in the internal affairs of developing countries. African states and their leaders are often well-placed to mediate and resolve conflicts because they command legitimacy, and sometimes cultural sensitivity, that can be lacking among third parties from other parts of the world. This is not always the case, but these potential advantages combine with the general desirability of having a variety of tools for responding to crises. If the UN fails, it is important to have other options.

The formal establishment of the African Union at the Durban Summit in 2002 sprang from a desire among African leaders to break with the continent's colonial past and forge a new, pan-African mechanism for promoting good governance, leadership, and security. The transition from the Organization for African Unity to the African Union marked a formal change, but the organization has often fallen short of its peace and security goals, mostly because of management problems and a lack of capacity to implement important measures, like the full standardization of training for peace support operations. Although, the AU Charter mirrors many core R2P principles, limited financial and institutional resources have fuelled difficulties in moving from rhetoric to reality. For example, lacking sufficient air lift capabilities makes it very difficult to deploy troops quickly and effectively. Nevertheless, despite the formidable challenges facing the relatively new organization, the African Union has demonstrated a substantial commitment to R2P and it is increasingly acquiring the support, legitimacy, and capacity required to mount meaningful responses to conflict situations on the continent.

The Peace and Security Council of the African Union, the organ tasked with providing guidance on all issues of security across the continent, lies at the core of plans for developing the African security architecture. The Council's real impact on security in Africa, however, should be measured by its ability to mobilize rapid reaction forces capable of mitigating violence against civilians. This capacity should be a priority because the achievement of the AU's other founding objectives, namely socio-economic integration and solidarity among African states, depends heavily on the maintenance of stability across the continent, and of security between and within states. Innovative solutions to tackle poverty and an overall lack of development can only be implemented if an atmosphere of security can be ensured and sustained.

The African Standby Force (ASF) is intended to provide a rapid reaction capacity, and to embody the logistical, strategic, and technical advantages of African security architecture.[6] Envisaged as a force ready for deployment to the continent's troubled areas by 2010, the ASF is meant to respond quickly and independently to situations of concern. Unfortunately, the ASF is not on schedule to fully meet this goal. Without enhanced external support and increased capacity in areas such as training and transportation, the ASF will not realize its full potential as an effective tool for implementing the principles of R2P over the next 5 to 10 years (depending on the sub-region).

For those sceptical of African states' willingness to assume greater responsibility for the protection of civilians, the statistics on troop contributions to United Nations missions tell an encouraging story about the active engagement of African states in peace operations. As of November 2008, three of the 10 countries contributing the most soldiers, military observers, and police to UN peacekeeping operations are African. Nigeria ranked fourth, Ghana sixth, and Rwanda eighth. This is part of a sustained pattern, with four out of the 2003 top 10 contributors also being African: Nigeria ranked third, Ghana fifth, Kenya ninth, and South Africa tenth.[7]

These statistics provide some indication of African states' willingness to engage in peace operations, but there are several case studies, including the South African-led mission in Burundi, that provide a more comprehensive illustration of the merits of African-led intervention in regional conflicts. The African Union Mission in Burundi (AMIB), composed of 700 South African troops as deployed in 2003 to monitor a fragile security situation, demonstrated the ability of the AU to intervene and establish stability. Meanwhile, despite a series of attempts, no mandate could be obtained from the UN Security Council to monitor the partial ceasefire. When eventually deployed in 2004, the UN Operation in Burundi (ONUB) commanded significantly more resources than its predecessor, but it

---

6   The African Union Commission was mandated, within the framework of Article 13 of the Protocol on the Peace and Security Council, to establish an African Standby Force (ASF). The ASF is intended as a rapid reaction tool to facilitate timely and efficient responses to conflict and crisis situations in Africa. Following meetings of African Chiefs of Defence Staff in 2003 and 2004, and a 2004 meeting of African Ministers of Defence, the policy framework of the ASF was approved. The force was designed to consist of standby brigades in each of the five regions (Northern, Western, Eastern, Central and Southern) and to incorporate a police and civilian expert capacity. Cilliers, J. and Malan, M. (2005) 'Progress with the African Standby Force', *Institute for Security Studies*, Paper 98, 1–3.

7   Global Policy Forum, 'Peacekeeping Tables and Charts – Troop Contributions to UN Peacekeeping Operations', http://www.globalpolicy.org/security/peacekpg/data/index. htm, accessed 23 February 2009.

was clear that AMIB had laid the foundation for the UN mission's subsequent success. Although a rapid reaction force would have been preferable in the case of Burundi, South Africa's contributions helped create a political and logistical base for ONUB, and AMIB showed that the AU was, in some instances, capable of responding more quickly and efficiently than the UN.

While cases like the deployment of AMIB provide encouraging stories of successful African-led intervention on the continent, the case of Darfur is a deeply uncomfortable reminder of this model's current limitations when it comes to halting and preventing atrocities on a large scale. Like in Burundi, contributors to the African Union Mission in Sudan (AMIS) were among a small group courageous enough to intervene early, and more quickly, than the United Nations, but the mission's limitations were evident. AMIS highlighted the lack of capacity, in areas like training and equipment, and the dearth of political support that can afflict African-led missions and prevent them from effectively providing security and otherwise fulfilling their mandates.

The United Nations – African Union Mission for Darfur (UNAMID) has subsequently set a precedent for the hybrid model, displaying its advantages along with its severe deficiencies. Major problems with this model include the Byzantine complexity of command and control, and the significant time lapse before deployment. Another failing is a lack of operational equipment and an ineffective logistical team to sustain the force in the field. While a political stalemate precluded the deployment of a conventional UN mission in Darfur and made the hybrid model a necessity, the case reminds us that the costs of excessive organizational complexity and slow deployment times can be measured in suffering endured by vulnerable civilians.

R2P is a shared responsibility, but a hybrid mission has proved a less than ideal means of sharing the work associated with intervention in Darfur and the UN alone is often prevented from taking appropriate action. There is no shortage, however, of imploding nations and humanitarian catastrophes left by outside actors that are less than engaged in the region. African-led missions have the potential to fill significant gaps in the implementation of R2P. However, a lack of capacity is the most common obstacle to responses at the regional level. This will have to be addressed if meaningful progress is to be made in enhancing and implementing an effective African security architecture.

Meeting the Demand for Intervention: Capacity-building and African Security Architecture

It is critical, from the international community's point of view, that African states assume responsibility for resolving conflicts within their region, and for protecting civilians from massive human rights violations. Leaders from outside the continent have periodically pledged to help develop a self-sufficient African security architecture through initiatives like the Joint Africa/G8 Plan to Enhance

African Capabilities to Undertake Peace Support Operations,[8] but formidable challenges remain.

Enhancing technical and institutional capacities, and improving management of security structures, must become and remain priorities if unrealized potential is to eventually yield entrenched and reliable tools for managing conflict at the regional level. Specifically, efforts to develop a rapid reaction force within the continent are heavily dependent on enhanced capacities for training, deployment, and logistics to get troops on the ground and sustain them in the field.

The idea of an African Standby Force (ASF) was first proposed at the second meeting of the African Chiefs of Defence Staff (ACDS), held in Harare in October 1997. African states and donors did not immediately act upon the recommendation from the ACDS that a brigade be formed from each of the five African sub-regions. However, in 2002 the G8 Kananaskis Summit in Canada provided a framework for the Africa Action Plan,[9] which included important provisions for technical and financial assistance to the African Standby Force. In the meantime, some progress has been made in areas such as doctrine development and the creation of training centres, but the deadline of 2010 for the full preparation of five regional rapid deployment brigades (Central, North, Southern, East, and West Africa), and a sixth at the African Union Headquarters in Addis Ababa, does not appear to be on track

Many questions remain surrounding training, equipment, logistics, force capacities and maintenance, as well as reporting channels among regional standby forces and the African Union. A variety of financial and management issues also require clarification if the ASF is to capitalize on its potential to provide more timely responses to crises than does the United Nations. United Nations efforts to reduce the amount of time it takes to deploy a mission have taken the form of the UN Stand-by Arrangements System. They have included the more successful Rapid Deployment Level of the system, which aims to achieve deployment within

---

8   The Joint Africa/G8 Plan to Enhance African Capabilities to Undertake Peace Support Operations grew out of the 2002 G8 summit in Kananaskis, and it was endorsed at the 2003 G8 summit in Evian. It is a key component of the G8 Africa Action Plan, which includes a commitment to provide technical and financial assistance so that African countries, the AU, and regional organizations are able to more effectively prevent and resolve violent conflict. The Joint Plan was formulated in collaboration with African partners and it outlines 'building blocks' required to help enhance African capabilities vis-à-vis peace support operations. Some of the 'building blocks' were identified by the G8. G8 (2006), 'Joint Africa/G8 Plan to Enhance African Capabilities to Undertake Peace Support Operations', *G8 Summit 2006 – S. Petersberg*, http://en.g8russia.ru/g8/history/evian2003/16/, accessed 29 July 2009.

9   The Africa Action Plan was adopted by G8 leaders at the 2002 Kananaskis Summit and it contains over 100 specific commitments to Africa that reflect the New Partnership for Africa's Development (NEPAD) framework document. Department of Foreign Affairs and International Trade Canada, 'G8 Africa Action Plan', http://www.international.gc.ca/ssa-ass/aap-paa/index.aspx?lang=eng, accessed 29 July 2009.

30 to 90 days from the issuance of a mandate by the Security Council. However, experience has shown that mounting rapid responses to situations of concern are still not a strong suit for the UN. Despite the challenges faced by the ASF, its proximity to conflicts and its potential for rapid deployment make it an attractive option, whether on its own or in conjunction with UN efforts.

In 1995, the Government of Canada released a report entitled *Towards a Rapid Reaction Capability for the United Nations*. Many of the recommendations made in this report are equally applicable at the regional level and should be implemented in the African context. Early warning capabilities should be pooled at the local, regional, and international levels to facilitate timely action, and operational-level headquarters should undertake generic contingency planning when early-warning mechanisms are triggered, all while liaising with concerned governments and organizations.[10]

Another element of the 1995 report that can and should be mirrored in developing a rapid-reaction capability for the AU is the development of rosters of senior military commanders who might serve as Force Commanders for ASF operations. These officers should come together periodically for discussions about contingency planning, mandates, operational guidance, the integration of humanitarian and human rights concerns in peacekeeping, and lessons learned from past operations. Furthermore, forces allocated for standby service should be organized according to 'capability components' (such as observation force, ceasefire monitoring, etc.), corresponding to function.[11]

Also transferable is the recommendation that Member States should establish readiness targets and develop 'a set of generic and mission specific training standards and "type" curricula applicable to all troop contributing nations'.[12] Furthermore, states contributing to the ASF could also incorporate the recommendation of providing annual training summaries outlining activities undertaken and proposed for those units identified for service with the ASF.

Implementing these measures, and generally enhancing the capacity of the ASF, depends heavily on increasing available resources, particularly for training African peacekeepers. Some training centres, including the Peace Support Training Centre in Kenya, receive training support from the UN Department of Peacekeeping Operations (DPKO) as well as funding from Western countries. This gives them the wherewithal to provide quality pre-deployment training to peacekeepers. For example, with support from Canada, 32 military officers drawn from 12 African countries completed a Tactical Operations Staff Course for peacekeepers at the Centre in Kenya in May 2009.[13]

---

10   *Towards a Rapid Reaction Capability for the United Nations*, op. cit., 70.
11   *Ibid.*, 69–70.
12   *Ibid.*, 70.
13   Government of Canada, 'Military officers from 12 African countries attend Peace Support Course conducted by Canadian Forces', http://www.canadainternational.gc.ca/kenya/highlights-faits/peace_course-cours_paix.aspx?lang=eng, accessed 29 July 2009.

Other centres are very much in need of additional support. The SADC Regional Peacekeeping Training Centre (RPTC) in Harare, Zimbabwe, typifies a potentially very useful training centre in need of additional funding. The RPTC reflects a recognition that African leadership of the ASF should not just be maintained at the top, but also at the grassroots level. There is a concerted effort at the Centre to ensure that most training takes place in Africa, and that training programmes rely heavily on African leadership and expertise. Although the concept of regional peacekeeping forces is relatively new, the participation of African peacekeepers in United Nations missions provides access to knowledge, skills, experience, and best practices that can be shared with African troops designated for action within the ASF.

Other important contributions to the training of African peacekeepers come from the Bamako Peacekeeping School in Mali and the Kofi Annan International Peacekeeping Training Centre (KAIPTC) in Accra, Ghana. The KAIPTC relies on its strong links with Western training centres, such as the Pearson Peacekeeping Centre in Canada and the Centre for Defence Studies at King's College in the United Kingdom. The exchange of information on lessons learned and experiences in developing curriculum have been central to KAIPTC's success since its establishment in 2004, but centres such as the KAIPTC need stable support and funding from donors that view their contributions as part of a long-term commitment. This is essential because a disconnect currently exists between the objectives of the ASF and the political, financial and logistical realities it is facing. Reliable funding provides the training centres with the autonomy and resources that will allow the ASF to act autonomously when necessary.

Conclusion

Chronic conflict produced by imploding nations, the *Responsibility to Protect* doctrine, and the repeated failures of outside intervention have created demand for an African security architecture and an African Standby Force capable of mounting effective responses to humanitarian crises. Other support is clearly required, including help from African civil society, local governments and regional organizations. As the world's largest peacekeeping organization, the United Nations relies heavily on its Human Rights and Civil Affairs section, as well as the Field Support Department for logistical support to peacekeeping operations. African security architecture would be incomplete without a similar civilian foundation to support military intervention, but in order to be credible, the ASF must develop a reliable rapid reaction capacity.

Responding appropriately to massive human rights abuses is a moral and legal obligation and our willingness to intervene when necessary is a direct measure of our commitment to the *Responsibility to Protect* doctrine. There are several advantages to African-led intervention, including proximity, shortened deployment times, local knowledge, and enhanced legitimacy. However, the primary obstacle for most African-led missions is a lack of capacity. The political will for intervention frequently exists at the regional level, but the capacity for independent and credible action will only develop with sufficient resources, a certain degree of financial independence, and under thoroughly African leadership. There are reasons for optimism, but a renewed commitment is required from the international community and donors, as well as African states and the African Union.

Chapter 1
African Solutions for African Problems and Shared R2P

Hany Besada, Ariane Goetz, and Karolina Werner

Background

Since the early 1990s, the world has witnessed profound and new challenges in the realm of peace and security. On the one hand, the dramatic rise of intra-state conflicts, particularly on the African continent, reflected an acute security vacuum that many less developed countries were facing due to the end of the Cold War and the 'sudden' withdrawal of military, political, and financial support by great powers, largely a result of superpower competition by the United States and the Soviet Union. On the other hand, and in response to this debasing security situation in many countries around the world, unprecedented national, regional, and global efforts were undertaken to address these severe imploding security conditions.[1] In fact, the often-weak political, socio-economic, and military capacities and capabilities of states or international organizations[2] in dealing with these security concerns yielded a push by national and international actors for adequate institutionalized solutions at the regional or international level. Consequently, a reconfiguration of

---

1   Given the fact that between 1945 and 1986, 125 (out of 127) major conflicts took place in the so-called "Third World" (Latin America, Africa, Middle East, and Asia), it would be wrong to label the Cold War era as an era of stability and security. In this context, Acharya (in Fawcett 2000) has pointed out that the "Third World" accounted for a majority 'of the over 20 million war-related deaths during this period' (Acharya in Fawcett 2000: 80). Nevertheless, the end of the Cold War did provide for an increase in the instability and insecurity of many less-developed countries due to the breakdown of domestic regimes whose survival had been closely related to superpower patronage (e.g. Cuba, El Salvador, Nicaragua, Cambodia, Somalia, Ethiopia), or due to the emergence of ethnic conflict and the lack of sufficient military self-reliance. See Acharya, Amitav (2000): Developing Countries and the Emerging World Order. Security and Institutions. In: Fawcett, Louise (2000): *The Third World beyond the Cold War. Continuity and Change* (Oxford: Oxford University Press): 78–98.

2   This refers particularly to the UN Security Council and its difficulty to react adequately in situations of severe crisis during the 1990s (e.g. Rwanda 1994) due to weak financial and military resources, normative inconsistency, lack of political unity and will, unrealistically mandated missions, and/or a lack of knowledge about the situation 'on the ground'.

existing institutions has taken place together with the creation of new elements and norms within the regional and international security architecture.

It is against this background of events that the authors in this book, assess the security architecture emerging under the new overarching international security and human rights norm 'Responsibility to Protect'. The chapters focus on a broad range of phenomena, covering not only the emerging African security architecture but also, more broadly, forms of international cooperation in the realm of peace and security. Additionally, case studies on Sudan, Burundi, and Liberia evaluate regional (EU, AU, or ECOMOG) and global (UN) actors and the particular modes of cooperation involved in African Peacekeeping. Central to our discussion about the emerging (African) Security Architecture on the regional and global level is the new concept and norm of a (shared) 'Responsibility to Protect'(R2P).

Global and Regional Developments in View of R2P

At the global level, the concept and norm 'R2P' was first introduced and promoted in 2001 by a correspondent report of the International Commission on Intervention and State Sovereignty (ICISS). The Commission had been initiated by the Canadian government as a direct reaction to the long and disreputable history of retroactively mandated 'humanitarian' interventions[3] by individual nations or so-called 'coalitions of the willing',[4] and the widely rejected 'right to intervene'[5]-principle underpinning them. Faced with the rise in intra-state wars and the related 'moral dilemma of non-intervention' (Thakur 2006[6]), the overall goal was to reconsider and further 'standardize' procedures, contents, and channels of intervention and global security cooperation. In doing so, the 'right to intervene'-principle was superseded by the 'responsibility to protect' of states towards its own citizens and of the international community to protect civilians in case a state fails to fulfil this responsibility.

The concept of R2P built on and complemented the notion of 'human security' that had been introduced into the international relations discourse as early as 1994, when a Human Development Report by the UNDP had tried to re-conceptualize

---

3   The latest example of such a retroactively mandated intervention is the US–Iraq War in 2003. Here, only at a later stage – under Resolution 1483 – did the US as occupier attain legal status according to international law.

4   'Coalition of the willing' is a term used to describe humanitarian and/or military interventions where the UN Security Council cannot agree or are unable to raise a peacekeeping force.

5   The concept of rushing to the aid of vulnerable populations in time of war or humanitarian crisis is not a new phenomenon. Hugo Grotius examined such an intervention in *De Jure Belli ac Pacis* (On the Law of War and Peace) in 1625.

6   Thakur, Ramesh C. (2006): *The United Nations, Peace and Security. From Collective Security to the Responsiblility to Protect* (Cambridge: Cambridge University Press): 264–65.

the notion of security in an attempt to provide for an analytical lens for intra-state conflict. Traditional IR discourses had focused primarily on inter-state conflict and security threats, mainly the nuclear threat, and had thus proven unable to analytically capture the phenomenon of intra-state conflict adequately enough for policy makers and politicians to act upon in cases of severe crisis.[7] Accordingly, the concept 'human security' comprised a wider range of issues, such as economic security, food security, health security, environmental security, personal security, community security, and political security, thereby merging the development and the security discourse. Both aspects seemed relevant for the achievement of peace.[8]

Similarly, the concept R2P expanded beyond military protection, and included a three-dimensional notion of responsibility to prevent, react, and rebuild. The promoters of the concept argued that the world needed a multilateral and principled security response in the face of mass atrocities, genocide and crimes against humanity. The response should reflect an obligation of all nations to provide for civilian protection in severe crises, and at the same time put more effort into non-military means of prevention. Thus, at the international level, the doctrine of the responsibility to protect, together with the establishment of an International Criminal Court (ICC),[9] were meant to provide for a widely accepted security approach in the face of gross internal human rights violation, thereby also acknowledging for the first time that the state itself could become a security threat for its population.

In 2005, still under the impression of the history of UN failures in form of intervention *or* non-intervention in situations of severe humanitarian crisis, massacre, or genocide (e.g. Somalia, Cambodia, Rwanda, and Srebrenica), the United Nations General Assembly unanimously endorsed the concept R2P at a summit meeting on its 60th anniversary, in September 2005.

At the same time, institutional and normative changes took place on the regional level. The African continent – the focus of this book – began restructuring its security architecture, with the failures and lack of reliability of the international security architecture (e.g. Rwanda in 1994) serving as contributing stimulus for change. In fact, normative and institutional changes

---

7   UNDP Human Development Report (1994): New Dimensions of Human Security (New York: UN).

8   See UNDP Human Development Report (1994): 23–4.

9   In the first ICC case against a sitting head of state, opinions in Africa are divided and fears of setting precedents run high. In July 2008, the prosecutor of the ICC, Luis Moreno-Ocampo, accused the Sudanese leader of crimes against humanity, war crimes and genocide in Darfur. In March 2009, the court issued an arrest warrant for the Sudanese leader. The violent conflict in Darfur has left more than 300,000 people killed and another 2.7 million internally displaced. As head of state and commander of the Sudanese armed forces, al-Bashir is accused of leading a five-year counter-insurgency campaign against three armed groups in Darfur.

took place. In 2002, the Organization of African Unity (OAU) was succeeded by the African Union (AU). The focus of the newly founded AU yielded a shift from non-intervention to non-indifference in the face of massive human rights violations within a member state. Its founding doctrine incorporated the R2P concept in form of a reinterpretation of the sovereignty principle. Moving beyond the legal restrictions of the OAU, the AU today has the potential to become an influential regional actor in view of civil strife and mass atrocities across the continent, and with regard to the R2P implementation In fact, new sub-institutions and agencies were created, such as the Peace and Security Council (PSC) to provide for institutional means to recommend and implement interventions in cases of severe crisis. At the same time, the responsibility to prevent has been strengthened through the creation of new structures such as the consultative Panel of the Wise and the Continental Early Warning System (CEWS). In addition, an African Standby Force (ASF) is being built up to ensure various missions, from observation to intervention.[10] While most of these innovative institutions are still in the build-up phase, in the medium term the higher degree of 'institutional preparedness'[11] of the continental organization could enhance its role as an important building block in the international peace and security architecture, as well as satisfy the widespread desire for greater continental self-reliance. However, similar to sub-regional groups and integration initiatives, such as the Economic Community of West African State (ECOWAS) and Common Market for Eastern and Southern Africa (COMESA), the AU still faces many hurdles in form of shortage of financial resources, very diverse members, as well as great challenges in view of the overall improvement of human security within the member states (particularly in view of security, economic development, environmental and health challenges).

Dilemmas and Prospects

In defence of the new concept, the proponents of R2P argue that the real choice has never been between intervention or non-intervention, but rather between a regularized, multilateral, and principled approach to intervention, conducted by the global security community in the face of mass atrocities, or an arbitrary, unilateral approach by world powers or a 'coalition of the willing'.

In fact, R2P is perceived as the best possible solution in the myriad of contradicting principles and norms such as an expanded notion of sovereignty, humanitarian intervention with military means, and responsibility in providing for an almost subsidiary understanding of responsibility, or the understanding of responsibility. Accordingly, the 'old' Westphalian notions of sovereignty as

---

10   Evans, Gareth (2008): *The Responsibility to Protect. Ending Mass Atrocity Crimes Once and For All* (Washington, DC: Brookings Institution Press), pp. 157–8.

11   Evans (2008): 158.

territorial 'control' by the state and the related principle of 'non-intervention' in state matters was re-phrased into sovereignty as a primary responsibility by the state to provide for the protection of its citizens. Only in cases where this primary responsibility was not met, the secondary responsibility by the international community to provide for the safety and protection of the respective population comes into being.[12]

Thus, R2P – according to proponents – does not undermine the state's sovereignty, but instead strengthens its role in the international community. Contrary to the 'right to intervene' with military means, R2P's focus on prevention and reconstruction are seen as valuable contributions to international peace and security.

At the same time, and quite to the contrary, opponents of the concept argue that the consequences of R2P and 'human security' *do* undermine sovereignty, the potential costs of which are hardly ever taken into closer consideration. Moreover, the asymmetric power distribution in the UN Security Council, and the UN more generally seemingly adds to the difficulty of potential host countries to trust in the concept. While there are regional differences concerning the perception of R2P, a fundamental – and valid – point of skepticism is sparked by the fact, that thus far R2P remains a rather top-down endeavour, one that puts particular emphasis on the second responsibility to *react*, while neither prevention, nor the comprehensive analysis of systemic causes or roots of a conflict are being given the attention they would deserve.[13] This is often less the result of a traditional understanding of sovereignty, but in fact a lack of political will of all parties involved.

---

12   Evans (2008): 31–3.

13   Efforts towards conflict prevention and comprehensive conflict analysis have suffered from several limitations: first, it has proven a difficult task for weak states to get the attention of the UN Security Council. Even in the face of severe crisis, the sense of individual responsibility of member states has often been 'undermined by the mechanics and compromises of committee decisionmaking, as well as spectacular council failings such as Rwanda, Somalia, Bosnia' (Malone, David M. (2004): *The UN Security Council. From the Cold War to the 21st Century* (Boulder, CO: Rienner): 7–8). A second challenge for sustained support and effective conflict prevention lies in institutional limitations, such as the limited resources available to the UN Security Council, as well as its limited interconnection with regional or sub-regional partners. (Malone 2004: 12) Third, the fact that the underpinning notion of human security is focusing primarily on the 'freedom from fear', and hardly on the 'freedom from want' has contributed to the strong emphasis on the *responsibility to react* (MacFarlane, Stephen Neil; Khong, Yuen Foong (2006): *Human Security and the UN. A Critical History* (Bloomington, IN: Indiana University Press)). In this context, it has been argued that the specific economic and social problems facing less developed countries need to be considered more closely when advising a strategy for peaceful development, conflict prevention, or post-conflict reconstruction (e.g. Evans 2008). For instance, when UNSAMSIL withdrew from Sierra Leone in 2005, economic, political, gender related and social violence in form of marginalization, exclusion, and impoverishment remained largely unaddressed. Instead, the main criterion for withdrawal

Besides, scholars such as McFarlane and Khong (2006) have pointed out that the R2P's complementary notion of human security might suffer from conceptual overstretch – while this not only raises false hopes and promises, it also creates a preference of military solutions to problems due to their *a priori* securitization. [14]

Discussions among academics have made it clear, that so far, there seems to be no common perception or agreement on the notion of a *shared* responsibility to protect. While it was argued by some participants that the most important normative shift took place from non-intervention to non-indifference, this shift was many times looked at very critically. Repeatedly, it was questioned, by whom and why the responsibility to protect should be shared. From a similar perspective, the question was raised regarding the role regional organizations, such as the AU and ECOWAS, have played and should play in the near future in the continent's security architecture. In a time of globalization, how realistic was the demand by some for 'African solutions to African problems'? And how adequate could global solutions be in providing for regional, national or local peace? Here, for instance, the UN-induced preference for negotiating comprehensive peace agreements was mentioned as an impediment rather than a stepping stone to sustainable peace, due to its unrealistic presumption that all parties would be interested in participating in a peaceful interaction or be interested in a peaceful resolution to a conflict(s). [15] This

---

was the establishment of peace as the absence of violent (physical) conflict, in spite of the report by the Truth and Reconciliation Commission (TRC) which had identified the whole spectrum of forms of violence to have prepared the grounds for the former civil war. Fourth, systemic factors of international governance remain largely ignored in the analysis of conflict. In this context, aid conditionality was mentioned by some to represent less 'a structural measure to address root cause problems but a kind of functional equivalent of broad-based economic sanctions' (Evans 2008: 76) Also the increasing securitization of development topics at the international level tends to blur that '[s]ecurity-focused strategies only ever take you so far: it is the broader based political ones that ultimately count most' (Evans 2008: 193). In a similar vein, it has been argued that the discrepancy between practice and ideals at the international level needs to be addressed (Stiglitz, Joseph (2003): Globalization and Development. In: Held, David; Koenig-Archibugi, Mathias (2003): *Taming Globalization. Frontiers of Governance* (Cambridge: Polity). Particularly, when looking at trade issues, it is obvious that the losses of trade are greater than the transfer of development aid for most less developed countries. Also, it has been criticized that systemic causes of crisis such as debt burdens or the legacy of colonial structures of production remain unaddressed; instead, the primary approach is to focus on the quality of governance of a country's government (Guttali, Shalmali (2005): The Politics of Post-war/Post Conflict Reconstruction. In: *Development*, Vol. 48 (2005): 73–81).

14   See MacFarlane and Khong (2006): 228–36.

15   For instance, in the case of Rwanda, the Arusha Peace Talks (1994) prior to the genocide were meant to provide for a peace settlement through means of preventive diplomacy. However, the existence of 'spoilers' was not taken into consideration, and thus the Arusha Peace Talks failed (Mayall, James (2007): Introduction. In: Sharp, Paul; Wiseman, Geoffrey (2007): *The Diplomatic Corps as an Institution of International Society* (Basingstoke, Hampshire: Palgrave Macmillan): 8). The case of Sierra Leone provides for

is particularly evident in situations characterized by a privatization of authority and polypoly of force.

In addition the 'shared R2P' concept was seen critically in the light of self-determination of the host country, given that the third component of R2P, the reconstruction process, implied the implementation of particular economic, social and political models on the ground.[16]

Scholars such as Thakur (2006) have rightly pointed out that these unresolved discussions often take the form of a 'North–South blame game', where the South blames the North over its dominant position in the international system, while the North refers to the South's failure to fulfil its international responsibilities.[17] Yet, at the same time, scepticism about and criticism of R2P point to important problems of the concept as a proxy of international norm creation. While, for instance, from

---

another example for unrealistic preventive diplomacy efforts (by omitting the potential of spoilers in the deliberations): the Lomé Peace Accord, signed in the Togolese capital in July 1999, aimed at ending the violent conflict and sustaining the ceasefire. The peace accord was the outcome of negotiations (under international auspices) between the elected Kabbah government and the rebel group Revolutionary United Front (RUF), and it included RUF members in the government. Yet, RUF did not adhere to its commitments outlined in the peace agreement and relaunched attacks against peacekeepers and the population thereafter.

16   The largely liberal normative presumptions underpinning reconstruction and peacebuilding efforts have become subject to critique. Some (e.g. Guttali (2005):73) accuse the current reconstruction model to represent a form of expansive neo-liberalism. Accordingly, instead of focusing on rebuilding 'lives and societies after periods of violent conflicts and crisis', the current hallmark of reconstruction is about establishing an unregulated market economy, and pushing for privatization and liberal democracy through economic structural adjustment programs, whereas the role of the state is primarily defined as facilitator and protector of free market conditions. This yields the effect that most of the created wealth in fact does not contribute to the social development of the post-conflict environment but is to a large part expropriated by private sector actors outside the country or concentrated among national elites. Besides, external actors in the peace building process often lack forms of external accountability, even though their programs have far-reaching implications for the host country and its population in the area of economic and financial development (e.g. World Bank and IMF); this is reflected in the fact that despite harsh criticism over Structural Adjustment Programs (SAP), the same economic growth model is underpinning the new Poverty Reduction Strategy Paper (PRSP) (see for instance Scholte, Jan Aart (2002): *Civil Society and Global Finance* (London: Routledge)). Also, while the importance of local ownership has become conventional wisdom in theory, in practice, civil society organizations and groups remain marginalized; for example, despite the inclusion of women in reconstruction efforts being acknowledged as important component for sustainable peace, women remain marginalized in formal processes, as the cases of Sudan, Congo (DRC) and Uganda show (Evans 2008: 140). Moreover (e.g. Uganda), oftentimes the Bretton Woods institutions dictate the final version of a rebuilding strategy, even though civil society has been included at the beginning (Scholte 2002: 51–65).

17   Thakur (2006): 264–5.

the viewpoint of R2P, external (international) concepts and actors (implicitly) are considered to be effective in reconstruction, prevention, and reaction efforts, from the host country's perspective they might be seen as troubled by their weak accountability, or their potential unreliability in the face of acute crises or long-term commitment.[18] Moreover, the current normative inconsistency and incoherence in the global security realm, and the pervasive case and norm selectivity undermine the trust by less developed countries further.

Thus, it seems that as long as these states are denied more active roles in the global norm creation processes, it is unlikely they would project a strong political will in support of international measures and concepts; yet, aside from leadership and mandate, political will has proven to be the most important factor for the success of any security cooperation.

One might conclude that difficult security problems, be they practical or normative in kind, require complex solutions. In order to find widespread approval and improvement of top-down security means, more emphasis should be given to prevention, actual analysis of roots of conflicts on the ground, as well as incorporation of systemic causes in the overall assessment and solution-finding process. This would imply not only scrutinizing the problems and actors of actual host countries, but also the programmes and actions of international organizations and actors. Also, normative implications or realities of the current society of states would need more open discussions and assessments. In this regard, R2P not only reflected a redefinition of the principle of state sovereignty; it also cemented the fact that in the current institutional architecture and economic practice of the system of (modern) states, 'self-determination' is at best 'limited self-determination'.

---

18   The UN Mission to Sierra Leone (UNAMSIL) provides a good example of long-term commitment problems: while the funding and decision making structure as well as interest of international organizations such as the UN tend to focus on short- to medium-term results (e.g. elections, peace agreement, restoration of state structures), important elements of peace building that exceed technocratic restoration efforts and imply working on individual capacities of actors have been neglected. Taking the post-conflict Demobilization, Disarmament and Reintegration (DDR) program as example, the time frame and funding structure clearly reveals an emphasis on the DD phase. While DD as an earmarked budget, Reintegration measures of former combatants depend on additional voluntary funding and support. In the case of Sierra Leone it has been additionally argued that a mere restoration of the state and its institutions to the status quo ante bellum is not enough to provide for positive peace; instead, an overarching governance framework would be needed that reconstructs power relations 'in a process oriented, participatory and accountable manner' (Fayemi, Kayode (2004): Governing Insecurity in Post-Conflict States: The Case of Sierra Leone and Liberia. In: Bryden Alan and Haenggi Heiner (eds) (2004): *Reform and Reconstruction of the Security Sector* (online publication): 23). Apart from limits of long-term commitment, recent cases such as Rwanda, where the international community failed to provide for security also show that 'the costs of being dependent on others can be unacceptably high' (Samkange, Stanlake JTM (2002): African Perspectives on Intervention and State Sovereignty. In: *African Security Review*, Vol. 1, No. 1 (2002): 21–34: 27).

This has several implications for African peace and security as well as the role of the international community in the further build up of a peace and security architecture. First, with regard to the international level, it seems important to reconceptualize the regional and international peace and security architecture and ambitions by taking into consideration that the 'playing field was never level'.[19] As Mayall (in Sharp and Wiseman 2007) has pointed out, '[e]ven before the end of the Cold War, the Western powers had begun to shape the 'developing' world to their own design by attaching economic conditions to their bilateral loans and debt relief and imposing structural adjustment programmes'[20] through the IMF and WB. After the end of the Cold War, good governance, democratization, and human rights were added to the economic conditionality of the 1980s, which is reflected by the ingredients of the actual comprehensive peace building toolkit. Here, the development prescriptions underpinning the responsibility to *rebuild*, as well as the international institutional landscape more broadly need to be reconsidered and a delinking of ends and means on a case-by-case basis has to take place to reduce the likelihood that less-developed countries might be committing 'themselves to ill-fitted policy approaches, creating resentment and opposition among national constituencies' (Kaul, Inge (2008): *Bye-bye Westphalian State; Hello Intermediary State – Why Fair Multilateralism Matters* (Online Publication, Berlin 2008): 6) and thus incorporating another factor of instability. The holding of elections, for instance, is often more of an exit strategy of external actors rather than a successful strategy yielding democratization.[21] At the same time, the marginalization of weak states in the international norm production has to be moderated.

Second, on a regional level, it seems important for *African* peace and security to further strengthen and expand the continental and sub-regional organizations to bridge the general divide between self-reliance and further internationalization of security. They would provide for regional and continental alternatives in form of organizations that reliably serve as building blocks within the international peace and security arena, enhance (e.g. AU and peer review mechanism) continental collaboration and coordination in security questions by providing for continuity and a (preventive) diplomacy platform, and strengthen the continent's own role concerning norm creation and diffusion.

This puts the focus on the third aspect of implications, i.e. the importance of African leaders for peace and security. After all, and with regard to crisis prevention efforts, as well as during and after crises, 'security-focused strategies only ever bring you so far', and political strategies and a common willingness to collaborate and coordinate remain to 'count most'[22], together with 'responsible' domestic politics.

---

19   Mayall in Sharp and Wiseman (2007): 8–11.
20   Mayall in Sharp and Wiseman (2007): 10–11.
21   E.g. Evans (2008): 132–4.
22   Evans (2008): 102.

Overall, a broad discussion seems necessary about the current liberal internationalist agenda and normative basis underpinning the existing peace and security architecture and the human security notion, particularly since the end of the Cold War. After all, both 'res[t] on a solidarist rather than pluralist conception of international society'[23] of states.

As the plurality of viewpoints at the *Potsdam Spring Dialogues 2008* has shown, it seems important to accept pluralism across the international community to reduce the danger of ill-fitting policy advices and enhance the development and establishment of regional and domestic institutions for conflict prevention and resolution, instead of aiming to establish a 'world society' of states, all of which share the same normative basis.

Moreover, as has been pointed out by MacFarlane and Khong (2006), the human security concept underpinning R2P needs revisiting. So far, it is still more of a slogan than an analytical concept,[24] and clearly part of the liberal agenda. In this regard, it might be valuable – from an analytical point of view – to follow the recommendation of MacFarlane and Khong (2006) to look for a better analytical framework that comprises 'freedom from fear' as well as 'freedom from want' in order to find sustainable solutions.[25]

Challenges and Lessons Learned

In light of the academic discussions taking place and the ensuing need for further debate on the issue of the emerging African Security Architecture and R2P, this volume offers a more detailed analysis of the outstanding challenges, prospects, and successes of the framework.

The next two chapters provide a broader overview of the African Security Architecture. In particular Chapter 2 compares the integration methods used by the AU and the EU, with a particular focus on security issues. The author, Siegmar Schmidt, argues that the federalist integration method chosen by the AU is not sustainable in the environment it functions, and that the Union itself does not have the broad support of the population, but remains an elite oriented institution. Schmidt contends that the lack of leadership and structural deficits created by the AU integration process negatively impact on the creation of an African security infrastructure even though peace and security were at the forefront when the AU was created, following several large-scale conflicts such as Rwanda. The author suggests that identifying the faults in AU structures may lead to a reform process which will benefit the security architecture as well as the Union as a whole.

---

23   Mayall in: Sharp and Wiseman (2007): 11.
24   MacFarlane and Khong (2006): 242.
25   MacFarlane and Khong (2006): 240–42.

In Chapter 3 Jakkie Cilliers provides an overview of the Peace and Security Architecture of the African Union. Cilliers argues that Africans have increasingly engaged in peacekeeping on their continent after the 1994 genocide in Rwanda. He points to the encouraging decrease in the number of wars and greater prosperity and stability many states in the region have shown. The author highlights the AU Peace and Security Committee as an organ with major achievements; however he also outlines the African Union's tendency to rhetoric and policy production over implementation. The chapter provides a short overview of mechanisms such as the Panel of the Wise, the Continental Early Warning System, and a more in-depth analysis of the African Standby Force.

Lack of state capacity, coordination, resources, and the Union's unwillingness to confront fellow leaders among others, means that Africa has not operationalized its peace and security architecture. However the author notes that progress has been made, and recommends further integration between the AU and UN as the way forward.

The following three chapters focus more on R2P and international interventions. The chapter by Ebo and Powell discusses Security Sector Reform (SSR) in the context of the changes in understanding of SSR in recent years from focusing primarily on state security to an increased focus on human security. The chapter outlines the role of the AU and UN, their concept of SSR, and the potential for both organizations to complement each other and partner on security sector reform in Africa. The authors recognize the challenges inherent in SSR, including its multidimensional character, the oft-criticized lack of national ownership, and its broad scope. However, the strategic partnership between the UN and the AU seems to hold the promise of a mutually beneficial outcome in tackling those challenges.

The chapter by Gaenzle and Grimm provides a detailed overview of EU involvement in and support for the emerging security architecture in Africa. The authors note the historical and economic ties between Africa and Europe, as well as the EU's unprecedented interest in African security both financially and in terms of troop support. The African Peace Facility as well as the Instrument for Stability are briefly discussed, both of which have provided substantial funding and streamlining strategic responses to stabilize conditions in times of both emerging conflict and peace. Gaenzle and Grimm argue that the EU security structures have become an example for newly forming African mechanisms. However, they also caution that overly westernized models may not meet the approval of African stakeholders and a balance will need to be found.

The following chapter by John Siebert discusses in great detail the role of IGAD in the African Security architecture and R2P. Although the author argues that IGAD does not subscribe to the traditional principles that many of the organizations founded after the AU do, it has developed in its own right, in tandem with the various policies that have resulted in R2P. Although the IGAD founding agreement cites non-interference and preservation of state sovereignty, the organization has take steps toward recognizing state responsibility to protect its citizens. While IGAD remains weak in the African security architecture, it is participating, with the continued support of international donors.

Chapters 7, 8, 9, and 10 feature case studies, with the first two focusing on Burundi, and the others on Liberia and Darfur respectively. Chapter 7 outlines the complexities of a peacekeeping mission involving both the UN and a regional organization such as the AU. Curtis and Nibigirwe discuss the relative success of the AU and UN missions to Burundi, while also providing a detailed analysis of the various dilemmas and challenges of coordinating peacekeeping activities across institutions and forming hybrid missions.

Among the main challenges listed, the African Union Mission to Burundi was plagued by ongoing violence, dealt with multiple ceasefire agreements, and suffered from lack of funding. The authors note that the Mission failed in its DDR mandate: however, it succeeded in stabilizing the situation and preparing for groundwork for the deployment of a UN mission. Furthermore it ensured the security of various Burundian leaders returning from exile. ONUB, on the other hand, oversaw a largely peaceful electoral process, which was very well received. Overall the authors argue that peacekeeping missions have unpredictable effects, and Burundi in particular was heavily dependent on the intervention of South Africa.

Youssef Mahmoud focuses on some of the lessons that can be gleaned from the partnership between the African Union, the United Nations, the Regional Peace Initiative and the Facilitation for Burundi. The author acknowledges the challenges in the partnerships, as well as the still precarious situation in Burundi. He also notes, however, that the determination and engagement of the African counterparts in particular, with the support of the UN, has resulted in undeniable progress. Among the key difficulties encountered the chapter outlines the significance of national ownership of the process and the time this consumes, the difficult balance between speedy reaction times and adherence to UN protocols, integration of the various efforts, as well as a focus on building sustainable peace.

The chapter by Jaye and Pokoo details the trials evident in Liberia's security sector reform processes. Focusing on the unique history of the country, as well as the elements common in so many other African states, the authors discuss the partial success of the DDR process as well as its challenges and lessons learned. Among others, the chapter proposes that although the process contributed to the peace and stability of the country, it remained unfinished, leaving many ex-combatants without tools to reintegrate into their communities. Furthermore, the lack of coordination between agencies involved meant that the mechanisms were underprepared and lacked clarity distinguishing the various elements of the process. An additional issue of local ownership and resources was also identified as in many of the other chapters in this volume.

In her chapter Ayesha Kajee focuses on Darfur, the key issues pertaining to the conflict, such as historical marginalization, political pressures, ethnicity, as well as international factors. Within this context Kajee explores the various peacekeeping interventions, including AMIS and later UNAMID. She also touches upon the issues of the International Criminal Court, which continues to be a controversial element which arguably will influence the delicate situation in Darfur. The author concludes by noting that few of the employed mechanisms have been successful, and suggests several next steps for the international community, including support for a deferral of the ICC indictment of Bashir, provision of funds and equipment to UNAMID, and actively support the implementation of the CPA, among others.

Finally the volume concludes with two chapters that provide lessons learned and policy recommendations on the issue of operationalization of the African Standby Force and accountability and oversight mechanisms. The chapter by Franke details the concepts behind, and current state of, the African Standby Force (ASF). The author argues that the ASF, Functioning as a rapid reaction force, has been considered in similar forms for decades, but is only now becoming a reality. As the force is operationalized challenges remain due to the decentralized nature of the body, which is spread across the various regions of the continent. As noted in the chapter by Schmidt, Franke also acknowledges the overall structural issues inherent in the AU Commission which result in challenges for the security force.

And finally, Chapter 12 identifies the struggle for public accountability at a global level, especially in the context of the Responsibility to Protect (R2P) doctrine. The author notes that without accountability we cannot be sure that the peace and security goals established for countries in conflict are in line with the needs of people affected by the conflict. Furthermore, the involvement of the international community, often through various regional organizations in an ad hoc fashion, risks promoting political goals of individual institutions ahead of international legal standards. Lack of accountability to global organizations such as the United Nations, as well as the public and civil society, means that there is no oversight ensuring contradictory activities are eliminated or corrupt organizations are held in check. The chapter concludes that currently peace and security governance does not live up to democratic standards due to the lack of public accountability.

The author recommends that global and regional organization, as well as governments and multilateral institutions establish clear accountability procedures; that parliaments focus on strengthening and increasing their roles as oversight mechanisms; and that governments and multilateral institutions raise awareness on the importance of accountability among their own staff, parliamentarians, and civil society.

Bibliography

Acharya, Amitav: Developing Countries and the Emerging World Order. Security and Institutions. In: Fawcett, Louise (2000): *The Third World Beyond the Cold War. Continuity and Change* (Oxford: Oxford University Press): 78–98.

Evans, Gareth (2008): *The Responsibility to Protect. Ending Mass Atrocity Crimes Once and For All.* (Washington, DC: Brookings Institution Press).

Fayemi, Kayode (2004): Governing Insecurity in Post-Conflict States: The Case of Sierra Leone and Liberia. In: Bryden Alan and Haenggi, Heiner (eds) (2004): *Reform and Reconstruction of the Security Sector.* (Available at http://se2.dcaf. ch/serviceengine/FileContent?serviceID=21&fileid=B0EA7833-62AD-2215-99BF-182ADF9F413A&lng=en.)

Guttali, Shalmali (2005): The Politics of Post-war/Post-conflict Reconstruction. In: *Development*, 48 (2005): 73–81.

International Commission on Intervention and State Sovereignty (ICISS) (2001): *The Responsibility to Protect: The Report of the International Commission on Intervention and State Sovereignty* (Ottawa: International Development Research Centre).

Kaul, Inge (2008): *Bye-bye Westphalian State; Hello Intermediary State – Why Fair Multilateralism Matters* (Online Publication, Berlin 2008).

MacFarlane, Stephen Neil and Khong, Yuen Foong (2006): *Human Security and the UN. A Critical History* (Bloomington: Indiana University Press).

Malone, David M. (2004): *The UN Security Council. From the Cold War to the 21st Century* [a project of the International Peace Academy] (Boulder, Colorado: Rienner).

Mayall, James (2007): Introduction. In: Sharp, Paul and Wiseman, Geoffrey (2007): *The Diplomatic Corps as an Institution of International Society* (Basingstoke, Hampshire: Palgrave Macmillan).

Samkange, Stanlake J.T.M. (2002): African Perspectives on Intervention and State Sovereignty. In: *African Security Review*, Vol. 1, No. 1: 21–34.

Scholte, Jan Aart (2002): *Civil Society and Global Finance* (London: Routledge).

Stiglitz, Joseph (2003): Globalization and Development. In: Held, David and Koenig-Archibugi, Mathias (2003): *Taming Globalization. Frontiers of Governance* (Cambridge: Polity).

Thakur, Ramesh C. (2006): *The United Nations, Peace and Security: From Collective Security to the Responsibility to Protect* (Cambridge: Cambridge University Press).

UNDP Human Development Report (1994): *New Dimensions of Human Security* (New York: UN).

Chapter 2

Through the Lens of European Integration Theory: African Peace and Security Architecture as a Framework in Transition

Siegmar Schmidt

Introduction

The aim of this chapter is to discuss the path of African Union (AU) integration[1] against the background of experiences from the European integration process. My intention is to bring integration theory back into a largely under-theorized debate. Insights from integration theory and experiences from integration processes in other geographical spheres can enlighten our understanding of the path of the AU. The limited space available in this volume and its overall direction does not allow for a comprehensive systematic comparison. Therefore, the findings of this chapter should be regarded as tentative hypotheses and an invitation for further discussion.

The chapter starts with a brief overview of the history and characteristics of the AU with emphasis on the AU right to intervene. A brief comparison to the European Union (EU) during the Balkan wars follows. The lion's share of this chapter compares the EU and AU integration logic and the different sets of institutions and decision-making structures. The central hypothesis is that the AU chose a federal type of integration but lacks the preconditions for realizing this ambitious approach. The members' reluctance to grant power to supranational institutions, the lack of political coherence and the rather vague consensus on norms produce several grave deficits which hamper the building of an effective institution. In fact, the AU is largely an elite project and lacks broad support. One example of a prematurely built and ill-designed institutional component of the African Union is the Pan-African Parliament (PAP) that was established in March 2004, reflecting the 'vision to provide a common platform for African peoples and their grass-roots organizations'.[2] An even more ambivalent case concerning design and build-up is the AU Commission. The absence of committed leadership is an

---

1   This chapter does not discuss the various African regional arrangements and the difficulties of integrating them into a continent-wide institutional framework.

2   See the website of the Pan-African Parliament under <http://www.pan-african-parliament.org/> accessed on 10 November 2009.

additional deficit which could postpone institution-building further. Overall, these structural deficits and lack of leadership slow the AU integration process, thereby hampering progress in the process of building an African security architecture.

Therefore, this chapter can, on the one side, be understood as a warning against unrealistically high hopes and expectations concerning an African Peace and Security Architecture. On the other side, the identification of current deficits might offer the chance for reform. In particular, stronger ties with civil society and, most importantly, the formation of an avant-garde group of like-minded states committed to regional integration, could increase the likelihood of necessary African security architecture reform.

From the Organization of African Unity (OAU) to the AU

For a long time, the issues of state security and human security[3] were neglected by regional and continent-wide African institutions as well as external powers. On the one hand, during the Cold War era (i.e. until the end of the 1980s), traditional state-centred security concepts were obsessed with strategic interests; on the other hand, African institutions and governments rejected any form of conflict intervention for principle reasons: the main aims of the OAU were to promote the unity and solidarity of the member states and act as a collective voice for the African continent. In addition, the OAU tried (unsuccessfully) to keep African states from being entangled in international wars. The focal point of activity was in fact the struggle against colonialism in the form of the so-called settler regimes in Zimbabwe, South Africa, Namibia and (up to the mid-1970s) Angola and Mozambique and the preservation and protection of existing borders. Although most borders in Africa are artificial products of colonialism, the newly sovereign states and the OAU jealously guarded the inherited borders by refusing to accept any secessionist tendencies (e.g. during the Biafra war 1967–70). Any removal of borders was regarded as dangerous for the stability of African regimes and states, even if some of the borders were, at least from an economic point of view, dysfunctional and hindered trade, in particular in West Africa.

Due to a combination of factors, such as the historically shallow stateness[4] and in most cases ill-designed development strategies – by African governments and donors – and poor governance, most African states remained. Moreover, after

---

3   The UN promotes a concept of human security that offers a much broader understanding of security than the traditional understanding of security which focuses heavily on military security. Human security includes issues of access to health facilities and education, as well as the absence of domestic violence and food security, in particular for vulnerable groups. Concerning the relevance of the concept for Africa, see related articles in the *African Security Review*, vol. 16, no. 2, June 2007.

4   The condition of shallow stateness refers to feudal states with limited control over territory, and weak central administrations.

the end of the Cold War the continent lost its strategic importance; Sub-Saharan Africa became increasingly marginalized in international relations, especially in the global economy,[5] with the exception of some resource rich countries such as Nigeria and South Africa, which are more integrated into the world economy. At the same time, a number of extremely violent conflicts (e.g. Zaire, Sierra Leone, Liberia, Rwanda), some of which were fuelled by the increase of commodity prices, affected probably 20 per cent of Africans directly or indirectly in 2000 according to estimates.[6] The threat of becoming a marginalized continent and the destabilization of states and regions as a result of intra-state wars spreading to neighbouring states were some of the most pressing challenges of the 1990s, alongside the classic questions of how to overcome underdevelopment and poverty. To reintegrate the continent into the global economy and to draw new attention (and aid) from Western countries, enlightened African leaders launched the New Partnership for Africa's Development (NEPAD) in 2001,[7] and they replaced the OAU with the AU in 2002. By the time the new millennium had arrived, African leaders had accepted that the OAU was unable to deal with Africa's most pressing problems such as internal wars and the erosion of states' steering capacities leading in some cases to state failure. The new continent-wide cooperative institutions of the AU can be interpreted as 'tool[s] for the continent to face the "multifaceted challenges" posed by globalization'.[8]

Although there are many similarities between the OAU and AU, the AU is not the OAU without an O. There are fundamental differences between the organizations.[9] The set of institutions of the AU is much more differentiated and includes a parliament and civil society representation. This is in marked contrast to the OAU which did not establish any institutions for participation of the African peoples. In addition, the AU agenda is much more ambitious and incorporates issues of good governance, democracy and human rights. Also, the AU has given priority to the peace and security field, long ignored by the OAU which only as late as 1993 had installed a Mechanism for Conflict Resolution. This Mechanism led to some security related efforts in the form of conflict mediation, or fact-finding and observer missions (e.g. in Burundi, Mozambique, Guinea, Lesotho, Eritrea).[10] The focus was clearly on soft instruments such as diplomacy; the military dimension was largely excluded.

---

5   Sub-Saharan Africa's share in international trade is around 2 per cent.

6   See Department for International Development (DFID) (2001): 1.

7   NEPAD is widely regarded as an extensive development programme aiming at economic reform and a new partnership with industrialized northern hemisphere countries. The centrepiece of NEPAD is the African Peer Review Mechanism (APRM), a voluntary self-monitoring system to improve governance. Currently, 30 countries have become members of the APRM.

8   Makinda and Okumu (2008): 35.

9   For a comparison see Mwanasali (2008).

10   There is still no systematic evaluation of these missions available.

However, following the disaster of the US led UN-intervention in Somalia in the early 1990s, which resulted in Western powers' retreat from the continent, and still under the impression of the genocide in Rwanda in 1994, African states were left with no alternative other than to take up responsibility for peace and security. Therefore, security issues were of central importance to the AU from the very onset. The most striking difference between the OAU and the AU lies in their principles and aims. In in marked contrast to the OAU, the AU reflects a radical departure from the principle of non-interference.

The AU – a New Beginning for Africa

We have the privilege to be witnesses of a revolution in Africa. It is both a revolution in thinking and in acting. Compared to its predecessor, the AU reveals a historically unprecedented progress. Indeed, the AU means a clear departure from the past in many respects. At the heart of the new thinking lies the curtailment of state sovereignty, one pillar of the system of Westphalia which emerged after 1648, spreading from Europe across the globe and introducing the nation-state as the most important actor in international relations.

The founding document of the AU, the Constitutive Act of 11 July 2000, defines a wide range of aims: promotion of peace, stability and security, guarantee of territorial integrity, sovereignty and interdependence.[11] These aims are very much in line with the macro-theories of international relations, i.e. realism and neo-realism. According to these theories, states first and foremost seek their survival in an anarchic system of states in which states are the only actors guaranteeing security. From this perspective, borders are sacrosanct. But Article 4 of the Constitutive Act breaks with this classic understanding of international relations and the role of the state in giving the AU the right to intervene 'in respect of grave circumstances, namely war crimes, genocide and crimes against humanity'.[12] Or, in the words of the first AU Peace and Security Commissioner Said Djinni: 'we are replacing the principle of non-interference with the principle of non-indifference'.[13] In 2004, Article 4 of the Constitutive Act was amended, now also giving the AU the right to intervene in cases of serious threats to the legitimate order of states. In comparison with the OAU and other regional or international organizations, such as the Organization of American States (OAS), the AU Article 4 provisions are currently the most far-reaching. No other organization has given itself such a mandate, nor can a similar principle be found in the statutes of any other international organization, not even the UN Charter, according to which it is up to the Security Council to identify (on a case-by-case basis) which threats to international security and peace necessitate an intervention. Therefore, much

---

11   See Constitutive Act of the African Union (2000), Art. 4 (a–k).
12   See Constitutive Act of the African Union (2000), Art. 4 h.
13   Cited in *Business Day* (Johannesburg), 25 May 2004.

scholarly and political attention focuses on Article 4 of the AU Constitutive Act and its provision of a legal justification for intervention; most observers regard it as a watershed in African thinking about security. There is no doubt about the revolutionary character of the AU's curtailment of state sovereignty, but revolutions can fail. Historians can name many failed attempts to replace an existing order by a new regime, or new ideas that never were put into practice.

The Quest for Security in Africa and Europe

Eight years after the founding of the AU in Durban, South Africa in 2002, and six years after the Peace and Security Council (PSC) was launched in 2004, it is still not clear whether the AU can cope with the tremendous challenges to peace and security in Africa. Meanwhile, the euphoria that prevailed in academic and political circles about the new beginning in African continent-wide integration has disappeared and has been replaced by a more realistic and sometimes even pessimistic perspective. Most observers point to the AU's limited capacities, shortage of funds, and lack of experience in peace-keeping and peace enforcement operations. For instance, Appiah-Mensah commented on the African Union Mission in Sudan (AMIS): 'From its inception, AMIS's operations have been characterised by persistent shortfalls in logistics and funding.'[14] Despite these serious impediments, the AU took action and intervened in a number of the most violent and difficult conflicts.[15] AU missions were sent to Burundi, Darfur (Sudan) and Somalia. While the AU-led Burundi mission managed to maintain peace, and can be described as a success, the Somali mission suffered from a lack of troops and a weak mandate. However, both missions clearly underlined that the AU was not a paper tiger and that a new security actor has emerged in Africa.

The experiences with AU peace enforcement missions are mixed. As this volume reveals, there are successes but also many lessons to be learned. Compared to peace-enforcement in Europe, notably during the Yugoslav wars, it can be said that although the AU missions were originally planned as peacekeeping forces they were courageous in the sense that the troops fought bravely against well-equipped and government-supported militias (e.g. Darfur).

This is remarkable because the centrepiece of the African security architecture, the Peace and Security Council (PSC) and the military dimension (i.e. the African Stand-By Force, regional brigades) are still in their infancy.[16] EU member states, on the contrary, despite having obtained the necessary resources, logistics and

---

14   Appiah-Mensah (2006): 8.

15   As Makinda and Okumu (2008: 39) correctly observed, the focus of the AU lies on conflict management rather than on the prevention of conflict or on post-conflict peace building. This means that civil society could become less incorporated.

16   For an overview about the institutions and its context see: van Nieuwkerk (2006).

troops, proved unable and partly unwilling to stop the most brutal war in Bosnia where massive human rights violations, including mass rapes, cost approximately 200,000 lives between 1992 and 1995.[17] From a European perspective, it was humiliating that it was a North Atlantic Treaty Organization (NATO) intervention led by the US that brought the fighting to an end in 1995. But even the debacle in Bosnia did not lead to the development of adequate peace enforcement mechanisms and strategies. The Kosovo crisis in 1999,[18] with mass killings and ethnic cleansing, demonstrated again the helplessness of the EU against large-scale atrocities, and the US had to step in once again for an intervention which was not based on an explicit UN Security Council Resolution. The negative experience in Kosovo pushed the EU to develop both conceptual frameworks and capacities. The European Defence and Security Policy (EDSP)[19] gained momentum and a military and civil infrastructure was established in Brussels despite criticism from the US, which feared that NATO would lose its central role as the sole security agency in Europe. The EU also announced in 1999 the build up of a 60,000 troop strong European rapid reaction force.[20] The EU established 14 multinational Battle Groups for emergency situations, i.e. in case of acute danger to the population in form of mass killings or genocide. Each of them has 1,500 combat troops and can be deployed on short notice in approximately two weeks.[21] In 2004, the EU took over the NATO Stabilization Force (SFOR) mission in Bosnia and Herzegovina which then became the European Union Force Operation 'Althea' (EUFOR – Operation ALTHEA). At the time of writing, over 10,000 European

------

17   The violence started after the Bosnian population overwhelmingly voted for independence in a referendum. Bosnian Serb militias supported by the Serb army pursued strategy of 'ethnic cleansing', killings, torture and mass rapes were systematically used to lead to an exodus of Bosnians from their homes.

18   Before 1990, Kosovo was an autonomous province of Yugoslavia, with a 90 per cent majority of ethnic Albanians (10 per cent Serbs). In mid-1998, Serbian militias started to attack villages in Kosovo. After a guerilla movement was defeated by the Serb army, the expulsions and killings started. Massive NATO air strikes against Serbia began in March 1999. Finally, Serbia agreed to a peace plan for Kosovo in June 1999 and a semi-sovereign state Kosovo emerged.

19   The EDSP consists of different institutions with the Political and Security Committee (PSC) as a permanent body. In cooperation with additional military institution the PSC is able to conduct military operations, if the European Council has decided so. See Salmon (2005).

20   The Rapid Reaction force consists of troops from the member states. Sixty thousand troops should be deployable in case of a crisis within 60 days and of maintaining a presence for one year at maximum. The national governments decide on military actions. Due to technical (lack of capabilities) and political obstacles (resistance from some states which prefer NATO) the Rapid Reaction Force has still not reached its intended capacities.

21   See http://www.consilium.europa.eu/uedocs/cmsUpload/MILITARY%20CAPAB ILITY%20COMMITMENT%20CONFERENCE%2022.11.04.pdf, accessed 9 November 2009.

troops are deployed in former Yugoslav countries, and 17,000 NATO troops[22] are deployed in the tiny semi-sovereign state of Kosovo with only around 2 million inhabitants. The European Union experiences in the Balkans[23] not only reveal the enormous challenges which accompany peace enforcement operations in general but also show that there is no guarantee that states will learn from past failures and/or change policies subsequently or in a timely fashion. The EU reaction to the succession wars in collapsing Yugoslavia between 1992 and 1999 was a case of too little, too late and inadequate instruments. That is, in the case of the Balkan wars, diplomacy and even economic sanctions did not work. To make matters worse, the endless diplomatic conferences provided the Serb militia with the opportunity to continue with their operations and to conquer large parts of Bosnia. The three years between 1992 and 1995 clearly revealed that diplomacy without a credible threat of force cannot stop war, especially if the political and military leaders calculate that violence is the most successful instrument to reach their aims.

In the case of the AU, it is too early to judge whether the PSC and thereby the Heads of States and Governments will take the necessary steps to make African peace-enforcement more effective.

The AU and EU Paths of Integration in Comparative Perspective – Some Tentative Findings

The main hypothesis of this chapter is the following: the AU's difficulties with peace-keeping and peace-enforcement consist, on the one hand, of an overall shortage of resources and a lack of experience.[24] On the other hand, there are structural reasons which are deeply engrained in the AU institutional architecture and the logic and mode of its federal type of integration. The most serious problem lies not in the federalist approach per se but in the absence of necessary preconditions for a workable federalist structure: many difficulties and the malfunctioning of some central AU institutions are the result of an intergovernmental logic paired with weak institutions, an unrealistic time frame, a heterogeneous membership with little consensus on core values, and an absence of committed leadership.

To highlight the structural characteristics and deficits of the AU, a comparison with the EU helps to identify shortcomings and achievements.

---

22 To compare: the UN Mission into the Democratic Republic of the Congo (DRC) (MONUC) has only slightly more troops for a country with over 40 million people, i.e. about eight times larger than Germany.
23 See Blockmans (2004).
24 For more information on the PSC, see Cilliers and Sturman (2004).

The Time Dimension

European integration started with six states signing the Treaties of Rome in 1957. These founding states – Italy, France, Germany, the Netherlands, Belgium, and Luxembourg – started a sector-wide cooperation as early as in 1952 with the European Coal and Steel Community (ECSC).[25] The European Community (EC) increased its membership in five rounds of enlargement (in 1973, 1981 (1986), 1995, 2004, and 2007) from six to 27 states.[26] Five decades of integration established a dense network of relations between political leaders, bureaucracies, and the civil societies of European member states. The centuries' long hostility and mistrust among Europeans was gradually replaced by trust. The European institutions in Brussels and in other countries worked as an agency for Europeanization in the sense that cooperation was learned,[27] and communication became routine and led to a shared understanding about the necessity of a united Europe. It took 22 years to replace the European Parliamentary Assembly, which had consisted of delegates from the member states' parliaments, with a directly elected European Parliament (EP) in 1979. Thirty-five years after the European Community was born, the Maastricht Treaty in 1992 gave birth to a (still relatively weak, because decisions need unanimity) European Foreign Policy. The Common Market[28] was completed at the beginning of the 1990s and the Euro became the single currency in 15 countries by 2002.

Against these historical experiences of the relatively similar European countries, the AU time frames are overambitious if not utopian. It will take time for AU institutions to build trust, learn cooperation, and socialize its members to certain principles, norms and values. An example of an overambitious time frame is the premature founding of PAP.[29]

Although political visions are needed to motivate actors by defining the overall direction, they must be anchored in reality or they will not be taken seriously, yielding a loss of credibility.

---

25   The ECSC placed the production of coal and steel, the most important resources building up military forces, under a common High Authority. This supranational institution successfully controlled the German military potential and enhanced trust.

26   In 1973, the UK, Ireland and Denmark became EU members; in 1981, Greece and Spain, and Portugal in 1986; in 1995, Austria, Sweden and Finland; in 2004, Poland, Hungary, Czech Republic, Slovakia, Malta, Cyprus, Latvia, Lithuania and Estonia; and in 2007, Romania and Bulgaria joined the EU.

27   In addition, the institutional design is characterized by checks and balances between supranational and intergovernmental institutions. Many decisions require extremely high majorities or unanimity and make consensus inevitable. See also: Hanf (2007).

28   The Common Market was completed in the early 1990s. It allows the *freedom of movement of people, goods, services, and capital* between all 27 members, with only few exceptions and an transitional agreement with respect to labour migration.

29   For more information, see below and Hugo (2008).

A Federal Type of Integration Based on Shaky Ground

The AU integration is following the federalist[30] path of integration. The federalist theory of integration[31] makes the following core arguments about the European integration process:

- the integration process starts with a grand design, an overall framework such as a founding treaty or a constitution;
- a federal type of integration is based on the common will of states and peoples sharing a leading ideology or vision to form a federation;
- the most important actors are individual statesmen and the peoples which should not only be included to provide legitimacy for the process but who should also foster it;
- in a federation, a Union government is responsible for a common foreign and defence policy but the subsidiary principle gives member states the right to act autonomously in most spheres. In this regard, a federation is a voluntary union with a supranational[32] government in certain fields. The federal government must recognize and accommodate different interests, identities and cultures;
- the logic of integration can be characterized as a 'function follows form – approach'. The integration steps fill in the overall framework step by step.

Both the Pan-Africanism of the first Ghanaian President Kwame Nkrumah[33] and the AU path of integration fit into the federal model of integration. Against the background of Africa's diversity a federal model is an adequate structure for the diversity of African states and peoples. The AU Constitutive Act and the many protocols establishing the various AU institutions define the framework for further integration. Whether concrete steps are being taken depends on the willingness of African Heads of State to give up or to pool sovereignty. Currently, there are no signs that African leaders are willing to give substantial powers to supranational

---

30 The discussion about federalism is blurred by the contradicting use of the term: especially in the UK public discourse. Federalism is often misunderstood as a process of political unification, even centralization. This chapter shares the common understanding of federalism as a specific form of political order and rule, as a way to diffuse power between central government and regional units.

31 For an overview on different theories of integration, see Diez and Wiener (2004); on federalism, see Burgess (2004).

32 Supranational means that decisions can be taken independently; there is no veto for governments of the member states but political lobbying to influence these decisions.

33 See Nkrumah (1963: 216–22). Nkrumah envisaged a continental government with a common market and currency and an African defence policy. Libya's leader Muammar al-Gaddafi borrowed heavily from Nkrumah's ideas. They were an impressive manifestation of pan-Africanism but remained vague on concrete steps to be taken. He also underestimated the significance of European integration by arguing it was doomed to fail.

institutions (see below). Rather, African leaders approved and even embraced the federal model because it guaranteed that the nation-states would not lose control over the extent of cooperation.

One disadvantage of federalism in general is that there are no immediate benefits. The existence of an overall framework in form of a constitution has to be filled with concrete steps – such as, for example, a common market or a tariff union – before states and societies will gain from it. Benefits from economic integration are easier to receive in case of a neo-functionalist integration path. Accordingly, integration is understood as a gradual process, starting in more uncontroversial areas and initiating a functional spill-over to other areas that also include political aspects. European integration followed this path most of the time. The benefits of a common market, of guaranteed prices for agricultural products, among others, created support and legitimacy for the European integration process.[34] Although European integration was for decades more an elite project than people-driven, the benefits of integration created a 'permissive consensus'[35] among the people, a kind of low level of interest and general trust in the integration process.

The United States of Africa?

The European Union is still avoiding discussing the final point of integration. The so-called finalité-discussion emerged in the wake of the discussion over the Constitutional Treaty[36] after 2001 and revealed in the end how much the member states differ on fundamental questions. There is no consensus among the member states about the aim of the integration, whether it should be a United States of Europe, a loose federation, or a continuation of the present status that reveals both elements of statehood and a cooperative federation. Similarly, in the case of the African Union the Constitutive Act does not give a clear answer to the final destination of the process. There are two main competing visions about the final point of African integration. The first formula takes up Nkrumah's vision of the United States of Africa.

The most outspoken advocate of this idea is Libya's leader Muammar al-Qaddafi.[37] From his perspective, the formation of a single African state would put an end to the division of the continent and is therefore regarded as a precondition for Africa pursuing its interests successfully in a globalized world. With the

34   An advantage for European integration had been the dominance of the US in the security field after European efforts failed in 1954. Although Europe was dependent on US security export, it could concentrate its energy on other fields.

35   Lindberg and Scheingold (1970).

36   The Constitutional Treaty was negotiated by a European Convention representing delegates from the member states and members of the national parliaments. It was adopted in 2004 by the Heads of States and Governments and rejected by referendum in France and the Netherlands in 2004.

37   See for the discussion Mwanasali (2008): 41.

Libyan leader becoming the Chairman of the AU in February 2009, the idea of the United States of Africa will continue to be included on the agenda. The problem of this vision lies mainly in the fact that neither a concrete programme of action nor a clear institutional design exist. In addition, most African leaders have been reluctant even to discuss the idea and there is not much response outside of academic circles. The realization of such a far-reaching formula is therefore very unlikely in the foreseeable future.

The less utopian, more realistic vision is represented by former South African President Thabo Mbeki, who became the architect of NEPAD[38] and the AU[39] in their formative years. His vision can be summarized in the words of Makinda and Okumu (2008): 'Mbeki's mission was to create a continent ruled by like-minded African democrats who shared his goals of competitive markets, technological advancement, progressing economy, and industrious populations.'[40] This approach found acceptance among Africa's leaders and was translated into NEPAD and the AU institutional design. It is an inclusive approach because membership is open for all African states and governments could choose the depth of integration by signing different protocols, and/or become a member of the African Peer Review Mechanism (APRM[41]), or stay away. The inclusiveness of the AU has been realized, with the exception of Morocco, which criticized the AU's position on the West-Sahara conflict and did not become a member. The inclusive approach of the AU brought together not only states with different cultural background or levels of development but also states with different political systems.

Out of the 38 states from Sub-Saharan Africa, 22 are more or less democracies, 13[42] classify as autocracies, and three are regarded as failed states, according to the Bertelsmann Transformation Index (BTI) which covers the political and economic developments.[43] In contrast, the EU has always been a 'club of democracies'. As

---

38   NEPAD was born in 2001 in Abuja, Nigeria. It consists of numerous ambitious development aims and proposes a new partnership between the rich North and Africa. As preconditions for development, good governance, peace and security, and respect for human rights are defined. In 2002, it became the development programme of the AU.

39   Mbeki's ideological starting point had been the idea of Africa's renaissance, see Landsberg (2007); and Olivier (2003).

40   Makinda and Okumu (2008): 33.

41   The APRM is a voluntary self-review mechanism of African states. The main idea is to identify achievements and deficits through a national dialogue including civil society and to initiate reforms. So far 29 African states have become members. The NEPAD review teams, visiting the countries under review, steer the whole process.

42   The BTI defines several subtypes of the general categories democracy and autocracy. The result of the 2007–2009 round will be published in November, see www.bertelsmann-transformation-index.de/16.0.html?&L=1. The index covers 125 transformation and developing countries. The ranking and classification is based on country reports. The download of the approx. 20 pages long reports (in English) is free of charge.

43   There are also a number of fragile states (e.g. Chad, Central African Republic etc.) which are too weak to implement major reforms.

early as in 1961, the European Parliamentary Assembly unanimously adopted the report of Willi Birkelbach, a German politician of the Social Democratic Party, defining democratic principles and the respect for human rights as a precondition for the accession to the EC. The provision that only democratic states are members of the Union became one of the founding ideas of an EU-identity. Greece, Spain, Portugal and the East-Central European countries had to become full fledged democracies before they could become members of the EC and EU respectively.

The heterogeneity of the AU members means that the basic consensus on values and norms is much weaker than in the case of the EU. The lack of a general consensus on basic values explains the passivity of the AU in the Zimbabwe case. The AU handed the Zimbabwe case over to the South African Development Community (SADC) and South Africa, but failed to encourage the South African government to modify its 'quiet diplomacy' approach which proved unsuccessful, prolonging the suffering of the people of Zimbabwe for years.

The practice in many states contradicts the values enshrined in the AU Constitutive Act and the NEPAD founding document. This may affect the credibility of the AU within Africa and on the international stage.

African Integration as a Top-down Process

Among the preconditions for a federation is the participation of the people. It provides the integration process with legitimacy and support and reduces mistrust against governance structures remote from the peoples' daily reality. At the very onset of European integration, a pro-European integration movement, the European Federalist Movement, lobbied actively for a united Europe. The members of the federalist organizations[44] belonged to different political camps but they shared the basic assumptions that lasting peace and the reconstruction of Europe would only be possible in a united Europe. Once the European integration process started, the Federalist Movement lost momentum. Ernst Haas has demonstrated that organized interest groups played a highly significant role for the European integration process.[45] There is no similar development in the African integration process. The lack of support from African societies is one of the weakest elements in the current African integration process. The African integration process both on the continental and regional level are top-down processes. The AU is widely perceived as an elite project.

In many African countries, AU and NEPAD are only known by a small portion of the population, mostly urban elites. As empirical surveys reveal, the low awareness of African integration and the lack of will to support the integration

---

44   The federalist movement still exists with 17,000 members in Germany alone, but has lost momentum, see for further information Union of European Federalists <http://en.federaleurope.org/>, accessed 12 November 2009.http://en.federaleurope.org/.

45   Haas (1958).

process is even common among the elites.[46] Currently, also the links between civil society and the African Union institutions are underdeveloped. In 2005, the Economic, Social and Cultural Council (ECOSOCC) met for the first time; its functions are still hampered by organizational difficulties and inadequate funding.[47] For the time being, ECOSOCC cannot fulfil its task to serve as a bridge between the people and the AU. This is also the case with regard to AU peace operations. Especially in conflict prevention and post-conflict peace building, civil society plays an important role as recent experiences demonstrate.[48] However, the potential of civil society and other non-state actors has not been recognized fully in the emerging African security architecture.

The Lack of Committed Leadership

What holds true for political processes is also true for integration processes. Both require committed leadership fostering integration by diplomatic activities or even material concessions to reluctant partners.[49] Between the 1970s and 1990s, it was the German-Franco cooperation which worked as a motor for European integration. In cases where both countries agreed on certain policies they commonly tried to lobby for their projects among the other member states. In the case of the AU, the close cooperation and even partnership between South Africa and Nigeria played a similar role at the beginning of the integration process. Nigeria and South Africa became the driving force behind core ideas of NEPAD and the AU. The leaders of both countries, Thabo Mbeki and Nigeria's former President Olusegun Obasanjo, met before important meetings and coordinated their policies to push the African integration further.[50] One example for such a successful cooperation is the establishment of the PSC with a rotating membership and without a veto.[51] Even the diplomatic services worked together and formulated common positions.

However, the axis between Nigeria and South Africa as promoters for African security came to an end when President Obasanjo stepped down after he had served his two terms in office and when Mbeki resigned after losing the intra-party fight against Jacob Zuma, the current president of South Africa. Neither Mbeki's successor Zuma, who had never shown serious interest in foreign policy, nor the new Nigerian president Umaru Yar'Adua, who came to power following highly contested and controversial elections, seem able or willing to play a leading role and push for further integration. It remains to be seen whether the current chairman

---

46   See for the first years Kotzé and Steyn (2003).

47   See Mutasa (2009).

48   Paffenholz (2010).

49   In the case of European Union integration, Germany sometimes (e.g. 1992 Maastricht Treaty) used side-payments for weaker EU members to accept the deepening of the Union.

50   Adebayo (2007): 229.

51   Landsberg (2007): 201.

of the AU, 'Brother Leader' Qaddafi can accommodate the different interests and take the integration further. The chequered diplomatic history[52] of Qaddafi, who has held his country in an iron grip for the last three decades,[53] is not promising.

The Institutional Setting of the AU and EU Compared

The set of AU institutions mirrors the EU institutional structure, as the following table shows:

Table 2.1   **Comparison between AU and EU institutions**

African Union institutions	Functional logic, Decision-making	EU institutions	Functional logic, Decision-making
Assembly of Heads of States and Governments	Intergovernmental, two-thirds majority	EU Council (Heads of States and Governments)	Intergovernmental, unanimity
Executive Council	Intergovernmental, two-thirds majority	Council of Ministers/The Council	Intergovernmental - Absolute majority - Qualified majority - Unanimity
Pan-African Parliament (PAP)	Supranational, two-thirds majority	European Parliament (EP)	Supranational, absolute majority in most cases Co-decision Veto position
The Committee of Permanent Representatives	Negotiating body	The Committee of Permanent Representatives (COREPER)	Negotiating body
African Court of Justice	Supranational, but limited responsibilities	European Court of Justice	Supranational "Guardian of the Treaties"
African Union Commission	Secretariat	European Commission	Supranational
Economic, Social and Cultural Council (ECOSOCC)	Advisory body	Economic and Social Committee	Advisory body

52   Libya's foreign policy was often unpredictable in the past because its leader, Muammar al-Qaddafi opted for an unrealistic merger with neighbouring countries believed to finance terrorist activities and terror groups across Africa and elsewhere, and tried to build up nuclear capability.

53   Many in the West and in Africa regarded Libya's leader becoming Chairman of the AU as a black day for democracy in Africa and a wrong signal.

Set of Institutions

Although the set of AU institutions mirrors the set of EU institutions, they differ greatly in their underpinning logic. While EU institutions are a mix of supranational and intergovernmental, the AU-institutions are organized along an intergovernmental logic, as the following argumentation will demonstrate.

Accordingly, and in contrast to the EU, the AU is clearly an intergovernmental organization, despite the fact that it has some supranational institutions included in its institutional setting. In comparison with the EU's supranational institutions, the AU's institutions[54] are extremely weak for two reasons: first, they are still in a process of institutionalization, whereby intergovernmental institutions, (especially the Assembly of the African Union, which comprises Heads of States and Government of the member states) dominate the political process. Second, the distinctive competencies of the different bodies, such as the PAP and the AU Commission, are not defined clearly. For example, it is not clear how the PAP should carry out its oversight function and how the legislative process will work precisely. In addition, the merger between the African Court on Human and Peoples' Rights (ACHPR) and the Court of Justice of the African Union (with limited competencies (compared to the European Court of Justice (ECJ)[55]) is still incomplete. The main reason for the delay is that there are different ideas among AU members and institutions about the role and competences of the envisaged court.[56]

The Pan-African Parliament

This point of incomplete institutions with vaguely defined competences will be made clearer by some observations about the PAP which is in Midrand, South Africa. According to the Constitutive Act and the protocol giving birth to the institution in 2004, the PAP should evolve into an institution with full legislative powers after a transitional period of five years with only advisory and consultative powers. This would have been the case in 2009. However, due to the unwillingness of political leaders to grant powers to the PAP, it remains largely powerless. Currently, there are no fixed time frames for the transitional period. As of today, the PAP cannot make laws, amend or improve old laws; it has no oversight function and no budgetary powers.[57] To make matters worse, it is not clear how the PAP

---

54   Supranational institutions can be defined as institutions capable of making decisions autonomously and even against the will of member states.

55   In the EU case, for example, the EU Commission can bring non-compliance of member states to the European Court of Justice (ECJ). The court can rule out national legislation contradicting EU law and sanction member states by fines in case they violated the Treaties.

56   See Motala (2008).

57   For an interim evaluation, see Hugo (2008).

exactly relates to other AU institutions.[58] Many resolutions stemming from the PAP and recommendations passed by the parliament have largely been ignored by the other AU institutions. Thus far, the PAP, which has many active members, serves as a broad platform for discussion fostering the exchange of views. Even if the Assembly were to delegate substantial powers to the PAP, the design of the institution will make it difficult for it to be accepted by the people and thereby to increase the Union's legitimacy.

The PAP is designed according to the senate principle, i.e. equal representation regardless of the size of the population of every country. Every country is represented by five MPs, 'whether Nigeria or the Seychelles – resulting in a democratic inequality in terms of the value of each vote of more than 1000:1'.[59] In contrast, the EU adopted a system of degressive proportionality: countries with large populaces elect more MPs than smaller countries but smaller countries are overrepresented (a German Member of the European Parliament represents approximately 800,000 citizens, a Member of Parliament (MP) from Malta only 80,000).[60] In addition, the PAP's work is hampered by a severe lack of resources. Its budget for 2007 stood at only US$6.4 million,[61] far too little for a continent-wide institution. The most serious problem for the PAP might be its structural deficit. It is hard, in fact, to imagine that non-democratically elected PAP members will hold the executive leaders accountable when they cannot do this in their own countries.[62] Direct elections of PAP members, who are currently delegates of the national organs of representation, are also hard to imagine in countries such as Eritrea and Libya where no elections have taken place so far and where only one party exists.

The current situation therefore demonstrates that the PAP is an example of a prematurely established and not thoroughly designed institution, regardless of certain achievements, such as passing resolutions and giving recommendations on the Darfur crisis, that the PAP has made in the process of constituting itself and developing workable procedures.

The AU Commission

A different development can be noticed with respect to the AU-Commission. The AU Commission consists of 11 Commissioners and the Chairperson. While the EU Commission is a supranational institution owing its loyalty to the Union as a

58   See Makinda and Okumu (2008): 47.

59   Gottschalk and Schmidt (2004): 142.

60   If there were to be an exact proportionality, countries such as Luxembourg with fewer than half a million inhabitants would hardly be represented at all.

61   Makinda and Okumu (2008): 45.

62   Hugo (2008): 9.

whole and having important functions,[63] the AU Commission obtains only modest functions.

According to the Constitutive Act (Article 20), the AU Commission is the Secretariat of the Union, a mere administrative institution. Yet, in reality the Commission developed into an executive body, even implementing peace and security policy. Makinda and Okumu (2008)[64] explain the extension of the AU Commission's power which actually go beyond the constitutional regulations as, on the one hand, due to the weakness of the PSC members to formulate and implement policies, and on the other hand, the Commission and its respective Chairpersons in particular have developed ambitions to expand their powers and strengthen the visibility of the Commission. The communication between the Commissioners and the PSC is still weak. The Commission tries also to fulfil the role as an agenda setter: the three volumes of the 2004–2007 Strategic Plan of the Commission of the African Union, published in 2004, offered a wide range of future activities and made concrete recommendations. For example, the AU Commission strongly advocated the end of the 'institutional cacophony' in the form of many overlapping regional institutions and proposed concrete measures and schedules.[65] The Assembly has widely ignored the many proposals by the Commission and other AU organs, and member states are concerned about the activities of the Commission.

The AU Commission also benefits from donor funds.[66] It receives direct financial and logistic support from the EU Commission. The EU Commission established a 'Support Programme to the African Union' in October 2006, with an amount of €55 million, to overcome the institutional weaknesses of AU institutions.[67] The emphasis of the EU Support Program lies on the support for the AU Commission. One core objective is that the AU Commission should become 'the engine of the Union and the integration process'.[68] The EU programme also includes an exchange of senior staff for a maximum of two years, similar to the Twinning-Programs which supported the accession of the Central and Eastern European candidate states up to 2004.

---

63   The EU Commission serves as a 'Guardian of the Treaties', an exclusive actor in certain policy fields (foreign economic relations, common market) as well as an initiator of legislation.

64   Makinda and Okumu (2008): 49–51.

65   See the Commission of the African Union (2007), vols 8–12.

66   See for an overview on donor funding for AU and NEPAD, Klingebiel et al. (2008).

67   See the document at http://www.africa-union.org/root/AU/Conferences/Past/2006/October/EU-AU/060828%20AU%20Supp%20Prog%20summary%5Bfinal%5D.pdf, accessed on 12 November 2009.

68   http://www.africa-union.org/root/AU/Conferences/Past/2006/October/EU-AU/060828%20AU%20Supp%20Prog%20summary%5Bfinal%5D.pdf.

Decision-making in the AU

Vast differences between the EU and the AU exist also in their decision-making structures. Decisions by both the Executive Council and the Assembly of the AU can be made by a two-thirds majority. It is remarkable that even decisions in the security field, the centrepiece of state sovereignty, can theoretically be made by two-third majorities.

In contrast, the veto right is still a core element of the European Council, and in the Council of Ministers states still have a veto on many issues. In the EU foreign policy (CFSP) decisions by majority or qualified majorities[69] are only possible in selected areas. EU defence policy decisions require unanimity in all cases of military questions (for example conflict management). The threat of a possible veto in EU foreign and defence policy makes compromises essential. As a result, should a compromise be reached, the chance that the EU member states will respect this compromise is high.

In many cases EU decisions requiring unanimity are not only time-consuming, but are often reflecting the lowest common denominator between the member states. In comparison with the EU decision-making, the AU regulations require only a two-third majority in key decisions. Theoretically, this could increase the effectiveness of its peace and security policy by making quicker decisions than is possible in the EU, where the search for a consensus, often reflecting the lowest common denominator, is the daily routine. But there are other factors which might qualify the significance of decision making by two-third majority. A public defeat by outvoting would mean that states, or Head of States, could lose face. This is difficult for every politician but especially in Africa with the high degree of personalization of politics and a more consensus oriented culture. In cases, where AU member states, especially larger states, are outvoted by a majority, it remains to be seen whether they will respect a majority decision even if they opposed it originally.

This could be the case with respect to decisions on human rights or humanitarian interventions because of the heterogeneous membership of the AU. There are no procedures in place, except for the suspension of membership, on how to deal with states that are not complying with AU decisions. An additional problem could emerge if the AU were to take a decision to intervene but lacked the necessary capacities or funds. So far, if international donors do not step in and provide the necessary resources, large-scale actions are impossible (e.g. AMIS). However, it is also possible that the AU and the donors may have different preferences.

The case of the AU and the Darfur crisis illustrates the largely theoretical nature of the progressive decision-making by a two-thirds majority. During

---

69   In cases where the European Council has established a 'Common Strategy', decisions can be made by qualified majority. However, the possibility for member states to refuse such an outcome with qualified majority remains in place (veto). In practice, it will be difficult for a state to block a decision under the framework of a Common Strategy because of informal pressure by other member states.

the negotiation process, the Sudanese government blocked the deployment of an AU force and due to the resistance of the government it took years before the deployment of UN and AU troops (AMIS Mission) was possible. The AU also failed to reach a more robust mandate. Instead of outvoting the Sudanese government, the AU tried to find a compromise, resulting in endless negotiations. There are two reasons for the reluctance to vote on the issue of Darfur/Sudan. First, the AU wanted the Sudanese government to accept the deployment of troops and thereby reduce the dangers for the AU mission. Second, it would have been too risky to vote on an intervention because it was not clear whether a two-third majority could be reached; some states could have simply abstained from voting or even voted against the mission. Overall, the scarcity of resources, which makes enforcement difficult, in combination with structural deficits such as the heterogeneous membership, will result in selective engagement, even though the principles laid down in the Constitutive Act promise something different.

Summary and Perspectives

The AU is an unprecedented experiment. Great progress has been made in the peace and security fields. Despite a severe shortage of resources and capacities the AU intervened courageously in some of the most difficult conflicts. The lack of funds and capacities means that the AU will need partners. Hybrid missions such as the one in Sudan, with all their practical problems and difficult questions of ownership and dependency, will therefore continue. The development of the African Union more broadly has not been as successful. Many institutions are still in their infancy. Besides the well-known resource and capacity problems, structural problems are responsible for the disappointing record in building strong and effective institutions and stopping the large-scale violence in the Democratic Republic of the Congo (DRC) and Darfur/Sudan.

The federal model of integration is an appropriate structure for a continent's diversity, but it is questionable whether the necessary preconditions to realize this integration path are existent. The AU lacks a common vision, there is only limited agreement on core values, most states are reluctant to strengthen supranational institutions,[70] and the people (civil society included) are largely excluded from the integration process. The grandiose programmes, inherent promises, and strong rhetoric do not match the real developments.

There is a danger that Christopher Hill's[71] dictum of an emerging capabilities-expectation gap, which he formulated for the EU at the onset of the 1990s when the Maastricht Treaty gave birth to the EU foreign and security policy, will also come true for the African integration process as a whole. The danger of that gap between

---

70   The belief in problem-solving capacities of institutions is in general much weaker in Africa than in Europe, African politics are traditionally much more personalized.

71   Hill (1993).

reality and vision could result in a loss of credibility and disappointment on the side of civil society, the donor community (with a lot of good will toward African integration), and reform-minded African governments. The current absence of an energetic and committed AU leadership could be an additional problem and postpone the integration process further. What can be done? First: the participation of civil society in the whole process is crucial for gaining legitimacy, especially because the PAP cannot act strongly. Second: more realism is needed. To overcome the structural problems, heterogeneous membership with limited agreement on core values and political reform is needed. One solution could be the formation of an avant-garde group of states moving ahead and deepening the integration process. Against the background of diversity of African states, Kwame Nkrumah noted in 1963: 'We might erect for the time being a constitutional form that could start with those states willing to create a nucleus, and leave the door open for the attachment of others as they desire to join or reach the freedom which would allow them to do so.'[72]

Bibliography

Adebajo, Adekeye, Adedeji, A. and Landsberg, Chris (eds) (2007), *South Africa in Africa. The Post-apartheid Era* (Pietermaritzburg: University of KwaZulu-Natal Press).

Adebayo, Adekeye (2007), 'South Africa and Nigeria: An Axis of Virtue?', in Adebajo et al. (eds).

African Security Review (2007), Vol. 16, No. 2, June.

Akokpari, John et al. (eds) (2008), The *African Union and its Institutions* (Johannesburg: Jacana).

Appiah-Mensah, S. (2006), 'Monitoring Fragile Ceasefires. The Challenges and Dilemmas of the Role of AMIS', ISS Paper, September 2006 (Pretoria: Institute for Security Studies).

Blockmans, Steven (2004), 'EU Conflict Prevention in the Western Balkans', in Kronenberger et al. (eds).

Burgess, Michael (2004), 'Federalism', Chapter 2 in Diez et al. (eds).

Cilliers, Jakkie and Sturman, Kathryn (2004), 'Challenges Facing the AU's Peace and Security Council', *African Security Review*, Vol. 13, No. 1, 97–104.

Commission of the African Union (2007), *2004–2007 Strategic Plan*. Vol. 2: 2004–2007 Strategic Framework.

Constitutive Act of the African Union (Lomé, Togo, 11 July 2000), http://www.au2002.gov.za/docs/key_oau/au_act.htm, accessed on 12 November 2009.

Department for International Development (DFID) (2001), *The Causes of Conflict in Sub-Saharan Africa* (London: DFID).

72 Nkrumah (1963): 220–21.

Dickow, Helga and Molt, Peter (eds) (2007), *Kulturen und Konflikt im Vergleich* [*Comparing Cultures and Conflicts*] (Baden-Baden: Festschrift for Theodor Hanf).

Diez, Thomas and Wiener, Antje (eds) (2004), *European Integration Theory* (Oxford: Oxford University Press).

Gottschalk, Keith and Schmidt, Siegmar (2004), 'The African Union and the New Partnership for Africa's Development – Strong Institutions for Weak States?', *International Politics and Society (IPG)*, No. 4, 138–58.

Haas, Ernst (1958), *The Uniting of Europe. Political, Social, and Economic Forces 1950–1957* (Stanford: Stanford University Press).

Hanf, Dominik (2007), 'The European Union: A Consensus-based Federation', in Dickow et al. (eds).

Hill, Christopher (1993), 'The Capability-Expectations Gap, or Conceptualizing Europe's International Role', *Journal of Common Market Studies*, Vol. 31, No. 3, 305–28.

Hugo, Gerhard (2008), 'The Pan-African Parliament: Is the Glass Half-full or Half-empty?', ISS Paper 168 (Pretoria: Institute for Security Studies).

Klingebiel, Stephan et al. (2008), *Donor Contributions to the Strengthening of the African Peace and Security Architecture* (Bonn: German Development Institute).

Kotzé, Hennie and Steyn, Carly (2003), 'African Elite Perspectives: AU and Nepad', Konrad-Adenauer Foundation Occasional Papers, Johannesburg.

Kronenberger, Vincent and Wouters, Jan (eds) (2004), *The European Union and Conflict Prevention. Policy and Legal Aspects* (The Hague: Asser Press).

Landsberg, Chris (2007), 'South Africa and the Making of the African Union and NEPAD: Mbeki's "Progressive African Agenda"', in Adebajo et al. (eds).

Lindberg, Leon N. and Scheingold, Stuart A. (1970), *Europe's Would-be Polity. Patterns of Change in the European Community* (Englewood Cliffs: Prentice Hall).

Makinda, Samuel M. and Okumu, Wafula F. (2008), *The African Union. Challenges of Globalization, Security and Governance* (London: Routledge).

Motala, Ahmed (2008), 'The African Court on Human and Peoples' Rights: Origins and Prospects', in Akokpari et al. (eds).

Mutasa, Charles (2009), 'A Critical Appraisal of the African Union–ECOSOCC Civil Society Interface', in Akokpari et al. (eds).

Mwagiru, Makumi and Oculli, Okello (eds) (2006), *Rethinking Global Security: An African Perspective?* (Nairobi: Heinrich Boll Foundation).

Mwanasali, Musifiky (2008), 'From Non-inference to Non-indifference: The Emerging Doctrine of Conflict Prevention in Africa', in Akokpari et al. (eds).

Nkrumah, Kwame (1963), *Africa Must Unite* (New York: Panaf Books).

Nieuwkerk, Athoni van (2006), 'Correlating African Regional and Security Initiatives to an Emerging Global Security Agenda', in Mwagiru et al. (eds).

Olivier, Gerrit (2003), 'Is Thabo Mbeki Africa's Saviour?', *International Affairs*, Vol. 79, No. 4, 815–28.

Paffenholz, Thania (ed.) (2010), *Civil Society and Peacebuilding: A Critical Assessment* (Boulder: Lynne Rienner).

Salmon, Trevor (2005), 'The European Security and Defence Policy: Built on Rocks or Sand?', *European Foreign Affairs Review*, Vol. 10, 359–79.

Chapter 3

Hopes and Challenges for the Peace and Security Architecture of the African Union

Jakkie Cilliers[1]

Introduction

The political behaviour of people in the majority of African countries is distinctly derived from the continent's material poverty. Poor countries do not have the means (armed forces, law enforcement agencies and the like) to enforce state authority, while local groupings have few constraints to assert their relative autonomy. It has been well established that the higher the per capita income a country enjoys, the lower its risk of armed conflict. This is why most wars take place in very poor countries and why Africa is the most violent continent.[2] This violence has resulted in a stream of refugees on the continent, massive displacement and immense suffering.

The evidence for this war–poverty association is reflected most starkly in the basic coincidence of instability and war that coexist with poverty and underdevelopment globally. Also, the lower a country's per capita income and the lower its growth rate, the greater the risk of a coup d'état. Africa's low economic growth rates (at least until the mid-1990s[3]) and extreme poverty made it particularly coup prone, and in a sort of self-fulfilling prophecy, a history of past coups increases the risk of future coups – just as a past history of armed conflict increases the risk of future conflicts, and conflict in a neighbouring country increases regional instability.[4]

Beyond poverty and lack of development most analysts agree about the centrality of the nature of the African state in explaining instability – and the

---

1   Executive Director, Institute for Security Studies, Extraordinary Professor in the Department of Political Sciences, Faculty Humanities at the University of Pretoria. Dr Cilliers also serves on the International Advisory Board of the Geneva Centre for Security Policy (GCSP) and as independent non-executive director of the South African Banking Risk Information Centre (SABRIC).

2   http://74.125.95.132/search?q=cache:4bB1SP0okGMJ:www.africanyouth.dk/docs/index.php%3FvcFile%3Dafricanyouth_pres_2.pdf+%22Africa｜is｜the｜most+violent+continent%22&cd=5&hl=en&ct=clnk&gl=ca&client=firefox-a (last accessed 18 September 2009).

3   http://www.africafocus.org/docs05/eca0505.php.

4   Human Security Report Project (2007).

reasons are evident. Modern African states were created by outsiders and held in place first by colonialism and then, during the Cold War, by superpower rivalry before the external scaffolding was removed shortly after the collapse of the Berlin Wall. Already the continent was at the mercy of the neo-liberal prescriptions of the international financial institutions and together with the mismanagement by the continent's own leaders, the 1980s and 1990s were a difficult time for Africa. To compound matters, in the aftermath of the Cold War large sections of the state-run networks that were engaged in transport, training, provision of arms and equipment, money laundering and the like were ostensibly disbanded, but often effectively privatized – not only in the hope of a more peaceful globe, but as part of the downsizing of the defence and security sectors by the two opposing power blocks that followed the collapse of the Berlin Wall. In search of sustenance, these networks served to lubricate resource competition in Africa. While there are only a few collapsed or failed states in Africa,[5] most African states are still weak, because governance in many has contracted rather than expanded for several decades in parallel with the acute economic crises experienced by the continent till recently.[6]

From the mid-1980s the lack of development and the weakness of states has been[7] deepened through rising external debt, structural adjustment programmes, the disengagement of Cold War patrons, and the advance of democratization. These factors combined to challenge the prevailing political order. In many cases, these changes disrupted the stability of African state formations, increasing resource competition, and accentuated the unsustainable character of the post-colonial social system.[8] That has started to change in recent years. While freedom of the press, the rule of law and government transparency remain weak, and corruption is widespread at many levels of politics and the economy, literally all indices show strong improvements over the last decade. The large majority of African countries enjoy rising levels of prosperity, stability, and the normalization of fragile state situations. More than 19 presidential and parliamentary elections were held in 18 African countries in 2007, although often marred by low turnouts, particularly in Nigeria and Egypt, and abstention (in Algeria). Most elections are peaceful. Incumbent heads of state are often re-elected by wide margins, as are new presidents. Even in Zimbabwe, amid substantial intimidation and manipulation, the governing party maintained a charade of electoral process – a façade that fellow dictators of a decade earlier would have dispensed with at an early stage.[9]

The March 2005 Report of the Commission for Africa found that 'Africa has experienced more violent conflict than any other continent in the last four

---

5 http://www.globalpolicy.org/component/content/article/173/30486.html.

6 Cilliers (2004).

7 http://ideas.repec.org/a/eaa/aeinde/v2y2002i2_5.html.

8 Authors such as Mark Duffield (1999) argue that the criminalization of African economies can partly be interpreted as the use of and adaptation to globalization and market deregulation.

9 Cilliers (n.d.): 117–18.

decades'.[10] Most of the world's armed conflicts now take place in sub-Saharan Africa and at the turn of the twenty-first century more people were being killed in wars in this region than in the rest of the world combined. Most of the 24 major armed conflicts recorded worldwide in 2001[11] were on the African continent, with 11 of those conflicts lasting eight years or more.[12] Estimates show that wars stripped about US$18 billion a year from African economies between 1990 and 2005[13] and there is serious concern that the impact of climate change will accentuate the propensity for conflict in Africa. Yet, by 2006, conflict in Africa had declined substantially from the extraordinary high levels that followed immediately[14] upon the end of the Cold War. Generally unreported in a world where bad news (such as that relating to Darfur, Somalia and Zimbabwe) crowds out the good, recent years have witnessed dramatic improvements in stability in Africa. The Human Security Report Group has, for example, recently recognized the reduction in open armed conflict in the region. By 2006, it reported, the annual battle-death toll in sub-Saharan Africa was just 2 percent of that of 1999 and the number of conflicts had fallen by half.[15] 'Between 2002 and 2006,' it found 'non-state conflict numbers have also dropped by more than half across the region, and their death tolls had fallen some 70 percent.'[16]

Four factors explain these remarkable trends. The first is the growth in democracy and human rights in the continent during the global 'third wave' of democratization in the 1990s – a development that has admittedly stalled in recent years. Although Africa remains the least democratic region in the world second to the Middle East, many countries aspire to regular elections. Evidence from studies such as that done by Afrobarometer in some 18 countries indicates that the demand for democracy remains strong.[17] The second relates to recent positive trends in economic growth. On the back of improved macroeconomic management, strong commodity prices and reduced debt, Africa grew at an impressive 6 per cent in 2008 and 5.8 per cent the previous year[18] – although growth is set to decline by

---

10   Commission for Africa, *Our Common Interest: Report of the Commission for Africa*, 14 March 2005.

11   http://www.iss.co.za/index.php?link_id=4056&slink_id=7259&linktype=12&slink_type=12&tmpl_id=3.

12   Human Security Report Project (2005): 4.

13   IANSA, Oxfam and Safer World (2007).

14   http://www.iss.co.za/index.php?link_id=4056&slink_id=7259&linktype=12&slink_type=12&tmpl_id=3 (last accessed 18 September 2009).

15   Human Security Report Project (2007): 5.

16   Ibid.

17   Afrobarometer (2006). Freedom House only categorized eight of 48 countries in Sub-Saharan Africa as liberal democracies at the end of 2008, compared to one of the 20 countries in the Middle East that it monitors. Barkan (2009): 3.

18   http://books.google.ca/books?id=mnyUL7Fql0MC&pg=PT120&lpg=PT120&dq=Africa+grew+at+6+percent+in+2008+and+5.8+percent&source=bl&ots=75R5Gwh8cf&

half in 2009 in line with the global downturn.[19] This growth is no flash in the pan, for the majority of the continent's member countries have experienced steady growth for almost a decade. A third factor in the improved capacity of African governments and hence their ability to provide security – and crush efforts to test their monopoly on the tools of coercion. The most recent report of the Mo Ibrahim Foundation, for example, found improvements in governance for 2006 in 31 out of the 48 countries that it measures.[20] Hence the government in Kinshasa has virtually no ability to control events in Kivu province of the Democratic Republic of Congo (DRC) (four hours flying time distant to the east), where a local warlord, Laurence Nkunda, set up an alternative administration in 2008.[21] Greater government capacity translates into the ability to provide services, education and roll out governance in territories at some distance from the capital.

A final factor, the focus of this chapter, is the greater activism by African leadership and the international community in the pursuit of African stability through peacekeeping and peacemaking organizations such as the United Nations and the African Union.

African conflicts often spill across state boundaries from a sub-region in one country to another next door. These clashes generally occur in areas outside formal state control. In the eastern DRC, for example, the conflict over access to the lucrative coltan and tantalite mining is between local militias, backed by business interests and foreign governments. In extreme cases (such as between Central African Republic, Chad and Western Sudan), insecurity and instability is a single, complex and interrelated problem that is an intrinsic part of the lack of state capacity and the absence of development.

Without administration and the application of rule of law – the nexus between the legitimate and illegitimate activities of business – government, criminals and conflict triggers are often difficult to distinguish from one another. Thus arms flow across national borders and involve numerous national and international actors as is evident in reports in December 2008 that detail how the Mugabe regime obtained arms through Kinshasa in the face of global outrage about suppression in that country.[22]

---

sig=BW8pe5D; WRNSVxqVh7tsKjrX1k&hl=en&ei=gTZaStPZBYvyNKSaufoC&sa=X& oi=book_result&ct=result&resnum=7.

19   See, for example, Economic Commission for Africa, Economic Report on Africa (2008): 38 and Statement on the Global Economic and Financial Crisis to the 12th Ordinary Session of the Assembly of Heads of State and Government of the African Union by Mr Abdoulie Janneh, UN Under-Secretary-General and Executive Secretary of ECA available at http://www.uneca.org/.

20   http://www.iss.co.za/index.php?link_id=4056&slink_id=7259&linktype=12&slin k_type=12&tmpl_id=3. See Mo Ibrahim Foundation (2008).

21   http://www.iss.co.za/index.php?link_id=4056&slink_id=7259&linktype=12&sli nk_type=12&tmpl_id=3.

22   http://www.iss.co.za/index.php?link_id=4056&slink_id=7259&linktype=12&sli k_type=12&tmpl_id=3.

Internationally, the most vivid example of the challenges presented by a collapsed state is the extent of piracy off the shores of Somalia, a country that has not had a central government since 1991. In 2008, there were 124 incidents of piracy off Somalia's coast and about 60 successful hijackings. As a result, nearly 400 people and 19 ships were held along the Somali coast at the end of 2008.[23] Generally, human-induced action serves to accentuate nature. Hence heavy rains in Zimbabwe over the 2008–09 Christmas season extended the cholera crisis[24] created largely by the collapsing administration system of the Mugabe regime.

The matter of what needs to be done to move from instability and insecurity in Africa to development and peace is deceptively simple. African governments, organizations such as the African Union (AU) and Africa's international friends need to prevent conflicts from occurring, manage those that do break out and, once stability has been restored, prevent a return to conflict. Most important of all, African leadership should set the basis for sustainable peace – a condition only possible in the long run if based on solid sustainable economic growth and development.

The Establishment of the African Union

Much of the initial praise lavished on the African Union (AU) after its inauguration in Durban in 2002[25] was motivated not only by the fact that it represents the start of a new political, judicial and economic vision for the continent but also by the prominence provided in its Constitutive Act to the principles of human rights, democracy, good governance and therefore to human security. These commitments permeate the Act and key associated legal commitments such as the Protocol on the AU's Peace and Security Council (PSC). Thus Article 3(g) commits the Union to promoting democratic principles and institutions, popular participation and good governance and 3(h) to the promoting and protecting human and peoples' rights in accordance with the African Charter on Human and Peoples' Rights and other relevant human rights instruments. Respect for democratic principles, human rights, the rule of law and good governance and the promotion of social justice now constitute a key(?) principle of the Union.[26]

Today Africans are heavily engaged in making and keeping the peace on the continent on the initiative of the African Union, in partnership with the international community and in numerous other ways, some of which could hardly have been

---

23   Foreign staff, Chinese ship uses Molotov cocktails to fight off Somali pirates, http://www.telegraph.co.uk/news/worldnews/piracy/3849969/Chinese-ship-uses-Molotov-cocktails-to-fight-off-Somali-pirates.html (accessed 19 December 2008); http://www.globalsecurity.org/military/world/war/somalia.htm.
24   Canadian Red Cross.
25   http://www.au2002.gov.za/.
26   Article 4.

Since 1999 a series of summits and ministerial meetings were key moments in the establishment of the African Union (AU), notably:*

Sirte (9 October 1999) OAU Special Summit
- Libyan proposal for a federal United States of Africa with a US-Congress Sirte Pan African Parliament (PAP) as the apex organization
- Declaration on the establishment of the AU

Abuja (May 2000) Conference on Security, Stability, Development and Cooperation (CSSDCA's) 1st African Ministerial meeting
- Called on African leaders to implement the Sirte Declaration and establish the AU, the Pan-African Parliament (PAP) and accelerate the implementation of the Abuja Treaty establishing the AEC (African Economic Community)

Tripoli (June 2000) Ministerial Conference on the Establishment of the AU
- Clarification of the relationship between the OAU, AU, AEC and PAP
- Finalization of draft documents for the Lomé Summit

Lomé (11 July 2000) 36th OAU Summit
- Constitutive Act of the African Union is approved
- CSSDCA Solemn Declaration approved
- Entry into force of the Constitutive Act (26 May 2001) – one month after it was ratified by the 36th Member States

37th Lusaka (July 2001) OAU Summit
- Asked Secretariat to prepare the establishment of the AU and make proposals for this to the Durban Summit
- Year from Lusaka to Durban designated as a transition year
- Adopted the New Partnership for Development in Africa (NEPAD)

Durban (July 2002) 38th and last OAU Summit and 1st Summit of the AU
- OAU disbanded and AU formally established in its place
- First year was designated as an interim year to allow the now Interim Commissioners to finalize proposals for the structure and financing of new Commission and the election of new Commissioners
- Issued a NEPAD Declaration on Democratic, Political, Economic and Corporate Good Governance

Maputo (July 2003) 2nd AU Summit: Major results
- Elected AU Commissioners for a first 4 years term of office
- Approved the budget and financing proposals
- Approved the Structure of the African Union Commission and programmes for the launch of the other organs
- Adopted a Declaration to integrate NEPAD into the African Union

*   African Union (2004a): 21–2.

foreseen a few years ago. Clearly Africans are doing more for and by themselves – and often in unexpected ways. For example, after several months of sanctions and mediation made no progress, a coalition of willing African countries (Tanzania, Sudan and Libya), supported the Comorian armed forces removed self-styled 'President' Mohammed Bacar from power in the island of Anjouan during March 2008.[27] The AU did so at the request of Ahmed Abdallah Sambi, the President of the Union of Comoros.[28]

Events in Zimbabwe provide the alternative perspective where African leaders, South Africa in particular, aided and abetted the suppression by Robert Mugabe of his people. Years of unwavering support to Mugabe's ZANU PF Party had delivered few tangible results for South Africa's purported quiet diplomacy and eventually the country staggered towards an imperfect agreement on 15 September 2008 that took several months before continued economic collapse led to its partial enactment early in 2009. Events in Zimbabwe appear, according to some, to portent a wider trend first evident in Kenya in January 2008, when regional leaders looked on with hardly a murmur as Kenyan leaders thwarted the popular will of their people through the manipulation of electoral processes and the constitution – although not through the barrel of a gun as had been the case earlier. But the trend towards improved accountability and democracy appears strong. Early 2009 saw Ghana's New Patriotic Party (NPP) peacefully cede power to the opposing National Democratic Congress party of Professor John Evans Atta Mills with an electoral loss of less than 0.5 per cent. In a recent briefing document, ISS Senior Researcher Berouk Mesfin wrote:

> [i]t is simply amazing just how quickly democracy has come to monopolise the political landscape in Africa … [t]wo decades ago, there were still respectable arguments in favour of one-party rule and authoritarian leaders, either military or civilian. Today, notwithstanding few exceptions, almost all African states legally allow multi-party politics and have routinely carried out multi-party elections; these and more recent elections, albeit of significantly varying qualities and frequency, have provided a vital opening for millions of Africans to actively involve in government affairs …. One determinant factor is the engagement and commitment of the African Union (AU) to strengthen its own governance and conflict management architecture and the role of elections in democracy building in Africa.[29]

---

27   allafrica.com.

28   The operation was in response to the appeal for assistance made by the Comorian Government and in conformity with decision Assembly/AU/Dec.186(X) adopted by the Assembly of the Union at its 10th Ordinary Session held in Addis Ababa from 31 January to 2 February 2008. AU military engagement occurred despite the protestations of the most powerful and richest country on the continent, lead negotiator on Comoros, South Africa, who continued to favour negotiations.

29   Presentation on the roundtable workshop on 'Elections and Conflict Management in Africa', that was held in Addis Ababa, Ethiopia, 16 April 2008.

The AU Commission

The organizational audit on the African Union that was commissioned by the then Ghanaian president John Koufor in 2007 and reported early in 2008[30] shone a sharp spotlight on the challenges that confront the Union and its various organs.[31] The audit was, in fact, a comprehensive assessment of all AU structures – a no-holds barred organizational review that spoke candidly about the manifold problems that beset the continental organization.

Like most enquiries of this nature the origins of the audit were deeply political – part of the efforts generally led by Southern African countries to counter the grandiose ambitions of former Malian President Alpha Konare, until recently the Chairperson of the AU Commission, towards rapid African integration – backed by Libya's ever mercurial Muammar al-Gaddafi. Konare and al-Gaddafi's vision alarmed many countries who believe that integration should commence at a sub-regional level and only once substantial progress is evident here, should it translate into substantive steps at the continental level. These tensions came to a head in January 2009 during the AU Summit in Addis Ababa, where they lead to the extension of the Summit for an additional day and ended in an effective stalemate as members were locked in a bitter and sometimes acrimonious debate.[32]

Summarizing its assessment in 2008, the chairperson of the audit committee Nigerian Professor Adebayo Adedeji, had presented the challenges thus: 'Although the Commission, as the nerve center of the AU architecture, has lifted the profile of the Union globally, it is handicapped at three levels. First, there is lack of clarity in the set up of its leadership. Second, its activities are spread too widely for it to be effective in playing the role envisaged for it; and thirdly, the management needs to be improved.'[33] Evident from the challenges is that the Commission has an approved staffing structure of 912 available positions[34] – yet of these only 60 per cent have been filled with most vacancies for professional staff.[35]

---

30   http://www.iss.co.za/index.php?link_id=4056&slink_id=7259&linktype=12&slink_type=12&tmpl_id=3.

31   Adebayo Adedejii (chair), Audit of the African Union, 18 December 2007, Addis Ababa.

32   The only available candidate for the northern region, Libyan leader Muammar Abu Minyar al-Gaddafi, was appointed as Chair of the AU – a rotational position that carries little executive responsibility.

33   Elsewhere in their review Professor Adedeji's team write about the dysfunctional relationship between former chairperson Konare and his nine commissioners, with overlapping portfolios, unclear authority and responsibility, unwieldy and illogical division of areas of responsibility and the like. Audit of the African Union, 18 December 2007, Addis Ababa: 19.

34   http://www.regjeringen.no/nb/dep/ud/kampanjer/refleks/innspill/afrika/cilliers.html?id=533452.

35   African Union (2009a), Foreword by Jean Ping.

According to the Constitutive Act, the key Organs of the African Union are as follows:*

The Assembly of the Union, the supreme organ of the Union is composed of Heads of State and Government or their duly accredited representatives. This organ meets at least twice a year in extraordinary session. During 2009 it meets in Addis Ababa at the seat of the Commission and in Sirte (Libya) given the chair of the Assembly being held by Libya.

The Commission of the African Union, is the Secretariat of the Union located in Addis Ababa. It is composed of the Chairperson, his or her Deputy and Commissioners. It represents the Union and defends its interests under the direction of the Assembly and the Executive Council. It can initiate proposals for submission to the other organs of the Union and executes decisions taken by them. It assists member states in executing the policies and programmes of the Union such as NEPAD. It formulates common positions of the Union and coordinates the work of member states during international negotiations.

The Executive Council, composed of the Foreign Ministers or such other Ministers or representatives as are designated by the governments of Member States, is responsible for coordinating and taking decisions on policies in areas of common interest to Member States.

The Permanent Representatives' Committee, composed of Permanent Representatives or other Plenipotentiaries of Member States accredited to the African Union in Addis Abaa, is responsible for preparing the work of the Executive Council and acting on the latter's instructions.

The Peace and Security Council composed of 15 Member States is responsible for the promotion of peace, security and stability in Africa, preventive diplomacy and restoration of peace. It is also responsible for disaster management and humanitarian activities. It replaced the Central Organ of the Conflict Prevention, Management and Resolution Mechanism established in 1993 by the Heads of State at the Tunis Summit. To enable it to discharge its responsibilities with respect to deployment of peace support missions and interventions in the event of genocide, war crimes and crimes against humanity, the Peace and Security Council is served by early warning system, consult a Panel of the Wise composed of five African personalities, a Standby Force within the five regions of Africa, advised by a Military Staff Committee. The work of the PSC is funded through the Peace Fund

The Pan-African Parliament located in Midrand, South Africa, is unicameral but represented by all Parliaments of the countries of Africa. Currently only with advisory powers it will eventually adopt legislations by two-thirds majority of its members. **The African Court of Justice** is currently being amalgamated with the **African Court of Human and Peoples' Rights,** located in Arusha, Tanzania. The Court of Justice was intended to adjudicate in civil cases will be responsible for human rights protection and monitoring human rights violations. It will also constitute itself into a real criminal court in the long term. **The African Court of Human and Peoples' Rights** adopted at the Ouagadougou Summit in 1998 has jurisdiction in cases of human rights violation by any State party, the African Commission on Human and Peoples' Rights and African intergovernmental organizations. The Court can hear cases filed by individuals and nongovernmental organizations with observer status in the Union, when the State party concerned makes a declaration to this effect. It is composed of 11 Judges elected by the Assembly for a mandate of 6 years renewable only once.

The Economic, Social and Cultural Council is an advisory organ composed of different social and professional groups from Member States of the Union, particularly youth and women's associations but has no effective power.

The Constitutive Act also provides for three **Financial Institutions** namely the African Central Bank, The African Monetary Fund and the African Investment Bank.

Specialized Technical Committees composed of Ministers or senior officials responsible for the sectors falling within their respective areas of competence. Seven Technical Committees, number and composition of which are not limited, are provided for in the Constitutive Act of the Union; namely the Committee on: Rural Economy and Agriculture; Monetary and Financial Matters; Trade, Customs and Immigration Matters; Industry, Science and Technology, Energy, Natural Resources and Environment; Transport, Communications and Tourism; Health, Labour and Social Affairs; and Education, Culture and Human Resources.

*   Adapted and updated from African Union (2004b): 29, Table 11.

The focus of the AU on the development of appropriate norms and standards, often noted more by the absence in application than in adherence became particularly evident under Konare's leadership. Reporting to the Executive Council and the Assembly in January 2009, the new Chairperson of the Commission, Jean Ping wrote:

> Our Organisation is, indeed, endowed with a wide range and a relatively comprehensive set of documents (legal texts, decisions and recommendations) covering all spheres of human activity, documents that could make us the envy of other Continents. It must however be observed that the political will underpinning this wide range of documentary asset, an asset shaped by our good intentions, have not always been translated into concrete measures. Our peoples in their towns and villages gain nothing from these good intentions which are quite often relegated to the status of feasibility study and consigned to the dusty archives of our offices.[36]

---

36   *Ibid.*: 2–3.

By all indications, Ping has brought a necessary managerial focus to the AU Commission that has sought to consolidate the sometimes unrealistic and expansive vision of his predecessor.[37]

The budget of the Commission has already expanded several-fold in the last decade. In January 2009 the AU Summit approved a budget of US$140 million for the year consisting of US$106.6 assessed contributions from member states and an estimated US$32.4 million from partner organizations (the AU received US$66.1 million from international partners in 2008). Although the organization is still faced with membership arrears in the region of US$53.5 million, contributions have tripled in recent years.[38]

The AU's Peace and Security Architecture

The Protocol on the Peace and Security Council entered into force in December 2003. According to Article 2, the PSC is '… a standing decision-making organ for the prevention, management and resolution of conflicts. The PSC shall be a collective security and early-warning arrangement to facilitate timely and efficient response to conflict and crisis situations in Africa'.[39] The PSC is supported in its work by the staff of the AU Commission, a panel of five eminent or 'Wise' persons[40] for mediation purposes, a Continental Early Warning System (CEWS), an African Standby Force (ASF), and a Special Fund. The Organ is also authorized to establish subsidiary bodies as it deems necessary for the performance of its

---

37   For example, Ping has undertaken a review of the progress with the previous strategy and reported that: '… in spite of the numerous constraints, nearly half of the actions planned under the Strategic Plan 2004–2007 were implemented, 46% of the actions of the Plan were executed or well underway, and 37% were executed in full.' African Union (2009b): iii.

38   African Union (2009a): 2–3. The budget of the OAU in 2000 was around US$32 million.

39   The peace and security architecture of the African Union is not limited to the structures discussed in this article or those listed in the PSC Protocol alone. It also consists of a Military Staff Committee of the members of the PSC and a Peace Fund. There is the African Centre for the Study and Research on Terrorism in Algiers (ACSRT), the Committee of Intelligence and Security Services of Africa (CISSA), the African Committee of Experts on the Rights and Welfare of the Child, the Commission for Human and Peoples' Rights, the African Court on Human and Peoples' Rights, structures such as ECOSOCC, PAP, APRM, etc. These structures are supported by a plethora of decisions, statements and protocols that provide a comprehensive framework for conflict prevention, management and post conflict resolution in Africa.

40   http://www.africa-union.org/root/au/publications/PSCEarly%20Warning%20System.pdf.

functions. It may also, under Article 8(5), seek such military, legal and other forms of expertise as it may require for the performance of its functions.[41]

Article 3 confers on the Organ wide-ranging responsibilities for the prevention, the management, and the resolution of conflicts, and post-conflict peace-building. The promotion of democracy, the rule of law and good governance, are all regarded as part and parcel of conflict prevention of the mandate of the PSC. The Council is expected to coordinate and harmonize continental efforts in the prevention and combating of terrorism in all its aspects. It is also entrusted with the responsibility of developing a common defence policy. Finally, Article 4 of the Protocol reinforces provisions in the Constitutive Act under which the AU can intervene in the affairs of a Member State.

More than any other structure, the AU's African peace and security architecture can point to numerous achievements. In 2006, special PSC meetings were convened on the Sudan, the Central African Republic, the Democratic Republic of the Congo, Darfur, Chad, Comoros, Somalia and Côte d'Ivoire. For 2007, special PSC sessions have focused on Burundi, Comoros, Mauritania, Côte d'Ivoire and Darfur, and in 2008, on Zimbabwe, Kenya, Somalia, Eritrea/Djibouti, Côte d'Ivoire, DRC, Burundi, Comoros and other hot spots.

By the time of the most recent AU summit, in Addis Ababa (February 2009), the PSC had met more than 165 times and has sought to improve its workings along the way. For example, the 2008 organizational audit report referred to earlier, concluded with 159 substantive recommendations of which 10 related to the PSC – all of which were subsequently discussed and adopted at an extraordinary meeting of foreign ministers in Tanzania during May 2008 and are in the process of implementation.

African political engagement as regards peace and security today is at a different level to previous years. More importantly, the AU has moved from strict adherence to a policy of non-interference in the domestic affairs of its member states to one that its previous Commissioner for Peace and Security called one of 'non-indifference'. In the process, the continent adopted much of the language of the responsibility to protect prior to the adoption of the concept by the UN General Assembly in 2007. Though tentative at first (evident with the cautious engagement by member states to the spectre of Sudan as incoming chair of the African Union in 2007 – a process that would eventually see the Republic of Congo assume the chair), AU engagement is increasingly robust, of which the military engagement in Anjouan mentioned earlier is an important example.

Many challenges remain, of course, and it is naïve to assume that the AU is able to engage substantively on its own with conflicts such as that in Darfur, Somalia or between Ethiopia and Eritrea – three areas that are literally in the backyard of the AU commission in Addis Ababa. Despite its rhetoric, the AU remains a club of leaders rather than an assembly of its people. And although the number of democrats has increased steadily, key leaders such as those of Libya, Cameroon,

---

41   Adapted from paragraphs 265–66 of the Audit report.

Gabon, Burkina Faso, Uganda, Egypt, Zimbabwe, Nigeria, Kenya and Ethiopia have either not been elected or were elected under dubious circumstances where associated processes have been manipulated and often marred by substantial violence and abuse of state power.

On paper the AU has a number of structures and systems for the engagement of civil society, including the Economic, Social and Cultural Council (ECOSOCC), yet non-governmental engagement is weak and the predominant view remains that of elite and state security rather than human security. The AU lacks an effective sanctions regime through which it can deal with recalcitrant states and leaders – and even so, the will and willingness to engage with fellow leaders, many of who share a common democratic deficit, is limited. A collection of the world's poorest, and therefore most violent, countries, African politics often takes the form of the lowest common denominator – driven by consensus and accommodation rather than the confrontation, condemnation and isolation that most of its Western partners pressure it to adopt. In effect, the actual leverage that countries have over one another is constrained by the state of African armed forces, lack of control of borders, often limited territorial control of their own territory, domestic challenges and the often tenuous hold that leaders have on national power.

In this environment the 2003 decision by the European Union to establish the Africa Peace Facility[42] proved to be a catalyst in the ability of the Union to engage in active peacemaking. The Africa Peace Facility subsequently provided the AU with almost €400 million for peacekeeping and related capacity building by 2007, and has recently been renewed with an amount of €300 million for the period 2008 to 2011.[43] Other partners followed suit and eventually also the United Nations, which today spends more time on Africa at the UN Security Council than on any other region. For its part the AU commission itself has had to undergo a very steep learning curve on how to handle the massive budgets relating to African peacekeeping. For example, the AU's first peacekeeping operation, AMIB, had an approved budget of approximately US$130 million per year – at a time when the annual budget of the entire AU was about US$32 million. The second mission, AMIS, with close to 8,000 personnel, had an annual budget of approximately US$466 million.[44] As a rule the AU has sought the support of the UN Security Council for all missions, in part as this is a requirement for access to the financial

---

42   http://books.google.ca/books?id=jsTdKGnxkCgC&pg=PA73&lpg=PA73&dq =2003+European+Union+established+African+Peace+Facility&source=bl&ots=tefqk2 SQDZ&sig=J1N9SaY1PmhJM-YyTBrqs4AMOzc&hl=en&ei=bUBaSpLLBaTIMv_7- cAG&sa=X&oi=book_result&ct=result&resnum=3.

43   The instrument became operational with the first grant for the AMIS I operation in July 2004. See http://ec.europa.eu/world/peace/geographical_themes/africa/african_peace/ index_en.htm.

44   Background and concept paper for the brainstorming retreat between the AU and the regional mechanisms for conflict prevention, management and resolution, at Algiers, Algeria on 5 and 6 January 2008, para. 34.

resources from the African Peace Facility provided by the European Union as well as for much of the bilateral support available from individual partners.

The AU is also busy operationalizing other key components of its peace and security system, including the Panel of the Wise, meant to: 'support the efforts of the Peace and Security Council and those of the Chairperson of the Commission, particularly in the area of conflict prevention.' The members of the five-person panel (one from each of Africa's five regions[45]) were appointed in January 2007 and the modalities adopted in November 2007.[46] The panel has adopted a draft work programme, held its first two meetings and is in the process of establishing a secretariat. Rather than engage in the hot conflicts and challenges that make banner headlines, the intention is that the Panel focus on 'forgotten' and unresolved crises and the implementation of peace agreements. As such it intends to work with civil society and complement the work of the PSC. Whilst commentators have questioned the secretive and closed appointment process of its members that include serving government officials and the advanced age of others, the Panel would provide another important building block in the evolving security architecture of the Union.

Solid progress is also evident with the Continental Early Warning System that is tasked with providing the Chairperson of the Commission with information in a timely manner so that they can advise the PSC on 'potential conflicts and threats to peace and security' and 'recommend best courses of action.' Based on an open, networked system that includes an early warning module, a substantial amount of conceptual work on indicators, systems and processes has been concluded. Staffing is currently in process and the System should be fully operational by 2010 – although it is already providing substantial services to the Commission and Member States.

Most attention (and funding) has been towards the African Standby Force (ASF).[47] The purpose of the ASF is to provide the African Union with capabilities to respond to conflicts through the deployment of peacekeeping forces and to undertake interventions pursuant to article 4(h) and (i) of the Constitutive Act. The ASF is intended for rapid deployment for a multiplicity of peace support operations that may include, inter alia, preventive deployment, peacekeeping, peace building, post conflict disarmament, demobilisation, re-integration and humanitarian assistance.

---

45   http://www.regjeringen.no/nb/dep/ud/kampanjer/refleks/innspill/afrika/cilliers.html?id=533452.

46   Former OAU Secretary General Salim Ahmed Salim of Tanzania from the east; former Algerian president Ahmed Ben Bella from the north, Benin's constitutional court president, Elisabeth K. Pognon, representing the west, former Sao Tome and Principe president Miguel Trovoada for the central region, and the southern representative is South Africa's Independent Electoral Commission chief Brigalia Bam.

47   The following sections are taken from Cilliers (2008): 7, 17.

African Standby Force

In a reversal of thinking at international level, it has now become accepted that the AU can and should deploy in advance of the UN – demonstrated in Burundi (when AMIB was followed by UNOB in May 2004) during AMIS in Darfur (deployed in June 2004) and subsequently with the AU Mission to Somalia (AMISOM) in March 2007. Originally, the purpose of the ASF was largely 'never to allow another genocide like Rwanda', which was the rationale behind the need for quick response capabilities and the capability to mount a mission to cover the early days while the ponderous UN peacekeeping system lumbered into operational mode. Today it is accepted that the AU will deploy first, opening up the possibility for a UN follow-on multi-dimensional peace support operation. In this scenario ASF forces will therefore be deployed into a situation as part of the peacemaking process at an earlier stage than UN forces would be allowed to engage. They would thereby help to create the conditions on the ground that could lead to a comprehensive peace agreement and the deployment of UN forces. This was indeed the situation in Burundi with the AU and UN, and with the Economic Community of West African States (ECOWAS) and the UN in Liberia, Sierra Leone and Côte D'Ivoire. The exit strategy for ASF operations is therefore a transition to the UN – which could include the re-designation of ASF resources as UN contingents.

There are two practical challenges to this approach, however. The first concerns the relationship between UN and ASF operations, which could lead to a severe and early depletion of ASF forces available for deployment elsewhere. While the potential full standby strength of the ASF would come to 25,000 troops and up to 980 military observers, the UN had 55,980 troops, 6,995 police and 2,153 military observers deployed in MINORSO, MONUC, UNMIL, UNOCI, UNMIS, UNAMID and MINURCAT in January 2009.[48] As these numbers indicate, the re-designation of ASF forces as part of UN operations would quickly deplete the available ASF capacity even if that where fully developed. This could be exacerbated by the fact that African troop contributors obviously choose between deployment on better-paid UN missions and commitment to the less-well remunerated ASF. Given the disparities in resources available to the two types of missions, ASF also do not generally receive the same level of logistic and other support as that of UN missions – a challenge that has led to the appointment of the so-called 'Prodi' Report of the African Union-United Nations panel on modalities for support to African peacekeeping operations recently submitted to the UNSC.[49]

The second is the challenge of handing over control to the UN with its more restrictive entry criteria than those of the AU. In the aftermath of a slew

---

48   Calculated from data provided at http://www.un.org/Depts/dpko/dpko/bnote.htm, accessed 15 February 2009.

49   On 31 December 2008 as document A/63/666 S/2008/813.

of challenging missions, the 2000 Brahimi report[50] on peacekeeping emphasized the importance of 'there being a peace to keep' and set as a benchmark that the UN should not deploy forces unless a binding and overarching peace agreement was in place. The result is a marked UN reluctance to assume a peacekeeping responsibility before a comprehensive agreement is in place – an unrealistic and impracticable condition in fragile states where numerous fractured armed groups compete for dominance. In addition, once the UN has accepted such a role there are often extremely long delays in effecting the transition from an AU to a UN mission, as occurred in Burundi and Darfur.[51]

A lack of capacity at the level of the AU Commission has also complicated progress since in the absence of guidance from Addis Ababa, regions applied their own interpretation to the common roadmap that set out the way forward on the ASF. Today key arrangements in regions such as the South African Development Community (SADC), ECOWAS and in Eastern Africa regarding command, control, logistics, and planning differ from one another – a situation that complicates the deployment and use of forces from different regions. Hence SADC would like to authorize and control the deployment of SADC Brigade (SADCBRIG) under the authority of the SADC Summit whereas the Eastern African Standby Brigade Coordination Mechanism (EASBRICOM) more appropriately sees its function as largely that of force preparation, handing force deployment over to the African Union.

In preparation for an experts' working session in Algiers during January 2008, the Commission of the AU listed the following challenges about the key roles in future African peace operations: [52]

a. The likelihood that the UN will stage robust operations or enforcement missions under Chapter VII of the UN Charter remains small for the foreseeable future. The AU and the regional mechanisms will, therefore, continue to face the challenge of summoning the political will as well as the capacity to plan and execute robust missions.
b. While some of the ongoing situations of armed conflict will remain a challenge for some time to come, emerging trends suggest that such incidents of large-scale armed conflict will gradually decline in Africa. However, situations of low intensity conflict are likely to remain a challenge. While these situations do not necessarily pose significant threats to international

---

50   http://www.regjeringen.no/nb/dep/ud/kampanjer/refleks/innspill/afrika/cilliers. html?id=533452.

51   The Brahimi Panel on UN Peace Operations was convened by the UN secretary general in March 2000 to 'assess the shortcomings of the existing [UN] system and make frank, specific and realistic recommendations for change'. The report of the panel, which was led by Lakhdar Brahimi, a former Algerian foreign minister. was submitted on 21 August 2000 (UN 2000).

52   *Ibid.*, para. 31.

peace and security, they do constitute a threat to stability and sustainable development in the affected countries (and surrounding areas). As such situations of this nature will occupy the attention of the AU and the regional mechanisms and will be the focus of conflict prevention and management.

c. An operational African peace and security architecture will therefore need to develop effective early response systems and effective support for mediation efforts through, for example, preventive deployment.

d. A standby force implies that it consists of several components, including, for example, military, police and civilian dimensions. However, there has been more focus and attention on the military components. Although the AU has recognized this lack, there is a need for more targeted attention to rectify this shortcoming.

e. Training of future peace operations personnel (ie the ASF) must of necessity address the different dimensions of the challenges of conflict and post-conflict environments in which such persons will operate. This means that more attention should be given to the civilian dimension, including child protection, gender issues, human rights, civil affairs, economic recovery and HIV/AIDS issues, in addition to disarmament, demobilization and reintegration and security sector reform programmes.

f. African organizations have not demonstrated the ability to mobilize the financial resources required to address post-conflict, reconstruction, and development needs on their own. However, they can nonetheless set the agenda for external and other partners in terms of articulating priority approaches to peculiar needs of the targeted post-conflict environments. The AU policy on post-conflict, reconstruction, and development needs does articulate the principles and approaches, and the on-going process of developing operational guidelines will be particularly relevant in guiding the training of ASF personnel for future missions.

Conclusion

In reviewing the trends set out in this chapter, it is important to recognize the extent to which Africans have sought to assume leadership on intractable conflicts. In the aftermath of the genocide in Rwanda in 1994,[53] Africans sought to establish the structures and the systems for much greater engagement. Where the response of the international community has been found wanting, particularly in Burundi, Darfur and Somalia, Africa has been prepared to deploy its troops under an African Union mandate – not because clear solutions were in sight, but in the absence of effective international engagement, often under strong pressure from Western countries and with the haunting spectre of the Genocide in Rwanda always in the background. Eventually African engagement has served as a catalyst for international support

53   http://www.unitedhumanrights.org/Genocide/genocide_in_rwanda.htm.

(UNOB replaced AMIB in Burundi, UNAMID replaced AMIS in Darfur and the UN has started to plan a mission to replace AMISOM in Somalia) and the return of UN peacekeepers to Africa after the tragedies of Somalia and Rwanda in the early 1990s. Today Africa is the continent with the largest UN commitment on peacekeeping with eight of the 17 active UN peace missions in Africa,[54] largely funded by non-Africa countries[55] but with a significant contribution of African troops and police as well as the contribution being made by the new wave of engagement by Africans and the international community alike.[56]

Africa has not met the ambitious milestones to operationalize its peace and security architecture that it set for itself several years ago. Nevertheless, the progress made has been impressive. African conflict prevention, peacekeeping and post-conflict reconstruction will at some point have to be placed on a more sustainable basis. Arguably, the way forward in all of this is that a more integrated concept of peace and security should be developed between the AU and the UN. In effect, the degree of support and succour that the UN has provided to the African Standby Force has been a disappointment. Instead of leading, the UN has followed. Hence the Prodi report would find that: '[w]hile the United Nations Security Council clearly supports stronger cooperation between the United Nations and regional organizations, it has not considered this issue in a systematic way. Instead, it has focused on individual cases and, as a result, has not yet developed a clear framework for cooperation.'[57]

The African continent cannot close the security gap on its own and will continue to rely upon the international community, the UN in particular, for 'heavy lifting' and for anything beyond a temporary holding force. As noted in the Prodi report:

> It is important not to create the perception that the United Nations is subcontracting peacekeeping to the African Union. The objective should be to maximize the African Union's strengths in terms of its contribution to conflict prevention, mediation, its ability to address smaller-scale requirements such as mediation and restoration of constitutional order in the Union of the Comoros, and, finally, its capacity to act as the first response to larger-scale United Nations missions.[58]

---

54   UNMIS, UNAMID, MINURCAT, MINURSO, UNMIL, UNOCI, MONUC and BINUB.

55   At the end of 2008 the UN was deploying 91,382 personnel, including 77,349 troops; 11,494 police and 2,539 military observers.

56   Out of a total of 120 contributors, 38 African countries contributed troops, police and military observers to UN peacekeeping in January 2009.

57   Report of the African Union-United Nations panel on modalities for support to African Union peacekeeping operations submitted from the Secretary-General to the President of the General Assembly and the President of the UN Security Council on 31 December 2008 as document A/63/666 and S/2008/813, para. 38

58   Ibid., para 39.

Eventually, preparing the AU for the future is not only about providing vision and leadership to a Commission that has expanded its scope of work massively, but also to manage and restore the morale of an organization upon which many pin their hopes for an improved Africa. Former Tanzanian President Julius Nyerere cynically describing the OAU some decades ago as: "an opportunity for them [Heads of State] to congratulate each other for surviving coup plots in their countries and perpetuating themselves in power." Had he still been alive today, Nyerere would possibly have had to guardedly revise his opinion.

Chapter 4

From the Multilateralism of States to the Multilateralism of Peoples: The Roles of the African Union and the United Nations in Supporting Security Sector Reform

Adedeji Ebo and Kristiana Powell

Introduction

The past several decades have seen a dramatic shift in the parameters of international security agendas. The traditional security agenda – with its almost exclusive focus on ensuring the security of the state through the provision or threat of force – is increasingly being replaced by a broader security agenda, according to which the well-being of the individual and the community are fundamental. This broadening of the security agenda has been accompanied by corresponding shifts in the contours and components not only of what constitutes the 'security sector' but also in the focus of security cooperation more broadly. The security sector is now recognized as having moved beyond traditional security providers (e.g. statutory forces assigned the responsibility for the provision of state security including, *inter alia* the armed forces, the police, and paramilitary organizations) to include formal and informal security providers and oversight mechanisms, both state and non-state (e.g. ministries, legislative bodies and civil society organizations). In the same vein, security relations have expanded from a relatively narrow Cold War emphasis on gaining influence or providing support for proxy wars.

Security sector reform (SSR) is one of several items which have emerged on the post-Cold War security agenda.[1] In recent decades, approaches to SSR have become increasingly based on the assumption that the central objectives of the provision of security have moved beyond an exclusive focus on regime protection or preservation of the territorial integrity of the state to include considerations of the physical, economic and environmental security of citizens. Lessons learned from a variety of contexts revealed that effective and accountable security institutions

---

1   SSR is also often referred to as security sector transformation, development or governance. The debate on the appropriate terminology is itself ongoing and vibrant.

are essential for peace and development. The broadening of this agenda has led to a proliferation of engagement on the part of a diverse group of actors, both within and beyond states. There is widespread recognition in the literature that security is ultimately the result of various concentric circles which begins with the individual, and extends to the community, the state, sub-regional and regional organizations and ultimately the global level. Once largely governed by bilateral military partnerships, a range of political, development, and peacekeeping partners have now become engaged in offering SSR support to national authorities, particularly in the aftermath of conflict. While the bulk of this support continues to be provided through bilateral arrangements, multilateral organizations have also emerged as playing an essential and unique role in supporting the reform of the security sector, particularly in post-conflict contexts.

This chapter seeks to account for the role of the African Union (AU) and the United Nations (UN) as multilateral actors in the provision of SSR support and to identify the challenges inherent in this role, with a view to identifying discernible trends and useful lessons for the future. In the second part of the chapter, following this introductory section, we consider the background to the emergence and normative value of the SSR concept and in particular, the rationale behind the engagement of the AU and the UN in this specific area. In the third section, we identify the intersection of the AU and UN's approaches to SSR and we attempt an assessment of the relationship between the agendas of these two organizations. In the fourth section we discuss the significance of the strategic collaboration between these two multilateral organizations on SSR and the main challenges they will likely face moving forward. We then offer concluding remarks.

SSR and Shifting Security Paradigms

Conceptions of security have shifted radically in the past few decades. During the Cold War, the bulk of external assistance for reform of the security services took the form of training and equipping military, intelligence and police forces. Most of this assistance was provided through military partnerships and remained the almost exclusive domain of the military and political elite. Some actors lacked the capacity or mandate to provide support. Others had little interest in security issues or viewed security services as a cause of underdevelopment and conflict.

For the Organization of African Unity (the OAU), the precursor to the AU, security was approached mainly as an exclusive preserve of the state, with the armed forces and police as the main institutions under consideration. The military sought to perform this role, not by fulfilling their constitutional duty of protecting the territorial integrity of the state but often by taking over the government and administration of the country. Constitutions were routinely abrogated and parliamentary oversight habitually overruled. The security of the state (and at times the regime) was seen as synonymous with the security of the country. This approach cohered closely to the national security paradigm prominent in the Cold

War era in which security was perceived as the extent to which a state protected itself against foreign, hostile ideologies. The UN created one of the few spaces for negotiation between conflicting ideologies; those African (and other) states who sought to stay out of the East-West divide defined themselves as 'non-aligned'.

Following the end of the Cold War, the concept of security began to evolve dramatically. More comprehensive understandings of the security sector and the ultimate objectives of its reform began to emerge in SSR policy communities. By the end of the 1990s, SSR analysts and practitioners began to increasingly link SSR to the well-being of communities and the individual. While the security of the state still remained a central priority, the establishment of effective and accountable security institutions was increasingly seen as vital for the provision of physical security to communities and individuals. This thinking was reflected in and reinforced by a seminal World Bank study,[2] which revealed that a central concern of poor populations around the world is physical insecurity, including at the hands of statutory security forces. Accordingly, emerging SSR agendas became oriented toward building the capacity of the state to ensure the well-being of its citizens.

During the same period, security sector reform was increasingly linked to broader conflict prevention agendas. Practitioners argued that, on the one hand, poorly managed security forces could contribute to chronic insecurity, erode confidence in state institutions and create an environment conducive to the resolution of conflict through violent means. On the other, effective SSR that focuses on good governance of the security sector and civil-security sector relations, and a competent judicial and policing system may contribute to increased confidence in state authorities and to building a more peaceful society (Greene 2003). Many also argued that SSR can make an important contribution to peacebuilding by establishing more functional and accountable militaries that reflect national demographics, contribute to peace implementation and help prevent the resurgence of violent conflict.

SSR practitioners and analysts also began to identify the connections between military expenditure and poverty reduction, arguing that the reduction in military spending could free up funds to be spent on poverty reduction activities: that is, 'the peace dividend'.[3] It became increasingly evident that an effective security sector may reduce personal insecurity, the destruction of property and the outbreak of large-scale violence, all of which have negative effects on growth rates and undermine poverty reduction strategies. Furthermore, processes of reform may provide opportunities for broad-based participation in decision-making related to

---

2   The World Bank's 'Voices of the Poor' documented perspectives on poverty from 60,000 impoverished women and men in 60 countries around the world.

3   For a review of research supporting the notion of a 'peace dividend', along with relevant counterarguments, see Powell, Kristiana. 'The Impact of Arms Transfer on Sustainable Development: A Review of the Literature', Project Ploughshares Working Paper 04–3, September 2004. http://www.ploughshares.ca/libraries/WorkingPapers/WPlist.html.

security issues and may facilitate better access to security on the part of a larger segment of the population.

With empirical evidence and motivation provided by the post-Cold War experiences of many former Soviet regimes in East and Central Europe which revealed the utility of reforming security services to meet the needs to the population in addition to the state, many analysts also began to consider that SSR can be a core element of a governance agenda. Some argued that effective SSR can contribute to good governance by 'bringing the military under the ambit of parliaments, curtailing so called "off-budget expenses," and creating transparent methods of governance and management that filter into other areas of government' (Bellamy 2003: 109). Accordingly, SSR can play a critical role in redefining (often destructive) relations of power between security services and the population in post-conflict societies.

Policy debates underscored that the inverse is also true: effective SSR is not possible without wider governance reform (Hendrickson and Ball 2002). SSR agendas must build the capacity of central institutions of security sector governance – including the constitutional and legislative framework for civilian oversight and management of the security services. However, the success of these reforms is often not possible or sustainable, unless they are part of a much larger governance reform programme that strengthens good governance practices and addresses problems with corruption and the management of public expenditure.

In part in response to these increasingly broad understandings of the parameters and objectives of SSR, the past 10 years have seen the proliferation of policies and programming tools emerging from international organizations, donors, national authorities and a broad range of academics and practitioners. In addition, as the majority of conflicts have been internecine in nature, it became severally and increasingly clear that peace and security are not possible without fundamental changes in the security sector (Hutchful 2008). Thus, an increasing number of national authorities have requested assistance with the reform of their security sectors, particularly in the aftermath of conflict.[4] While a range of bilateral actors continue to provide the core of support to national authorities in this area, multilateral organizations have also developed normative frameworks and principles to guide the engagement of their members in the area of SSR. In the next section, we focus on the evolution and thinking of the involvement of the AU and the UN in supporting reforms of the security sector.

---

4   For example, in Burundi, national authorities requested that the United Nations Integrated Office in Burundi/*Bureau intégré des Nations Unies au Burundi* (BINUB) provide targeted assistance with a number of activities in support of police and military reform and other SSR-related activities, including civilian disarmament. The Government of Guinea-Bissau requested assistance from the United Nations (via the Department of Political Affairs) for SSR assistance. In the Central African Republic, the United Nations Development Programme has been provided support to nationally-led SSR mapping and programming.

The AU and the UN in SSR: Evolving Agendas

To be sure, the African Union and the United Nations have evolved in response to and as part of the more comprehensive agenda that emerged out of the Cold War and of the corresponding changing priorities and concerns of their Member States and the wider international community. There was broad consensus that states have rapidly become *necessary but insufficient* actors in the new security agenda in which several non-state actors play prominent roles.[5] At this juncture, it is appropriate to account for the institutional trajectory of the two organizations in SSR.

For the AU, its current recognition of the need for engagement in SSR can be traced to internal and external pressures on the African continent following the end of the Cold War. On the one hand, the end of Cold War rivalry enabled former allies to insist on marked reductions in military expenditure, eroding the very basis of many African states. On the other hand, the new wave of democratization in several parts of the world exacerbated similar pressures within African states for more accountable and participatory governance. This combination of internal and external pressures ignited a new wave of security thinking in Africa resulting in a body of overlapping normative instruments which seek a broader and more inclusive definition of the security agenda. Examples of these normative instruments include the Solemn Declaration on the Framework for an OAU Response to Unconstitutional Changes, the African Union Constitutive Act, and the Solemn Declaration on a Common African Defence and Security Policy.[6] This interlocking body of normative tools were themselves the product of important specific developments on the African continent. As Funmi Olonisakin (2007: 27) has noted, in the context of the ECOWAS Ceasefire Monitoring Group (ECOMOG) responded to the civil war and humanitarian crisis in Liberia:

> the experience of Liberia initiated a process of reform at the level of ECOWAS, which has gradually impacted some of its member States. The evolution of a culture of collective security in West Africa has had as a significant component, the creation of a normative framework, which presupposes democratic and good governance of the security sector.

Similar normative frameworks were starting to emerge in the southern part of the continent. The Southern Africa Development Community (SADC) set the scene also in the early 1990s when the end of the struggle against apartheid

---

5   Consider, for example, the Kamajors in Sierra Leone and the Bakassi Boys in Nigeria, which have provided security to specific constituencies.

6   For a detailed analysis of the evolution of regional normative instruments on the security sector, see Adedeji Ebo. 'Towards a Code of Conduct for Armed Forces and Security Services in Africa: Opportunities and Challenges', Policy Paper, Democratic Control of the Armed Forces, Geneva, 2005.

created the space to embark on long-term security and development. Indeed, the original Southern African Development Coordination Conference (SADCC) was transformed into the SADC via an innovative treaty.[7] 'The new instrument went beyond requiring Member States to give preeminence to democracy and the rule of law (with a provision allowing intervention in states in cases of unfolding humanitarian crisis): it provided for intervention when regimes flagrantly violate the rights of the local population' (Olonisakin 2007: 27).

Africa's journey towards a continental approach to the governance and reform of the security sector achieved a major milestone with the adoption of the AU's Post-Conflict Reconstruction and Development Framework (PCRD) in June 2007. The AU's PCRD provides a strategic framework for addressing post-conflict reconstruction, security and growth on the continent. 'Security' is one of the six constitutive elements of the PCRD framework, and its objectives clearly demonstrate – for the first time – the AU's intention to take a regional approach to the governance of the security sector (para. 25):

> ... (e) pursue the transformation of the organs of the State, especially those relating to security and justice; (f) give priority to the (re)establishment and strengthening of the capacity of the security institutions, including defence, police, justice system, border controls and customs officials; (g) establish mechanisms for the governance and accountability of the security sector, as a means of restoring public confidence, and ... (q) facilitate security sector reform, including civil-military relations, right-sizing and professionalisation of the security sector as early as demobilization efforts are commenced.

While the PCRD expressly noted that SSR is an essential item on the agenda of peace, security and sustainable development in Africa, an exclusive focus and explicit mandate for a regional instrument on SSR was only later to be articulated; in further providing the AU Commission with the mandate to pursue and operationalize SSR, the January/February 2008 AU Summit expressly 'encourage(d) the AU Commission to develop a comprehensive AU policy framework on security sector reform' (Assembly/AU/Dec.117(X)).

At the African Regional Workshop on Security Sector Reform co-hosted by the AU and the UN in March 2009, AU Commissioner for Peace and Security H.E. Ramtane Lamamra articulated the need for Africa to undertake SSR: 'Some member states face huge challenges that make it difficult for them to fulfill their security obligations to their own citizens. In other member states, the security forces have, for one reason or another, become a threat to ordinary citizens. For these reasons, some African member states clearly need to reform their security sectors ....'[8]

---

7   The 'Declaration and Treaty of SADC' was adopted by Member States in 1992.

8   Unpublished speech delivered on 23 March 2009 at the African Union Commission in Addis Ababa.

At the explicit request of the African Heads of State, the African Union Commission is currently developing a comprehensive Policy Framework on Security Sector Reform in response to directives from its Member States. This Policy Framework builds on a number of existing frameworks, like the PCRD Framework as well as corresponding developments in other components of the African Peace and Security Architecture (APSA).

For its part, the United Nations has articulated its approach to SSR in the January 2008 Report of the Secretary-General on SSR and subsequent developments (discussed in detail below) which seek to provide a common, system-wide framework to enhance the Organization's capacity to support the SSR initiatives of Member States. Consistent with the African Union's approach to SSR, the United Nations has also adopted a broad conception of security. The Millennium Declaration (General Assembly resolution 55/2, para. 6) articulates a vision of security that extends beyond the narrow security of the state to include the notion that 'men and women have the right to live their lives and raise their children in dignity, free from hunger and from the fear of violence, oppression or injustice'. In 2001, former UN Secretary-General Kofi Annan in his 'Towards a Culture of Peace' noted that security could no longer be understood in purely military terms but '[r]ather, it must encompass economic development, social justice, environmental protection, democratization, disarmament and respect for human rights and the rule of law'.[9]

These shifts toward a broader understanding of security have coincided with an evolution in the nature and composition of UN peacekeeping operations. Over the past few decades, peacekeeping operations have evolved from narrowly focusing on supporting a specific activity (e.g. monitoring ceasefires and patrolling buffer zones) to deploying multidimensional operations, which are composed of a range of diverse civilian and military capacities aimed at addressing the myriad security challenges prevalent in conflict and post-conflict settings. For example, depending on the requirements of each mission, this expertise may include military and/or police personnel, disarmament, demobilization, reintegration experts, mediation support, elections expertise, courts and prison management, de-mining expertise, human rights capacities, among a range of other specialized capabilities.

Security sector reform has been a core element of a number of these multidimensional peacekeeping operations. However, while the United Nations has been engaged in SSR in all but name for close to two decades,[10] the first Security Council mandate to explicitly use the term 'security sector' was not issued until 2002 in relation to the UN's engagement in Sierra Leone. [11] Since then, the

---

9   See Kofi Annan. 'Towards a Culture of Peace'. Available at: http://www.unesco.org/opi2/lettres/TextAnglais/AnnanE.html 08/22/01.

10   For example, in 1989, the UN supported national authorities in reforming the armed forces and building a new army in Namibia.

11   In Security Council Resolution 1436 pertaining to Sierra Leone, the Security Council urged the Government of Sierra Leone 'to strengthen the operational effectiveness

demand on the UN system to support national authorities in the area of SSR has increased significantly. Currently, most of the UN's field Missions are mandated to undertake SSR-related activities and to provide support to national authorities in this important area. While not exclusively limited to Africa, many of these operations are on the continent, including for example in Burundi, the Democratic Republic of the Congo (DRC), Liberia, Sudan and Côte d'Ivoire. While the UN's engagement in SSR various from context to context, the UN provides support to national authorities in a number of SSR-related areas, including training and infrastructure development, capacity-building for management and oversight of security institutions, strategic advice for the development of national security policies, strategies and plans, assistance with coordinating international partners in support of national SSR priorities, among a range of other activities.

Yet, despite this experience, the Organization's support to national SSR efforts has been ad hoc. This is due in part to the fact that – until recently – the United Nations did not have a common UN definition and approach to SSR or the requisite capacity to deliver support in this area. In light of these weaknesses, including the lack of an overarching framework, in 2007, the Special Committee on Peacekeeping Operations (C-34) asked the Secretary-General to submit to the General Assembly a comprehensive report on United Nations approach to SSR. The Security Council also acknowledged the need for such a report. On the basis of this directive from Member States, the United Nations Secretary-General prepared a report on the UN's approach. The report, entitled 'Securing Peace and Development: the role of the UN in supporting security sector reform (A/62/659-S/2008/39)' (released in January 2008) provides an overarching framework for the UN's approach to SSR.

As the title of the Report of the Secretary-General suggests, the UN's approach to SSR extends beyond narrow conceptions of SSR to include a broader, more comprehensive security agenda, which has as its ultimate goal the achievement of peace and development. Accordingly, the UN's approach to SSR is broad. It is based on the assumption that SSR is more than narrow exercises like 'right-sizing' the security services or 'training and equipping' uniformed personnel; it involves a set of strategies, policies and activities that are – at their core – aimed at transforming states and societies in accordance with nationally defined goals, including the reduction of poverty, the consolidation of the rule of law and good governance and the extension of state authority.

The UN has also assumed a very flexible definition of the security sector on the basis of the understanding that there is no single definition of SSR. It is ultimately

---

of the security sector'. For a review of the historical use of the term 'security sector' and 'security sector reform' in UN mandates see Heiner Hänggi and Vincenza Scherrer. 'Recent Experiences of United Nations Integrated Missions Security Sector Reform' in Heiner Hänggi and Vincenza Scherrer (2008) Security Sector Reform and UN Integrated Missions: Experience from Burundi, the Democratic Republic of the Congo, Haiti and Kosovo, Geneva, Geneva Center for Democratic Control of the Armed Forces.

up to Member States to decide which institutions will be considered part of their national security sector. The UN does however provide broad parameters of a security sector. Specifically, as the Secretary-General's report notes (2008: 5 (para 14)):

> 'Security sector' is a broad term often used to describe the structures, institutions and personnel responsible for the management, provision and oversight of security in a country. It is generally accepted that the security sector includes defence, law enforcement, corrections, intelligence services and institutions responsible for border management, customs and civil emergencies. Elements of the judicial sector responsible for the adjudication of cases of alleged criminal conduct and misuse of force are, in many instances, also included. Furthermore, the security sector includes actors that play a role in managing and overseeing the design and implementation of security, such as ministries, legislative bodies and civil society groups. Other non-State actors that could be considered part of the security sector include customary or informal authorities and private security services.

The Secretary-General's report also provides a definition of SSR in relatively general terms. It notes that SSR is 'a process of assessment, review and implementation as well as monitoring and evaluation led by national authorities that has as its goal the enhancement of effective and accountable security for the State and its peoples without discrimination and with full respect for human rights and the rule of law' (2008: 6 (para. 17)).

These definitions may, at first glance, appear overly broad. However, such flexibility and the need to avoid a 'one-size-fits-all' approach to SSR is inherent in the composition of the UN itself, an organization made up of Member States with varying approaches and security arrangements. In an attempt to ensure this flexibility does not translate into chaos, the Secretary-General's Report provides a set of 10 basic principles which guide the Organization's provision of SSR support. At the core of these principles is the notion of national ownership. The report underscores that SSR should be nationally owned and should be undertaken on the basis of a national request, a Security Council mandate and/or a General Assembly resolution in accordance with the UN Charter and standards. In addition, support in the SSR area must be anchored on national ownership and the commitment of involved states and societies.

Other, equally important, principles are also guiding the UN's approach to SSR. These include the following: i) the goal of the UN in SSR is to support states and societies in developing effective and accountable security; ii) a UN approach to SSR must be flexible and tailored to the needs of specific environments; iii) a gender perspective is critical in all stages of a SSR process; iv) a SSR framework is essential at the outset of a peace process, in early recovery strategies and in post-conflict contexts; v) a clearly-defined SSR strategy is essential; vi) the effectiveness of international support to SSR will be shaped by integrity of motive, accountability, resources and capacity; vii) the efforts of national and international partners must be well coordinated; and viii) monitoring and evaluation are essential to track and maintain progress in SSR over time (2008: 13).

The Prospects for Strategic Collaboration and the Challenges Ahead

What then is the relationship between the SSR agendas of the AU and the UN? What is the significance of such a relationship and what challenges are likely to lie ahead?

The UN Secretary-General's report makes clear that partnerships with regional organizations – particularly with the African Union – are absolutely essential to the UN's approach to SSR. This commitment is guided, in part, by the recognition that regional approaches to SSR form the building blocs for the legitimacy and sustainability of the global SSR approach of the United Nations. The viability of a global approach to SSR is, to a large degree, dependent on the extent to which it is informed by, and responsive to regional approaches. Thus, the UN recognizes that while Chapter VIII of the UN Charter states that the UN Security Council has primary responsibility for international peace and security, regional organizations such as the AU are the main custodians of peace and security in their respective regions. Thus, the AU is uniquely positioned to ensure that its efforts to maintain peace and security align to the African vision and African aspirations across the entire spectrum of activity areas that are crucial for the consolidation of peace. Therefore, the UN is dependent on regional organizations as building blocs and for the legitimacy of its SSR framework.

On the other hand, there is potential benefit to the AU (and other regional organizations) in the lessons and experiences of the United Nations in the development of a multilateral approach to SSR. As discussed below, the experiences of the United Nations – along with the fact that it is often one of the first actors on the ground – set it aside as a vital SSR partner for national authorities. The UN is also uniquely positioned to support regional organizations, like the African Union, as it develops its own approach to SSR. Indeed, SSR is highly political and cuts to the core of sovereignty of state and to the physical security of its people. For this reason, SSR remains a contested concept, complicated by the multiplicity of interests of both states requiring reform and those offering such support. Particularly within the framework of contemporary strategic politics, many developing countries have openly categorized the global North as being part of the security *problematique* of the global South. In essence they see their countries as the arena for the War on Terror, increasingly questioning the sincerity of motive in bilateral security cooperation. In this regard, the global mandate, political neutrality and legitimacy of the United Nations uniquely positions the Organization as the most suitable partner to provide support to the AU, and other regional organizations, in this important but delicate area. For these reasons, a strategic partnership between the AU and the UN is mutually beneficial to both organizations.

The intersection between the AU and UN's SSR agenda became more active and solidified around the preparation of the Report of the Secretary-General on SSR and the various related consultations. A major milestone in this regard is the international workshop on SSR held in Cape Town, South Africa, in November 2007. The International Workshop on 'Enhancing UN Support for SSR in Africa: Towards an African Perspective' was co-chaired by the Governments of Slovakia and South Africa and brought together 150 participants representing 47 countries, including 25 African countries, the African Union, including ECOWAS and SADC, and the United Nations system as well as several nongovernmental organizations.

The Cape Town workshop formed the basis of the February 2008 decision of the Assembly of the African Union, which, as noted earlier, called on the AU Commission to develop a comprehensive SSR Framework for the African Union. This statutory decision forms the basis of the United Nations collaboration with the AU Commission on SSR. Accordingly, towards the realization of the decision of this decision of African Heads of State, the AU Commission and the United Nations jointly held a regional consultation on SSR in Africa in Addis Ababa in March 2009. A major outcome of the event was the agreement of both organizations on a strategic collaboration on SSR through which the UN would support the AU to:

1. Develop a comprehensive AU policy framework on security sector reform and other SSR-related normative frameworks as may be decided by political authorities and as agreed with the AU Commission;
2. Enhance the AU's capacity to implement a continental SSR policy framework, in close coordination and collaboration with sub-regional entities and AU Member States;
3. Introduce and sustain annual regional consultation on SSR to serve as a mechanism for articulating, assessing and updating the African SSR agenda.

While both organizations continue to work to achieve these elements of strategic collaboration, it is useful at this point to consider the challenges which are likely to emerge.

First, the experience of the United Nations as a multilateral bureaucracy in the process of consolidating an institutional capacity to support SSR indicates that various inter-departmental and institutional architectural issues would need to be identified, negotiated, discussed and put in place by the AU Commission. That is, the UN is at a relatively advanced stage in the development of methodologies, tools and institutional mechanisms, which may be useful to the African Union. For example, the UN has developed a number of structures that seek to enhance the Organization's capacity to provide SSR support to national actors. In 2007, the Secretary-General's Policy Committee established a UN inter-agency SSR Task

Force, which brings together various SSR capacities and expertise. At present 11 UN departments, agencies, funds and programmes are members of this Task Force, which is chaired by the Department of Peacekeeping Operations (DPKO).[12] The Task Force meets regularly and serves as a forum for building coherence of UN SSR programming in specific contexts. Specifically, the Task Force is meant to provide a pool of system-wide expertise on SSR in a range of different contexts (e.g. peacekeeping through to early recovery, sustainable peacebuilding and development) and on the basis of broad expertise, including for example human rights, gender and governance).[13] The inter-agency SSR Task Force is also engaged in implementing a system-wide SSR capacity-building programme which includes the development of guidance on SSR, training, a community of practice, a roster of senior SSR experts, a repository of best practices and lessons learned in SSR, along with other elements.

DPKO's Office of Rule of Law and Security Institutions also hosts an SSR Unit, which serves as a SSR focal point and technical resource for the UN, national authorities and international partners. It serves as the chair of the UN inter-agency SSR Task Force, and manages the implementation of an inter-agency SSR capacity-building programme. The SSR Unit also provides direct support to UN Missions assisting national authorities with SSR. In the field, a number of Missions host a dedicated SSR capacity.[14] While the activities supported by these

---

12　The United Nations inter-agency SSR Task Force consists of members from the Department of Political Affairs, the Department of Peacekeeping Operations, the United Nations Office for Disarmament Affairs, the Office of the High Commissioner for Human Rights, the Office of the Special Advisor on Africa, the United Nations Development Programme, the United Nations Population Fund, the United Nations Children's Fund, the United Nations Development Fund for Women, the United Nations Office on Drugs and Crime, and the Peacebuilding Support Office.

13　In supporting SSR, different parts of the United Nations system have developed specific expertise and capacity. The Department of Political Affairs has focused on security sector reform in peacemaking processes and in the context of offices or missions led by the Department of Political Affairs, while the Department of Peacekeeping Operations concentrates on support for defence, police, corrections and, in a peacekeeping context, legal and judicial institutions. OHCHR addresses the reform of human rights institutions and capacity-building for security actors, and UNDP has expertise in supporting institutional development in the areas of justice and security, as well as in legislative and civil society oversight. UNODC has proven strengths in supporting the enhancement of crime prevention capacity, while UNIFEM brings knowledge and expertise on the gender dimensions of security sector reform. The United Nations is currently focusing on ensuring that all such SSR expertise and capacity form part of a coordinated United Nations approach, and it was largely towards this objective that the report of the Secretary-General on SSR was released in January 2008.

14　BINUB, the United Nations Mission in the Democratic Republic of the Congo (MONUC), the United Nations Mission in Liberia (UNMIL), the United Nations Mission in Nepal (UNMIN) and the United Nations Integrated Mission in Timor-Leste (UNMIT).

capacities vary from Mission to Mission, in general terms, support to national authorities falls into the following categories (A/62/659-S/2008/39: para. 50):

a. helping to establish an enabling environment;
b. supporting needs assessments and strategic planning as well as coordination and specialized resource mobilization;
c. providing technical advice to and building the capacity of security institutions and their oversight mechanisms; and
d. supporting national and international partners in monitoring and reviewing progress.

A major challenge for the AU Commission therefore is how to identify and establish the appropriate mechanisms for dealing with cross-cutting and multidimensional nature of SSR and to ensure coherence between them. Accordingly, the UN's experiences with the UN inter-agency SSR Task Force and the establishment of DPKO's SSR Unit may be useful.

A second central challenge relates to the seemingly omnipresent gap in the imperative of national ownership on the one hand and its implementation and realization on the other. Indeed, SSR has been severally criticized as being donor-driven, arguably reflecting more the preferences and dictates of external actors than the societies ostensibly undergoing reform. SSR support is also criticized for being based on models that represent a misreading of the political and cultural realities of reform contexts and adhere to external visions of reform priorities. The AU and the UN may be uniquely positioned to support national authorities in facilitating the process of developing a common national security vision for countries emerging from conflict.

However, a pan-African organization must be particularly sensitive to the challenge of national ownership if it is to be able to articulate an SSR agenda which is seen by all African States as being uniquely African and not a product of external pressure. While the AU Commission will necessarily continue to grapple with this challenge, its decision to launch a strategic partnership with the UN affords it a claim to a measure of neutrality. However, much will depend on the level of transparency and inclusive participation that goes into the articulation of the AU SSR policy framework. Closely associated with the challenge of national ownership is the question of financing SSR support by the AU, and the extent to which 'regional ownership' (in addition to national ownership) can be ensured in a context of dwindling resources.

At the time of writing, the United Nations Mission in Sudan (UNMIS) is in the process of establishing a dedicated team with SSR capacities.

Conclusion

Focusing on the AU and the UN, this chapter has sought to account for the increasing engagement of multilateral organizations in SSR support in a rapidly shifting context from a focus on the security of states to a focus on the security of peoples. The origins of each organization's SSR approach have been discussed. Both the AU and the UN stand to benefit from the strategic relationship that has evolved between them. The AU is veritable source of legitimacy and an essential building bloc for the global framework of the UN. On the other hand, the UN has valuable experience to share with the AU in the field of multilateral support to SSR processes. While the strategic collaboration on SSR between them is commendable, the chapter recognizes that significant challenges must be addressed moving forward, including challenges of national ownership and institutional coherence.

References

Annan, Kofi. 'Towards a Culture of Peace'. Available at: http://www.unesco.org/opi2/lettres/TextAnglais/AnnanE.html 08/22/01.

Bellamy, Alex J. 'Security Sector Reform: Prospects and Problems', *Global Change, Peace and Security*, Vol. 15, No. 2, June 2003.

Ebo, Adedeji. 'Towards a Code of Conduct for Armed Forces and Security Services in Africa: Opportunities and Challenges', Policy Paper, Democratic Control of the Armed Forces, Geneva, 2005.

Deepa, Narayan, Chambers, Robert, Shah, Meera K. and Petesch, Patti, *Voices of the Poor: Crying Out for Change*, New York: Oxford University Press, 2000.

Greene, Owen. 'Security Sector Reform, Conflict Prevention and Regional Perspectives: A Discussion Paper for Whitehall Policy Seminar on Security Sector Reform', *Journal of Security Sector Management*, Vol. 1, No. 1, March 2003.

Hänggi, Heiner and Scherrer, Vincenza (eds). *Security Sector Reform and UN Integrated Missions: Experience from Burundi, the Democratic Republic of the Congo, Haiti and Kosovo*, Geneva, Geneva Center for Democratic Control of the Armed Forces, 2008.

Hendrickson, Dylan and Ball, Nicole. 'Off-Budget Military Expenditure and Revenue: Issues and Policy Perspectives for Donors', CSDG Occasional Papers #1, Kings College London, January 2002.

Hutchful, Eboe. 'From Military Security to Human Security' in John Akokpari, Angela Ndinga-Muvumba, and Tim Murithi (eds) *The African Union and its Institutions*, Center for Conflict Resolution, Cape Town, 2008.

Olonisakin, Funmi. 'Pan-African Approaches to Civilian Control and Democratic Governance. Control and Democratic Governance', in Victor-Yves Ghebali, Alexandre Lambert (eds) *Democratic Governance of the Security Sector*

Beyond the OSCE Area: Regional Approaches in Africa and the Americas, Geneva Center for Democratic Control of the Armed Forces, Geneva, 2007.

Powell, Kristiana. 'The Impact of Arms Transfer on Sustainable Development: A Review of the Literature', Project Ploughshares Working Paper 04–3, September 2004. http://www.ploughshares.ca/libraries/WorkingPapers/WPlist. html.

United Nations Secretary-General, Report of Secretary-General. 'Securing Peace and Development: The role of the United Nations in supporting security sector reform'. 23 January 2008 (A/62/659-S/2008/39).

Chapter 5

The European Union (EU) and the Emerging African Peace and Security Architecture

Stefan Gänzle and Sven Grimm

International Responses to Africa's New Geostrategic Importance

When in the early 1990s violent conflicts and large-scale genocides like the ones in Somalia and Rwanda respectively had exacerbated Africa's image as a war-torn, 'dark' continent – if not a 'lost' one at the very end – the strategic interest of many international actors had sharply declined. In the midst of the Yugoslav war in the first half of the 1990s, Western actors very much concentrated on the European theatre. Furthermore, in a view to Africa, the United States had just suffered a severe blow in 1993 after the death of 18 US soldiers who were part of the United Nations Operation in Somalia I (UNOSOM 1), in Mogadishu in 1993. It appears to be a consequence of this particular experience that, in 1995, the US Department of Defence asserted in its US Security Strategy for Sub-Saharan Africa, that 'ultimately we see very little traditional strategic interest in Africa' (quoted in Ploch 2007, 2).

Since 2000, Africa's strategic importance had been recognized by many major actors. The US government, for instance, appointed Ambassador Cindy Courville to become the first non-African envoy to the African Union (in 2006), and established the African Command, a unified geographical combatant command of the US military focusing exclusively on the African continent (in 2007). In fact, since 2000, Africa is back on the agenda of most major players in the world including the United States, the European Union and new donors such as China and India. Also, Russia's energy giant Gazprom signed a US$2.5 billion deal with the Nigerian National Petroleum Corporation to form Nigaz, a new joint venture.

On the one hand, the renewed interest of these actors is certainly fuelled by self-interest, having identified Africa's abundance in natural resources as a key to provide long-term energy security by easing Western countries' dependence on the Middle East or Russia. According to estimates of the London-based World Energy Council, the continent harbours approximately 10 per cent of the world's reserves in crude oil and gas (see Gänzle and Grimm 2008). China's oil imports from Africa have been increasing at an annual compounded rate of 30 per cent.[1] In addition, Africa is becoming more important in other respects, too: China has evolved into Africa's third biggest trading partner, challenging the positions of number one and two, i.e. Europe and the United States. Chinese exports to Africa exceeded US$100 billion in 2008. Originally, the Chinese leadership had expected 2010 to be the target year for this trade volume. Another competitor to Chinese engagement is preparing in the wings: India. While its trade volumes and investments are still much smaller than the Chinese, the rivalry between these two Asian powers on the African continent (for energy sources, market shares, and international support) might exceed the current Western competition in the long-term. With China's adherence to non-interference in governance questions and the Chinese path for economic development as a new model, some African governments are starting to dream of alternatives to Western-style democracies and values.

Against this background, the United States, which already launched a number of important initiatives, such as the Millennium Challenge Account,[2] under the Bush government seems to have put diplomacy, development and defence *vis-à-vis* the continent into a higher gear. Some observers assume that the Obama administration has the ambition to eventually tackle thorny challenges such as peacekeeping in Darfur or how to overcome the Zimbabwean autocracy. Also the European Union (EU), the world's largest donor of development assistance (or rather: the world's largest donor system coalescing more or less around a set of policies), channels more than half of its development funding to Africa (Grimm 2006). In 2008, more than 60 per cent of all official development assistance to Africa actually came from the EU and its member states. On the other hand, the renewed interest of major powers in Africa's renaissance – an ambitious idea formulated by the former South African President Thabo Mbeki – has become instrumental in fostering bold steps towards closer political cooperation on peace and security matters on the continent. In this regard, new African initiatives were launched after 2000, such as the New Partnership for Africa's Development (NEPAD) and the African Peer Review Mechanism (APRM), both of which are meant to provide vision and strategic tools for the acclaimed renewal of Africa.

---

1   As of 2006, China consumed less than 10 per cent of Africa's oil production; more than 18 per cent went for instance to the US (compared to 17 per cent which are being imported from the Persian Gulf to the US). Overall, China imported more than 38 million metric tons of crude oil from Africa (York 2006), which amounted to over 31 percent of China's total oil imports (see Medeiros 2006a and 2006b). China now accounts for around 9 per cent of Africa's oil and gas exports, and comparable amounts pertaining to its other key mineral exports (such as copper, gold, platinum, manganese) (York 2006).

2   The United States' Millennium Challenge Account (MCA) is a bilateral development fund that was formally established in January 2004. The MCA receives funds appropriated by Congress on an annual basis. It is administered by the Millennium Challenge Corporation (MCC), a US government agency designed to work with some of the poorest countries in the world that are willing to adhere to a set of policy principles with the aim of forging good governance. It is meant to provide a premium for good governance to poor countries.

Contrary to previous attempts by the Organization for African Unity (OAU) to establish a Mechanism for Conflict Prevention in (June 1993), its successor organization, the African Union (AU), was ultimately successful in setting up an African Peace and Security Architecture (APSA) in 2004.[3] In doing so, the AU has come closer to realizing 'Kwame Nkrumah's dream of permanent and structured continental security cooperation' (Franke 2009a).

Five years into the existence of APSA, many international donors are highly active in supporting it via different channels, both bilateral and multilateral. However, as various modes of delivery and reporting standards on assistance to the African Peace and Security Architecture apply and little track is kept by central actors in Africa, it is extremely difficult to assess the exact financial scope of external support of APSA. The US, for instance, has provided support to peace missions (including in kind intelligence support), in particular to the Ugandan mission in Somalia. NATO, has provided logistical support to the AU Mission to Sudan (such as for airlift in Darfur) between June 2005 and 31 December 2007.[4] China is engaged with the AU in establishing new office buildings on the AU compound in Addis Ababa (since 2008). Last, but not least, Germany is contributing towards APSA through a number of activities, such as the building of a new Peace and Security Department (see African Union 2008), providing police training, and supporting the Kofi Annan Peacekeeping Training Centre and the German African Border Project (see GTZ 2009). Clearly, the EU is so far the largest funding partner of the AU[5] and has taken an active interest in supporting APSA (see Africa Clearing House 2008). Yet, the EU is not only important in financial terms; it is also unique because of its comprehensive approach as EU–AU relations are embedded in a multidimensional strategic as well as political approach to partnership, including the Common Foreign and Security Policy (not to speak of trade-related policies), as well as direct and indirect military and non-military support.

The EU is a highly complex actor which also includes individual policies of its member states, some of which still maintain 'special relations' with their former colonies. Thus, the African continent ultimately constitutes a fine benchmark for the EU's ambition to increase the internal coherence and coordination of its external policies. Obviously, the EU's motives are not purely altruistic: ultimately, the

---

3   Following the 'Sirte Declaration' of the Heads of State and Government of the Organisation of African Unity on 9 September 1999, the African Union was founded in 2002 to promote unity and solidarity of African states, to foster economic development, and to support international cooperation. The African Union (AU) replaced the Organization of African Unity (OAU).

4   NATO support ended on 31 December 2007 when AMIS was transferred to the hybrid United Nations/African Union Mission in Darfur (UNAMID) (see NATO 2009).

5   According to Africa Clearing House (2008), the EU has earmarked €55 million from the European Development Fund (February 2006–January 2010) for its support programme aiming to strengthen the operational and institutional capacity of the AU institutions.

European Union would like to see African states in a position to shoulder their fair share of responsibility for peace-keeping on the continent. Peace-keeping efforts in Africa, which take up by far the biggest part of the UN budget for missions, are also a political and financial burden to the EU, even more so as Brussels has engaged in a number of European Security and Defence Policy (ESDP) sponsored missions on the African continent.

In this chapter, we will make three closely intertwined claims: first, EU–Africa relations are growing out of the narrow (but certainly path-dependent) confines of their historic post-World War II matrix. Most of the EU's former colonial powers have increasingly 'europeanized' their national foreign policies *vis-à-vis* Africa, which means that they increasingly seek to align their national policies with EU policies as well as policy objectives and practices. Second, and consequently, the EU has become a key security actor, in particular by supporting African initiatives to establish an African Peace and Security Architecture. Third, this engagement has an impact on the EU itself by fostering new forms of inter-Union coordination, creating a dynamic which may lead to singing from the same hymn sheet – if not speaking with a single voice – in the Union's Common Foreign and Security Policy.

The Impact of Historic Legacies on EU-Africa Relations

There are deeply entrenched historic legacies in the relationship between Europe and Africa: from the early days of regional integration in Europe, Africa – or at least the former European colonies – has been viewed as a major concern and responsibility by most Europeans. In the Declaration of 9 May 1950, at a time when European colonial 'empires' still existed, the French foreign minister Robert Schuman proposed that:

> Franco-German production of coal and steel … will be offered to the world as a whole without distinction or exception, with the aim of contributing to raising living standards and to promoting peaceful achievements. With increased resources Europe will be able to pursue the achievement of one of its essential tasks, namely, the development of the African continent. (Schuman 1950)

In turn, European integration would help Europe's declining colonial powers, in particular France, Belgium, and later the UK and Portugal, to organize and 'overcome' the loss of their former colonial fiefdoms. It was important to these states that many aspects of their national agenda and responsibilities *vis-à-vis* Africa could be 'multilateralized' via the EU. At the same time, these countries, in particular the UK and France, would also be in a position to maintain or continue to forge a 'special relationship' with the increasing number of independent African states. Or, as a malevolent observer put it: for a long time, EU Africa policy used to be French policy writ large. Since the end of the Cold War, however, this has changed and post-colonial ties have gradually loosened. Given Africa's decreasing share in the European market,[6] the economic aspect of the special relationship is loosening, too. The relationship was once substantiated by different generations of agreements between the EU and the African, Caribbean and Pacific Group of States (ACP)[7] and now has shifted increasingly to the sub-regional level with the negotiations of Economic Partnership Agreements (EPAs) (see, for example, Makhan 2009). Since the second half of the 1990s, Africa has been increasingly targeted by the EU's foreign policy. In the wake of the European Security and Defence Policy (ESDP)[8] which came into existence in 1998–99, Africa has also become a testing ground on which to pull the EU's foreign policy trigger.

Geographical proximity and colonial legacy might be two reasons for Africa to be an arena for EU foreign policy, besides the increase of hard security interests, such as the fear of creating a breeding ground for terrorism in failed states, migratory movements, or energy security. Particularly, France has always assumed a decisive role in shaping EU foreign policy (e.g. setting up ESDP missions to Africa (Democratic Republic of the Congo, Chad/Central African Republic)) and has often taken the lion's share in terms of equipping contingents. In the case of the European Union Force (EUFOR) mission to Chad and the Central African Republic, for instance, 2,100 out of 3,700 soldiers were French (France Diplomatie 2008).

Almost half of the ESDP missions to date have been deployed on African ground[9] – often spear-heading new initiatives in this policy arena. Hence it comes as no surprise that the radius of operation for European battle groups is about 6,000 km, i.e. just enough to extend to the Cape of Good Hope. The first ESDP

---

6   In 1975, the share of the ACP group in global exports to Europe was 7.5 per cent. Despite preferential trade regime, this proportion of the EU market declined to 2.8 per cent in 2007. Much of this was commodities, not least oil (see Makhan 2009).

7   The ACP is currently comprising 79 member states: 48 African, 16 Caribbean and 15 Pacific states. In 1975, the share of the ACP group in global exports to Europe was 7.5 per cent. Despite preferential trade regime, this proportion of the EU market declined to 2.8 percent in 2007. Much of this was commodities, not least oil (see Makhan 2009).

8   With the Amsterdam Treaty of 1999, EU foreign policy was strengthened, *inter alia* by creating a 'High Representative' for the Common Foreign and Security in the Council. In the wake of the coming into force of the Amsterdam treaty, at a summit in the French beach resort of St Malo in 1998, the UK and France had agreed on closer cooperation in defence matters. This momentum was picked up upon at subsequent EU summits in Cologne and Helsinki in 1999, and led to the formulation of headline goals for a common security policy.

9   After the EUFOR mission to Chad/RCA was concluded on 15 March 2009, the number of operating ESDP missions was reduced to 12 (giving it a total of four in South-Eastern and Eastern Europe, including the Caucasus; three in the Middle East; one in Central Asia; four in Africa). The number of completed mission now is 10 (four in South-Eastern and Eastern Europe, including the Caucasus; one in Central Asia and five in Africa) – making a total of 27 ESDP missions to date (see ISIS Europe 2009, 1).

mission outside Europe ('Artemis') took place in the Democratic Republic of the Congo in 2003, and the first maritime ESDP mission ('Atlanta') was deployed in December 2008 to fight pirates in the waters just off the coast of Somalia. Although it is certainly true that some member states serve as driving forces at the EU level, it is important to note that the European Union as a collective body has increased its capacities to act *vis-à-vis* Africa. Security policy broadly conceived (thus including, for instance, concerns over the migratory pressure of Sub-Saharan Africa) has developed into the key unifying force in European capitals when it comes to devising European policy approaches towards the neighbours of the South. This political driver, however, does not mean that immediate unity has been achieved. Coastal countries; countries such as Greece, or Malta find themselves feeling overwhelmed by migrants arriving from the South. The migration pressure has led to cooperation with Libya and other North African states to coordinate efforts aimed at stemming the tide of illegal migrants to Europe, as well as deportation and repatriation efforts.

EU Cooperation with and Support to APSA

One of the key objectives of European security policy is to support African capacities in peace-keeping. This is done either through the AU or other sub-regional bodies such as the Economic Community of West African States (ECOWAS) or the Southern African Development Community (SADC). The EU and its member states are actively involved in strengthening the African Peace and Security Architecture within the AU. APSA is built around five core institutions such as a Peace and Security Council, Panel of the Wise, a Peace fund, a Continental Early Warning System and an African Standby Force (see Cilliers 2008; Franke 2009a for a general overview). The EU does not only aim at fostering the principle of African ownership, but also recognizes in these initiatives the opportunity not to have to deploy its own troops in the medium term. The EU has already financially supported a number of AU missions via its African Peace Facility, for instance in Burundi and Somalia, as well as logistically supported the African Union Mission in Sudan (AMIS), which is considered the AU's most ambitious operation to date.[10]

Most importantly, the European Union has included 'an important regional dimension in its Common Foreign and Security Policy (CFSP) and European Security and Defence Policy (ESDP)' (see Mubialia 2007, 114), which ultimately includes both a strategic vision and a concrete programme to address insecurity

---

10   See Center on International Cooperation (2009, 7): 'Since its creation in 2004, the African Peace Facility (APF) has financed African-led peace support operations (€360 million) and capacity building activities (€35 million) aiming to support peace, security and stability and to provide the preconditions for sustainable development. In total, the EU has provided €440 million to foster peace and security in Africa through the APF so far.'

in the world. The European Security Strategy, released in December 2003, has singled out Africa as a major concern for security in Europe as well as a common task for EU policy: 'State failure and organized crime spread if they are neglected – as we have seen in West Africa. This implies that we should be ready to act before a crisis occurs. Conflict prevention and threat prevention cannot start too early' (European Union 2003, 9).[11] Africa, which ever since the launch of the European integration project has played a role in EU policies, seems to become a point of reference in the making of a genuine strategic culture within the European Union.

Subsequently, the EU Strategy for Africa (2005) and the Joint Africa-EU Strategy (2007) and its associated Action Plan were fleshed out with a view of changing the very nature of relations between Africa and Europe.[12] The strategy was formulated in response to geopolitical changes, globalisation and the processes of integration in Africa and Europe respectively. At its core is a much more overtly political relationship (see Tywuschik and Sheriff 2009) and the desire to sketch out a relationship among 'equal partners'. The Joint Africa-EU Partnership, adopted in Lisbon in December 2007, established a 'highly complicated framework of interaction' (Pirozzi 2009, 19), which is probably the most complex and comprehensive framework the EU entertains with any of its strategic partners in foreign policy.[13]

Cooperation and Coordination

The Africa–EU dialogue is slotted to take place at different levels (including local authorities, civil societies, member states and European institutions) and in various institutional settings. Among the most significant levels are:

---

11   More often than any other continent and world region, 'Africa' is mentioned five times in the short strategic paper.

12   The Action Plan was agreed upon at the 2nd Africa–EU Summit in Lisbon. Africa–EU meetings were first started in 2000 in Cairo and were meant to comprise the entire continent (including North Africa), as opposed to the ACP group. Disagreements over the participation of Zimbabwean President Robert Mugabe (he is subject to an EU travel ban) prevented the meeting to take place until 2007. A connection might be drawn between the more flexible EU approach to Mugabe's participation in 2007 and the China–Africa summit in Beijing in November 2006. The increasing competition with Beijing might have softened the EU's stance on Mugabe. The agreed action plan comprises eight action areas, covering a vast range of topics, *inter alia* peace and security, democratic governance, the Millennium Development Goals (MDGs), trade, climate change, and cooperation in science and 'information society' (see fn 14). For more information, see: http://europafrica.net/jointstrategy/.

13   The AU is not the only institution to maintain a strategic partnership with the EU. In contrast, the EU has agreed upon strategic partnerships with a number of key partners, such as the US, Canada, India, China, Russia.

- Africa–EU summits, which are held every three years;
- complemented by periodical ministerial-level meetings;
- regular meetings of the EU Political and Security Committee and the AU Peace and Security Council;
- Commission-to-Commission meetings, which bring Presidents and Commissioners together; members of the AU and European Commission with similar portfolios also meet regularly on a bilateral basis. Staff from both Commissions meet twice a year (alternately in Europe and Africa) as the 'Joint Task Force', to review sectoral and institutional cooperation);
- Europe-Africa Research Network (EARN) (which links European and African non-governmental research institutions with the aim of providing independent political research);
- AU representation to the EU in Brussels and an EU Delegation to the AU; and
- joint expert groups, charged with the implementation of the eight areas for strategic partnership.

Thus, from a constructivist perspective, the framework of this relationship offers ample room for close interaction and socialization processes if utilized accordingly. Thus far, the real impact of these summits and meetings is hard to measure and actors privately express frustration with the slow pace of implementation and the limited commitment or capacity of all sides to taking an agenda forward.

A number of EU bodies and actors address issues of peace and security. While the Political and Security Committee exercises political oversight in the EU Council, it is the Directorate-General for Development (DG DEV), the Directorate-General for External Relations (DG RELEX) and the Europe Aid Co-Operation Office (AIDCO) within the Commission that are responsible for ACP countries, South Africa, and Northern African countries and policy implementation respectively.[14] In order to ensure coordination and coherence between these different Directorates-General (DGs) and eight priority areas,[15] an Africa Commission inter-service task force has been created (see Pirozzi 2009, 20). Eight implementation teams – composed by the European Commission and member states – have been set up to cover each of the eight partnerships. The EU Council Secretariat is in charge of facilitating the work of the implementation team dealing with peace and security. An Action Plan identifies three priority actions: 1) dialogue, led by the European Commission; 2) APSA, consisting of two components: military (led by France), and civilian and police aspects (led by Italy); and 3) peace support operations, led by the Commission and the UK (see Joint EU–AU Expert Meeting 2008).

---

14 See Pirozzi (2009, 20–21) for more details.

15 The eight priorities areas Africa-EU thematic partnerships are: 1) Peace and Security; 2) Democratic Governance and Human Rights; 3) Trade and Regional Integration; 4) Millennium Development Goals; 5) Energy; 6) Climate Change; 7) Migration, Mobility and Employment; 8) Science, Information Society and Space.

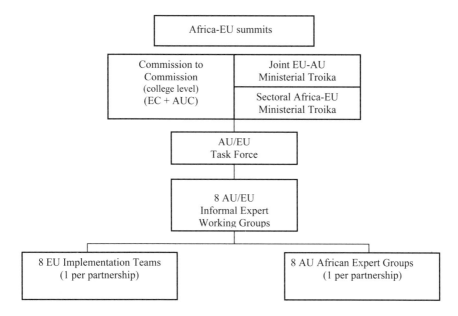

Figure 5.1   The institutional set-up of Africa–EU relations

On 18 November 2008, the first Joint EU–AU Expert Meeting 2008 on Peace and Security was held in Addis Ababa; the second meeting was held in Brussels on 27 April 2009, and an agreement was reached on a roadmap with clear deliverables and timelines, responding to the priority actions set in the joint action plan as adopted at the Lisbon Summit in December 2007 (see Joint EU–AU Expert Meeting 2008). However, there seems to be a problem due to the low attendance rate by African experts on the AU side and the large numbers of experts on the EU side. Given the constraints in terms of human resources, the eye-level partnership is facing some challenges in the near future.

In December 2007, the EU appointed the experienced Belgian diplomat, Koen Vervaeke, as both the EU Special Representative (EUSR) to the AU as well as the Head of Mission of the European Commission (EC) Delegation to the AU, thus combining the representation of Council and Commission in one person.[16] This is an important step towards strengthening the EU's presence in Addis Ababa and developing a single EU voice *vis-à-vis* the AU. As one Ambassador from a larger EU member state confirmed, 'coordination between the EU member states' ambassadors and the EUSR has been streamlined'.[17] In

---

16   This can be interpreted as a first test to arrangements under the Lisbon Treaty which foresees a European External Relations Service, combining Member States' diplomatic services and supranational European staff.

17   Author's interview in Addis Ababa, December 2008.

addition to improving coordination within the EU, the EUSR has the potential to strengthen the EU's visibility in other institutional settings which are of key importance to the AU in general and APSA in particular. The EUSR potential to strengthen the EU's visibility becomes obvious when looking at the African Union Partner Group (AUPG) – a loose network of donor countries including EU member states, USA, India, Brazil, China, Russia as well as other countries accredited at the AU. AUPG's major goal is to facilitate coordination among donor countries and to develop a common focus. Within the AUPG, the EUSR chairs the peace and security committee which can be seen as a first step towards stronger coordination between EU member states as well as a stronger position of the EU in similar networks, such as for instance the (G8++) Africa Clearing House.[18] The AUPG setting is 'the most inclusive framework in which donors to Africa can come together, exchange information on their respective activities and look at ways for improving coordination and cooperation' (Pirozzi 2009, 31). The AUPG permanent representatives at the ambassadorial level meet once a month. There are four sectoral working groups dealing with: a) peace and security (led by UK); b) capacity-building and institutions (led by Denmark); c) governance (led by Germany); and d) health and social issues (vacant): working groups meet according to need. Following several discussions with the Vice-President of the AU Commission, the Commission elaborated a proposal to structure the AU's work along four pillars matching – more or less – the structure of the AUPG working groups: a) peace and security; b) capacity-building and institutions; c) shared values ('good governance' etc.); and d) developmental issues (infrastructure, energy, climate change – cross-cutting issues).

Financial Support

Most importantly, the European Union provides financial support, however not in the form of budget support. At present, with the tenth European Development Fund between 2008 and 2013, the EU is funding a €27 million capacity-building programme for the Peace and Security Department.[19] The money is being used to develop liaison between regional economic commissions (RECs) and the AU; to foster the Continental Early Warning System (CEWS); to investigate into

---

18   In May 2004, following an initiative of the US European Command (EUCOM) which at that time still had responsibility for Europe and most of Africa, convened in Luxembourg with senior officers from NATO, the EU, European countries, the US and Canada. The conference was termed the 'Africa Clearing House'. Subsequently, in 2005, a G8-centered 'Africa Clearing House' emerged which regroups representatives from the G8, the AU, the UN and donors including Scandinavian countries, Russia, China, India.

19   From 2000–07, the European Commission managed a special programme to strengthen the institutional capacity of the AU organs of about €55 million. A key problem with this institutional support was the lack of planning capacity at the AU level; the funds could not all be used as no planning was possible in time.

telecommunication links on the continent and to support the RECs themselves. The two key financial instruments for funding APSA are the African Peace Facility and the Instrument for Stability (IfS).

African Peace Facility (APF)   In response to a request of the African Union (AU) summit meeting at Maputo in July 2003, the ACP–EC Council of Ministers of 11 December 2003 decided to establish a Peace Facility for Africa, which has been praised 'as the EU's single most significant financial support mechanism for Africa' (Abass 2008, 327), disbursing an initial amount of €250 million for a period of three years.[20] The Council of 11 April 2006 decided to extend this initiative for the period 2008–10, allocating €300 million under the tenth European Development Fund For instance, the EU has set aside an overall of €2.7 billion for the governance tranche. The amount can be used to finance expenses incurred by African countries deploying their peace-keeping forces in other African countries, including the costs of transporting troops, soldiers' living expenses and the development of capabilities, i.e. training for staff involved in planning and training. Yet, APF funding cannot be used to cover military and arms expenditure. The Peace Facility is based on the principle of African ownership subscribing to 'a logic of self-responsibility' (Grimm 2006, 11) and EU-spurred efforts to strengthen regional as well as sub-regional organizations in Africa. It supports AU-led peacekeeping operations as well as capacity-building for the emerging peace and security structure of the African Union (AU). It is the AU Peace and Security Council that will make recommendations for use of APF allocations. Yet, it is the EU Council that will ultimately make a decision. While the African Union is required to play a key role in the decision-making process relating to these peacekeeping operations (see Gänzle and Grimm 2008), they can also be launched and implemented by African sub-regional organizations such as ECOWAS or the SADC.

Instrument for Stability (IfS)   In 2007, the EC external relations instrument, the IfS, came into force. The IfS' main goal is to provide rapid assistance in cases of broadly defined (non-military) crises and has an annual budget of more than €200 million. Subdivided into a short- and a long-term component, the IfS pursues a threefold operational goal: first, in a situation of emerging political crisis or natural disaster, it seeks to contribute to stability by providing an effective response to help preserve, establish or re-establish the conditions essential to the proper implementation of the EC development and cooperation policies (Development Cooperation Instrument, European Neighbourhood Partnership Instrument, etc.). Thus, the IfS would: (1) address a new political crisis or natural disaster; (2) respond to a 'window of opportunity to pre-empt a crisis; (3) secure the conditions

---

20   €123.6 million was transferred from unallocated resources (reserves) of the 9th European Development Fund; the remaining €126.4 million came from each African ACP countries' contribution of 1.5 per cent from its allocated budget.

for delivery of EC assistance; and (4) be part of a joint approach involving ESDP operations (e.g. EUFOR Chad/CAR). Second, in the context of stable conditions, in turn, it aims to improve capacity to address specific global and trans-regional threats having a destabilizing effect, such as for instance proliferation of weapons of mass destruction and human trafficking, terrorism and organized crime; this can involve security sector reforms, for instance through (re-)training of personnel for instance with seconded police officers. Third, again in a situation of stable conditions, it seeks to ensure international and regional organizations, as well as state and non-state actors' preparedness to respond to pre- and post-crisis situations. It therefore also offers a political tool to address linkage areas between policies that aim at human security.

In 2007, Sub-Saharan Africa, one of the main targets of the IfS to date, received 43 per cent of the available funds, followed by the Middle East with 22 per cent, the Western Balkans with 11 per cent (primarily in support of the International Civilian Office in Kosovo), Latin America and the Caribbean with 10 per cent and the Asia-Pacific region with 6 per cent. In terms of thematic initiatives, the Commission distinguished 'short-term advice to develop and kick-start post-conflict security system reform' (in Democratic Republic of the Congo (DRC), Guinea Bissau, Lebanon), complementary measures in areas where ESDP missions are deployed (e.g. Democratic Republic of the Congo, Afghanistan, Chad), 'support to regional peace-building capacity' (African Union in Somalia (AMISON), AU-UN Mediation effort in Darfur), 'rule of law and transitional justice' (Afghanistan, Columbia, Haiti), with support to interim administrations (International Civilian Office (ICO)ICO Kosovo), 'conflict resolution and reconciliation' (Uganda, Zimbabwe, Myanmar, Southern Thailand), 'post-conflict needs assessments and rehabilitation' (Lebanese refugee camps), 'support to displaced populations' (Lebanon, Syria), and 'conflict resources' (Kimberley Process) (see European Commission 2008, 6–86ff).

The budgetary allocation for the IfS for the period 2007–13 amounted to €2,062 million originally, of which the lion's share, approximately 73 per cent or €1,487 million, was reserved for its short-term component and €484 million for its long-term component.[21] Given the tremendous costs of peace-keeping operations, this is not enough[22], and coordinated action with the United States and the UN is needed. Still, the Instrument for Stability remains the EC's most important crisis

---

21   See Gänzle 2009b. By its very nature, funding allocated to the short-term component is non-programmable thus making the instrument extremely flexible. From this perspective, it did not come as a surprise that, in December 2008, the Council and the European Parliament – supported by Commission President Barroso – decided to channel one eighth of the IfS total budget – or €240 million – towards the so-called Food Facility in order to respond to the global food crisis.

22   The UN remained the largest military deployer on the continent, accounting for approximately 87 per cent of all deployments there in 2008. When compared to other organizations, the UN provided more than 10 times the number of peacekeepers in Africa.

response tool operating between traditional foreign and development policies. Most importantly, the IfS regulation aims at bridging different policy areas and thus enshrines the obligation for EU institutions to ensure coherence in the external policies of both the European Union and the Community.[23]

CFSP/ESDP *vis-à-vis* Africa: Singing from the Same Hymn Sheet – at Last and at Least

The EU's African experience in peace and security has not been without effect. As a response to the 'Artemis' mission to the Democratic Republic of the Congo,[24] the EU Council decided in June 2004 to establish EU battle groups in order to increase crisis reaction capacities of the EU. Also, the EU provides financial and technical support to the AU's endeavour of building its African Stand-by Force, which is modelled along the lines of the EU rapid reaction force. The EU rapid reaction force units comprise up to 2,200 soldiers and are designed as pioneering missions with the task of preparing the ground for large-scale military operations, eventually led by the AU or the UN. Essentially, the African Standby Force is set to serve a similar purpose. One of the most recent actions, the EU mission to Chad, similar to the 2003 mission in Democratic Republic of the Congo, prepared for the arrival of a UN mission. The EU Support to the African Union Mission in Sudan (AMIS), which ended in December 2007, provided civilian and military support to the AU mission in Darfur (e.g. airlifts for AU troops in Sudan). Only through strategic thinking can Europe achieve a more coherent policy. The European Security Strategy of 2003 is not only a first step towards a more strategic culture of EU member states it also provides a clear expression of Europe's interest in Africa. All threats sketched out in the Strategy, such as terrorism, proliferation of weapons of mass destruction, regional conflicts and state failure, can be associated with some countries in Africa. Consequently, the EU has started to address those challenges which are commonly referred to as security-development nexus. It is focusing on the interfaces of economic development and peace-building and is henceforth getting increasingly engaged in Security Sector Reform (SSR) and Disarmament,

---

Large-scale UN deployments in Democratic Republic of the Congo, Sudan, Darfur, Liberia and Côte d'Ivoire made up the bulk of these troops.

23   For the first time ever, an EC external relations instrument transfers Art 3(2) TEU into secondary law: 'The Union shall in particular ensure the consistency of its external activities as a whole in the context of its external relations, security, economic and development policies. The Council and the Commission shall be responsible for ensuring such consistency and shall cooperate to this end' (Treaty of the European Union).

24   'Artemis' was the EU's first mission to Democratic Republic Congo between June and December 2003 in the Congolese province of Ituri. In accordance to the UN-mandate, EU forces were meant to stabilize the 'security conditions' and improve the humanitarian situation in Bunia, the province's capital, by means of protecting the airport and refugee camps. The mission was conducted mostly by France.

Demobilization and Reintegration (DDR). The EU Africa Strategy explicitly mentions peace, security, human rights and good governance as key objectives. More importantly, however, the Strategy – together with the European Consensus on Development of 2005 – has been signed by the Council, the Parliament and the member states. It thus provides a common framework for the entire body of Europe's multi-level foreign policy institutions. Although this loose form of policy coordination will still take some time to become effective, it is very likely to have a major impact on the coherence of EU foreign policy.

Conclusion

The European Union is the most significant donor to the African Peace and Security Architecture. It is most important not just because the sheer size of its financial allocations, but also because of the specific character of the EU as a political body and the place security and peace occupies on the EU's foreign policy radar. First, Africa has been a key concern to the EU herself, often linking major milestones in European integration with issues pertaining to the future development of Europe's southern neighbouring continent. Second, having gathered some operational experience on African ground, the EU's CFSP/ESDP has acquired a particular focus on Africa, which is also about to gradually trickle down into the Union's emerging strategic culture. In this context, the EU has been able to come up with a number of new and innovative financial instruments, such as the African Peace Facility or the Instrument for Stability, which have a significant impact on the EU's (or AU's?) capacities. Third, the development of African institutions in the area of security cooperation sits rather well with the institutional set-up of the EU. With regard to this stunning isomorphism, which in part results from a high level of dependency on EU assistance, in particular in peace and security matters, it is correct to caution that the EU is at the brink of 'Westernizing the AU to such an extent as to erode African support for it' (Franke 2009b, 4). The EU will thus have to support AU capacities at a pace that African member states can keep up with but that does not wait for the readiness of the slowest amongst them. The balance between legitimacy of decision-making and legitimacy via policy-results will have to be struck. However, given the proximity of EU-Africa relations, this is a challenge none of the partners can escape easily.

References

Abbass, Ademola (2008), 'EU Crisis Management in Africa: Progress, Problems and Prospects', in Steven Blockmans (ed.), *The European Union and Crisis Management. Policy and Legal Aspects* (The Hague: Asser Press), pp. 327–43.

Africa Clearing House (2008), 'Activity Program 2008 Onwards, Final Version', 18 April 2008, mimeo.

African Union (2008), 'Germany Signs Agreement with the African Union Commission to Construct New Office Building for Peace and Security', Press release No. 152/2008.

Blockmans, Steven (ed.) (2008), *The European Union and Crisis Management. Policy and Legal Aspects* (The Hague: Asser Press).

Center on International Cooperation (2009), 'Annual Review of Global Peace Operations 2009. Briefing Paper. A Project of the Center on International Cooperation at New York University. With the support of the Peacekeeping Best Practices Section of the UN Department of Peacekeeping Operations', <http://www.cic.nyu.edu/Lead%20Page%20PDF/GPO_2009.pdf>, accessed 9 November 2009.

Cilliers, Jakkie (2008), 'The African Standby Force. An Update on Progress', ISS Occasional Paper 160, 1 March 2008.

European Commission (2008), *Report from the Commission to the Council and the European Parliament, the European Economic and Social Committee and the Committee of the Regions: Annual Report from the European Commission on the Instrument for Stability in 2007*, Brussels, 09/07/2009, COM(2009) 341 final: (Executive Summary).

European Union (2003), *A Secure Europe in a Better World: European Security Strategy*, Brussels, 12 December 2003.

France Diplomatie (2008), 'France and Darfur', available at <http://www.diplomatie.gouv.fr/en/france-priorities_1/conflicts-and-crisis_1959/darfur_3538/france-and-darfur_6011/index.html>, accessed 9 November 2009.

Franke, Benedikt (2009a), *Security Cooperation in Africa: A Reappraisal* (Boulder, CO: Lynne Rienner).

Franke, Benedikt (2009b), 'EU–AU Cooperation in Capacity-Building', Mimeo.

German Agency for Technical Cooperation (GTZ), 'German-African Border Project' (online publication), Berlin, May 2009, available at <http://www.auswaertiges-amt.de/diplo/en/Aussenpolitik/RegionaleSchwerpunkte/Afrika/G8FriedenSicherheit/GTZ-GABP-Broschuere.pdf>, accessed 9 November 2009.

Gänzle, Stefan (2009a), 'Africa Command: "Pentagonisierung" oder integrierter Ansatz in der US-Afrikapolitik?', *Aus Politik und Zeitgeschichte* 34–5, 1–9.

Gänzle, Stefan (2009b), 'Coping with the "Security-Development Nexus": the European Community's Instrument for Stability; Rationale and Potential', DIE Studies 47 (Bonn: German Development Institute/DeutschesInstitut für Entwicklungspolitik (DIE)).

Gänzle, Stefan and Grimm, Sven (2008), 'Den Afrikaner kämpfen helfen' (Helping the Africans Fight), *welt-sichten* 7, 27–30.

Grimm, Sven (2006), 'EU Development Cooperation: Rebuilding a Tanker at Sea', Friedrich-Ebert-Foundation (FES) Briefing Paper, Dialogue on Globalization, Berlin.

ISIS Europe (2009), *European Security Review* no. 43, (bi-monthly news review), 43, March 2009.

Joint EU/AU Expert Meeting on Peace and Security (2008), Notes, Mimeo.

Joint EU/AU Expert Meeting on Peace and Security (2009), Peace and Security Roadmap (adapted from the official Draft Joint Roadmaps for the implementation of the 1st Action Plan (2008–2010) of the Joint Africa-EU Strategy, 28 April 2009), available at <http://europafrica.files.wordpress.com/2008/05/peace-and-security-roadmap.doc.> accessed 9 November 2009.

Makhan, Davina (2009), 'Strengthening the EU's Policies for Global Development: Lessons From The ACP-EU Negotiations on Economic Partnership Agreements', DIE Study 50 (Bonn: German Development Institute/Deutsches Institut für Entwicklungspolitik (DIE)).

Medeiros, Evan S. (2006a), 'China, Africa Forging Closer Ties', *Globe and Mail*, 10 November 2006.

Medeiros, Evan S. (2006b), 'Chinese Foreign Policy: The Africa Dimension', presentation held at the FLAD-IPRI Conference on 'Strategy and Security in Southern Africa', Lisbon, Portugal, October 2006, available at <http://www.ipri.pt/publicacoes/working_paper/pdf/10-Medeiros.pdf>, accessed 9 November 2009.

Mubilia, Mutoy (2007), 'Cooperation between the UN, the EU and the AU for Peace and Security in Africa,' *Studia Diplomatica* 60(3), 111–21.

NATO (2009), 'Topics: Assisting the AU in Darfur, Sudan', Brussels (website), available at <http://www.nato.int/issues/darfur/>, accessed 9 November 2009.

Pirozzi, Nicoletta (2009), 'EU support to African Security Architecture: Funding and Training Components', EU-ISS Occasional Paper No. 76, February 2009.

Plaut, Matin (2004), 'The Africa Clearing House', *African Security Review* 13(3), <http://www.iss.co.za/pubs/asr/13No3/CPlaut.htm#top>, accessed 9 November 2009>.

Ploch, Lauren (2007), 'Africa Command: US Strategic Interests and the Role of the US Military in Africa,' *CRS Report for Congress*, 6 July 2007.

Schuman, Robert (1950), Declaration of 9 May 1950, available at <http://europa.eu/abc/symbols/9-may/decl_en.htm>, accessed 9 November 2009.

Tywuschik, Veronika and Sherriff, Andrew (2009), 'Beyond Structures? Reflections on the Implementation of the Joint Africa-EU Strategy', ECDPM Discussion Paper 87 (Maastricht: ECDPM).

York, Geoffrey (2006), 'China, Africa Forging Closer Ties', *Globe and Mail*, 6 November, p. A12.

Chapter 6

R2P and the IGAD Sub-region: IGAD's Contribution to Africa's Emerging R2P-oriented Security Culture

John Siebert

IGAD's Silence on R2P

When considering Africa's security architecture and the responsibility to protect (R2P), the discussion about the role of sub-regional organizations is usually restricted to Southern African Development Community (SADC) in southern African and Economic Community of Western African States (ECOWAS) in western Africa (Weiss and Hubert 2001, pp. 168–70). The Intergovernmental Authority on Development, or IGAD, whose seven member states (Kenya, Sudan, Ethiopia, Eritrea, Djibouti, Uganda, and Somalia) comprise the Horn of Africa, is rarely mentioned in this context.

At one level this is understandable. Unlike the SADC and the ECOWAS, IGAD has no commitment in its founding document that would point toward sanctioning collective action under the second pillar of R2P (react), nor has IGAD made any formal statement specifically on R2P, positive or negative.[1] This is in spite of the fact that the principle of non-indifference and the imperative to intervene in certain circumstances marks both the Africa Union's Constitutive Act (Section 4H)[2] and subsequent AU statements in support of R2P to which all IGAD member states are party through membership in the AU (AU 2002). These commitments are reiterated in other African intergovernmental organizations – the African Commission on Human and Peoples' Rights (ACHPR), the East Africa Community (EAC), and the International Conference of the Great Lakes (ICGLR) – to which some or all IGAD member states also belong.

In contrast to the AU Charter, IGAD's founding agreement in 1996 explicitly cites the principle of non-interference and respect for the preservation of state

---

1 A review of IGAD public documents at www.igad.org and personal correspondence with IGAD Peace and Security Division staff confirmed that no explicit R2P discussions or initiatives have been taken by IGAD.

2 'The right of the Union to intervene in a Member State pursuant to a decision of the Assembly in respect of grave circumstances, namely war crimes, genocide and crimes against humanity.'

sovereignty (IGAD 1996). IGAD's being out of step on this point with the AU and other African organizations can be partially explained by timing. In 1996 when IGAD was being transformed from the intergovernmental Authority on Drought and Development (IGADD), the Organization of African Unity (OAU) was still some years away from its transformation into the AU with its Charter's normative declaration on non-indifference in 2002. More precisely, it can be explained by continuing recalcitrance by at least one of IGAD's member states, Sudan.

Sudan opposes R2P, considering it a pretext for the international community to inappropriately violate sovereignty generally, and its sovereignty in particular with respect to Darfur, under the react pillar of R2P. At the July 2009 UN General Assembly debate on R2P, Sudan reiterated its position:

> In the center of these controversial debates is the delicate balance of respect for state sovereignty and the need for intervention in state's affairs under the pretext of humanitarian intervention, and when legitimacy becomes responsibility to protect … My delegation strongly believes in the notion of non-interference as articulated by article 2 (4) of the United Nations Charter. (Sudan 2009)

There may well be other IGAD members that oppose R2P but have not made their opposition as demonstrable as Sudan.

In contrast to Sudan, Kenya has embraced R2P and credited international diplomatic intervention in response to its post-election violence in December 2007 as being a successful example of the first pillar of R2P, that is, prevention. Negotiations between the government Party of National Unity and the Orange Democratic Movement were successfully conducted by an AU Panel of Eminent African Personalities, headed by former UN Secretary-General Kofi Annan. The process was actively supported by the African Union, UN Secretary-General Ban Ki-Moon, and the US State Department. The Kenyan delegation to the July 2009 United Nations General Assembly debate stated:

> I would like to take this opportunity to express the appreciation of the people of Kenya for the personal initiative of the Secretary-General, to lend crucial support to the search for a negotiated solution to the problems in my country following the disputed December, 2007, General Elections … In order to enhance the crucial role that states, regional and sub regional organizations such as the AU, the EAC and IGAD can play in furthering the goals of Responsibility to Protect, it is important for the international community to assist in developing capacity for effective implementation of Responsibility to Protect obligations. (Kenya 2009)

With its silence on R2P, is there anything meaningful to be said about IGAD's contribution to Africa's security architecture and R2P? The answer is a qualified 'yes' if R2P is understood broadly as the crystallization of prior normative developments and international practice on 'humanitarian intervention' that was not necessarily subsumed into the norm-producing process leading to R2P.

In recent years, IGAD has taken important steps to construct its own sub-regional peace and security architecture for the deeply troubled Horn of Africa sub-region. In this process it has started to participate in the broader stream of normative development and institutional preparation for activities consistent with the three pillars of R2P: prevent, react, rebuild. Certain IGAD collective actions could be considered contributions to an emerging African security culture that is imbued with R2P principles, even if there are justified reservations about IGAD's (and AU, SADC, and ECOWAS) capacity and effectiveness. Said another way, IGAD is participating in an emerging African R2P-oriented security culture even without explicit IGAD affirmation of R2P. Advocacy by civil society organizations (CSOs) in the Horn of Africa has reinforced positive momentum in this direction.

R2P is Neither Stand-alone nor Narrow

Defining what R2P actually is can be seen as a work in progress. It is an evolving international norm, yes, but it also rests on a foundation of debate and practice preceding the International Commission on Intervention and State (ICISS 2001) Report. The 'Researchers' Preface' to the ICISS background documentation indicates that the R2P concept was founded on previous developments: 'The task given to us by ICISS was to lay out in straightforward and non-argumentative terms the main issues behind the debate about humanitarian intervention that has taken place over the last decade' (Weiss and Hubert 2001, p. x).

The existence of this previous stream of international practice and debate on 'humanitarian intervention' did not stop with, nor was it necessarily fully captured or superseded by, the 2001 ICISS report, or by the subsequent official recognition of R2P in the 2005 World Summit Outcome document, paragraphs 138 and 139. This raises the option of interpreting statements and actions by states or intergovernmental bodies such as IGAD as being consistent with the stream of practice and policy evolution that continues to flow without necessarily directly referencing R2P.

R2P also is broad in its encompassing of potential actions under the three pillars of prevent, react, rebuild. 'It is almost a "charter" or at least a multidimensional normative doctrine that can be used in various ways, depending on what component is primarily emphasized by its supporters or skeptics' (Helly 2009, pp. 46–7).

The striking difference introduced with the ICISS Report on R2P that distinguishes it from the previous 'humanitarian assistance' stream is characterized by commentators as: 1) a shift of focus from state sovereignty to state responsibility for the well being of its citizens; and 2) the obligation of the international community to intervene in the specific case of the four violations of international law (genocide, war crimes, crimes against humanity, and ethnic cleansing) where a country is unwilling or unable to protect its citizens (Evans 2006). As Brunnee and Toope (2006, p. 8) conclude, 'the responsibility to protect could well be of a different order. It could entail a fundamental conceptual shift, rooted in prior developments, but going much further'.

The previous stream of 'humanitarian intervention' and the broad scope of activities that could be interpreted as consistent with the three pillars of R2P provides the basis on which to say that IGAD is actually participating in the emerging African R2P security culture focused on the well being of member states' vulnerable citizens rather than state sovereignty.

IGAD's Developing Peace and Security Architecture

IGAD was created in 1996 with headquarters in Djibouti, replacing the IGADD which began in 1986. 'Early detection of recurring droughts, and timely alarming and mobilization of the international community were the primary supportive tasks of IGADD' (Terlinden 2004, p. 1). In a summary of its predecessor, the IGAD (2009a) website notes:

> The recurring and severe droughts and other natural disasters between 1974 and 1984 caused widespread famine, ecological degradation and economic hardship in the Eastern Africa region … The magnitude and extent of the problem argued strongly for a regional approach to supplement national efforts. In 1983 and 1984, six countries in the Horn of Africa – Djibouti, Ethiopia, Kenya, Somalia, Sudan and Uganda – took action through the United Nations to establish an intergovernmental body for development and drought control in their region.

In a leap of aspiration over reality that is not uncommon for intergovernmental organizations, IGAD's (2009a) stated goal is to 'promote peace and stability in the region and create mechanisms within the region for the prevention, management and resolution of inter-State and intra-State conflicts through dialogue'.

The post-colonial history of IGAD's member states seemingly would argue against the proposition as it includes a complex set of violent conflict dynamics that remain largely unresolved, even if the number of wars and other violent conflicts in the sub-region has decreased (Project Ploughshares 2009) in the past decade (see Table 6.1).

> Today, two clusters of conflicts continue to destabilize [the Horn]. The first centers on interlocking rebellions in Sudan, including those in Darfur and southern Sudan, and engulfs northern Uganda, eastern Chad, and northeastern Central African Republic …. The second cluster links the festering dispute between Ethiopia and Eritrea with the power struggle in Somalia, which involves the fledgling secular government, antigovernment clan militias, Islamic militants, and anti-Islamist warlords. (Prendergast and Thomas-Jensen 2007, p. 59)

Table 6.1   Conflicts in Africa

	# of conflicts	# of host countries
*1999	16	17
2000	17	18
2001	14	14
2002	14	14
2003	15	14
2004	14	13
2005	13	12
2006	12	11
2007	12	11
**2008	11	10

* The worldwide figure was 40 armed conflicts in 36 countries.
** The worldwide figure was 28 armed conflicts in 24 countries.
Table 6.1: Project Ploughshares, *Armed Conflicts Report*; see www.ploughshares.ca.

IGAD has been referred to as an organization of 'hostile brothers' (Terlinden 2004, p. 6).

In terms of institutional and normative advances to enhance peace and security, IGAD has understandably been held back by the intense conflict dynamics at work among member states. But over time IGAD has also made crucial contributions to supporting peace processes in its local neighbourhood, as in the cases of Sudan and Somalia.

The Agreement founding IGAD (1996) puts its activities, including the advancement of peace and security, firmly within the context of sovereignty and mutual non-interference. Article 6A states:

> The Member States solemnly reaffirm their commitment to the following principles:
> a) The sovereign equality of all Member States;
> b) Non-interference in the internal affairs of Member States.

The IGAD Agreement also contains commitments that reflect the rising African security culture of responsibility as opposed to strictly harping on sovereignty. One part of Article 7 in the IGAD founding Agreement points toward a responsibility that transcends member state borders where the well being of citizens is threatened by food crises or natural disasters:

> 7 r) at the national level and in their relations with one another, be at all times guided by the objectives of saving lives, of delivering timely assistance to people in distress and of alleviating human suffering. In this regard, Member

> States shall facilitate the movement of food and emergency supplies in the event
> of man-made or other natural disasters from surplus to deficit areas.

This commitment naturally flows from the earlier focus of IGADD.

In 2006 IGAD took further steps in the direction of state responsibility for its citizens, initiating a number of formal and CSO accompanying processes to develop a Peace and Security Strategy. Its goal is 'to actively contribute to developing and maintaining a robust peace and security order throughout North-East Africa' (p. 2). IGAD endorsed the three-year research process on creating an IGAD peace and security architecture headed by the Nairobi-based Africa Peace Forum, and entered into an agreement with the Institute for Security Studies (ISS). These are described in more detail below.

Like the aspirations expressed in Article 7r) of its founding Agreement, the Terms of Reference for the Peace and Security Strategy aims to reach beyond respect for state sovereignty and non-interference to matters internal to each member state. It is 'to contribute to democracy, good governance, economic development, and the social and economic integration of the IGAD sub-region and the African continent' (p. 2). Here we have aspirations that could be understood as preventive in nature for the evolution of IGAD member states themselves into functioning democratic and developed entities to preserve peace and build security in the sub-region.

IGAD also has responded positively to the initiatives of CSOs to participate and constructively support its development of a peace and security strategy. In one of several parallel civil society research projects, the Nairobi-based Africa Peace Forum (APFO), with funding from Canada's International Development Research Council (IDRC) and technical assistance from a Canadian NGO, Project Ploughshares, conducted a series of roundtables to discuss papers by scholars from the region. These papers were critiqued with the participation of IGAD Secretariat staff and member state representatives, and gathered into a book, *Human Security: Setting the Agenda for the Horn of Africa* (2008).[3]

The topics covered in this APFO publication highlight a complex web of related sources of human insecurity in IGAD's member states that underlie the conflict dynamics:

- human rights are systematically ignored or abused;
- good governance practices are the exception rather than the rule and people are marginalized from political participation and economic development;

---

3   I participated in this project, attending the roundtables in Nairobi, Addis Ababa, Kampala, Djibouti, and Mombasa between 2005 and 2008. The project's endorsement by IGAD facilitated the direct participation in roundtables by diplomats from member states with responsibility for IGAD. Participation in the roundtables was further enhanced by the presence of officials from other African organizations including the AU, the EAC, and COMESA.

- military, police, and intelligence state agencies too often fail to protect and serve the interests of ordinary citizens, or worse;
- illicit small arms and light weapons have flooded conflict areas and fuel violence;
- large numbers of people have been displaced internally or become international refugees due to armed violence – approximately 8 million in 2008;
- natural resources have been exploited in a way that makes conflicts worse rather than increasing the opportunities and well being of citizens;
- pastoralist communities, occupying large areas of the Horn of Africa, are increasingly impoverished and plagued by gun violence;
- the role of women as victims of insecurity and as fully-fledged partners in creating peace too often is ignored.

The research leading to the AFPO publication indicated that the search for an effective and comprehensive IGAD peace and security architecture has been complicated by historical and contemporary realities:

- the absence of a common external enemy or internal threat around which to rally all member states' allegiance;
- the lack of a recognizable leading power among IGAD states, unlike ECOWAS with Nigeria and SADC with South Africa, that can readily step forward to fund or act on collective decisions;
- few shared political values and goals, and little in the way of uniting historical experiences between IGAD states;
- mixed governance patterns among IGAD's members that range from democracies of varying strengths to autocracies, and, in the case of Somalia, a non-functioning state structure since 1991;
- North African Arab and Sub-Saharan African social realities and political ties represented within and among IGAD states;
- inherited colonial borders, which, while generally accepted, leave unresolved rivalries in multi-ethnic states and across porous national borders;
- pervasive poverty–all seven countries are at or near the bottom of the UNDP Human Development Index list of low-income countries, which points to a significantly greater statistical risk of hosting violent conflict;
- competition for scarce water in pastoralist areas and potential disputes between countries over water in areas such as the Nile basin.

Another serious handicap is that IGAD remains dependent for many of its activities on the contributions of international donors rather than the commitment of time and money by the member states themselves. The following countries and organizations are members of the IGAD Partners Forum: Austria, Belgium. Canada, Denmark, France, Greece, Germany, Ireland, Italy, Japan, Netherlands, Norway, Sweden, Switzerland, United Kingdom, United States of America,

European Commission, International Organization for Migration, United Nations Development Programme, and the World Bank. These 'partners in development' provide significant financial support for IGAD initiatives and projects. Terlinden (2004, p. 4) observed, 'The low priority attributed to IGAD by member states is also reflected in the defaulting payment of dues'. This has not changed significantly since 2004.

IGAD's modest capacity is clear and acknowledged by the Secretariat, but that has not stopped it from making contributions to increased peace and security in the Horn of Africa. This does not extend to IGAD's being able to launch a military intervention consistent with R2P. In 2004 General Daniel Opande (p. 2), Force Commander for the second United Nations Mission in Liberia (UNMIL), commented:

> IGAD is a sub-regional political organization which, unlike ECOWAS, has no functional security and defense arrangements. It is currently involved in sponsoring the peace talks within the region for Sudan and Somalia. While some IGAD member states like Kenya, Tanzania [sic], Uganda and Ethiopia have developed cooperation over the years on defense and security matters, the ability to match ECOWAS is yet to be realized.

What IGAD does have is a Peace and Security Division that is mandated to deal with security and humanitarian issues. The division has three main programme components: Conflict Prevention, Management and Resolution (CPMR), Political Affairs, and Humanitarian Affairs. CPMR is involved in activities and programs 'in Post-Agreement follow up of Peace initiatives of both Sudan and Somalia conflicts, development of counter-terrorism strategy, Coordination of the Eastern Africa Standby Brigade (EASBRIG), Small Arms and Light Weapons, Landmines, Civil Society, Inter-parliamentary Union of IGAD Member States and Conflict Early Warning and Early Response Unit' (IGAD 2007).

The Division also coordinates the activities of two IGAD institutions based in Addis Ababa, Ethiopia: the IGAD Capacity Building Programme Against Terrorism (ICPAT) and the Early Warning and Early Response Mechanism secretariat (CEWARN). ICPAT was launched in 2006 'to implement the decision of the Heads of State of IGAD member states meeting in Khartoum, Sudan in 2002'. It aims to build 'national capacity to resist terrorism' and promote regional security cooperation. It carries out research, convenes meetings to share information, and provides counter-terrorism training for law enforcement officers (ICPAT 2009). CEWARN's mission is 'to establish itself as an effective and sustainable sub regional mechanism that undertakes conflict early warning and response, fostering cooperation among relevant stakeholders so as to respond to potential and actual violent conflicts in the IGAD region and contributing to the peaceful settlement of disputes in the sub region'. While the CEWARN Protocol indicates a wide scope for the gathering of information, it has been mandated to begin by monitoring 'cross-border pastoral and related conflicts, providing information to

Member States concerning potentially violent conflicts as well as their outbreak and escalation in the IGAD region' (CEWARN 2009).

Ad hoc mechanisms and consultations also have been organized, such as the Mombasa Workshop, 'Lessons Learned from the Sudan and Somalia Peace Processes', held from 9–11 July 2007. Papers were prepared by various participants in these peace processes and were discussed by officials from IGAD member states.Consideration was given to the establishment of a 'mediation/conciliation' unit within the IGAD Secretariat, but concrete steps in this direction have yet to take place.

The Humanitarian Affairs Section of IGAD works to enhance disaster risk management capability through training, resource mobilization, and implementation; as well as the alleviation and mitigation of humanitarian crises, including those of refugees, returnees, and internally displaced persons. For example, the IGAD Secretariat serves as the host of the Eastern Africa Migration Route Program, which trains officials, conducts mass media campaigns on the dangers of irregular migration, operates a migration resource centre, and facilitates regional consultations. (IGAD News 2008). These activities, and the early warning function of CEWARN, fit with the 'prevent' first pillar of R2P.

Further evidence of the IGAD Secretariat's willingness to work with donors and CSOs to increase its effectiveness on security matters is the August 2009 Memorandum of Understanding (MOU) with the Institute for Security Studies (ISS), based in South Africa but with an office in Nairobi, in which they agreed to strengthen cooperation. The announcement of the MOU's signing (IGAD 2009b) lists activities that indicate the scope of the IGAD Secretariat's growing ambitions for a more secure Horn:

- finalize IGAD's peace and security strategy;
- ratification and domestication of existing international as well as continental conventions and protocols on peace and security;
- conflict analysis and early warning;
- conflict prevention, mediation support and peace building;
- combating terrorism;
- sustainable livelihood and pastoral security;
- combating money laundering, corruption and organized crime;
- arms management;
- peacekeeping/peace monitoring;
- security sector transformation, demobilization and reintegration.

Given the earlier description of the Horn of Africa's conflict dynamics, supporters and sceptics of IGAD might be excused for asking how realistic it is for an effective peace and security architecture to be put in place when IGAD member states are in varying degrees of active armed violence, either within their borders or with each other, or are on the verge of it, or are supporting proxies engaged in it. This neatly captures the struggles and contradictions within IGAD and, more broadly, Africa.

An IGAD peace and security architecture cannot on its own be the solution to the complex and entrenched conflicts in the Horn, but if properly structured for incremental growth and implementation it may provide ever stronger incentives for peacebuilding and disincentives for armed solutions, not only for states but non-state actors as well. Sustainable politics, diplomacy, institutions, and processes, within and among IGAD member states, over time can provide greater momentum for alternatives to violence in response to conflicts.

In this light, IGAD's achievements are worth highlighting. It has been credited with playing an instrumental role in both the Sudan and Somalia peace processes, although the still holding but tenuous Comprehensive Peace Agreement in Sudan trumps the accomplishments to date of action related to Somalia. Terlinden's (2004, p. 15) review of IGAD characterizes IGAD's role as providing 'good offices'. It has also assisted in eliminating 'at least some spoiling factors in the conflict management of the region: efforts were bundled and made more transparent under the umbrella of the [sub-]regional organization' (Terlinden 2004, p. 19). Again, IGAD's capabilities do not extend to the point where it could initiate or take the lead in an intervention under the second, or react, pillar of R2P. 'IGAD has made tremendous progress in conflict management and prevention but has yet to develop the instruments for comprehensive peace support operations' (Opande 2004, p. 2).

Inclusive intergovernmental bodies such as IGAD (and the AU) are not performance based but aspirational in nature. All the states in a region or sub-region are by definition included. States join based on their stated commitment to adhere to the principles and goals of the organization, but do not have to demonstrate the attainment of those goals or the implementation of the principles prior to joining. Moving from aspiration to implementation isn't a unique challenge for IGAD. All intergovernmental organizations face this. What needs to be borne in mind are the inherent security challenges, which are so great in IGAD. As a result, its accomplishments and advances in norms and institutions that move beyond non-interference should be recognized and supported by the international community.

Africa's Evolving R2P Security Culture

IGAD's evolving peace and security architecture fits not only within the broader international stream of 'humanitarian intervention' that preceded the ICISS, but is a specifically African tributary of that stream. In the 1990s African intergovernmental organizations were part of a developing security culture marked by a normative affirmation of the primacy of the needs of citizens. Musifiky Mwanasali (2006, pp. 90–91) identifies a number of factors influencing this changing security culture:

- emphasis on the protection of civilians in international humanitarian law;
- the democracy movement promoting the rule of law, personal freedoms, and renewed political institutions; and
- citizen demands for participation and transparency in governance.

The 1990s also witnessed the accelerated passing from the scene of the political 'grand old men' of Africa's immediate post-colonial period: Kenneth Kaunda of Zambia (1991), Moussa Traoré of Mali (1991), Félix Boigny of Côte d'Ivoire (1993), Hastings Kamuzu Banda of Malawi (1994), and Mobutu Sésé Seko of the Democratic Republic of Congo (1997). In the wake of their passing a newer generation of African politicians, public servants, and military leaders surveyed the littered landscape of non-democratic leadership with its fixation on regime survival rather than the security and prosperity of Africans more generally. They were working for more responsive and accountable national and intergovernmental leadership.

A Sudanese diplomat and scholar, Francis Deng (1996), helped to define this transformation with normative advances centered on transforming the principle of sovereignty as non-interference to 'sovereignty as responsibility.' Algerian diplomat Mohamed Sahnoun (2009), a former top UN official and one of the co-chairs of the ICISS, recently wrote that 'unlike other regions, our [i.e. African] legal systems have long acknowledged that in addition to individuals, groups and leaders having rights, they also have reciprocal duties. So the responsibility to protect is in many ways an African contribution to human rights'.

One result of this African affirmation that states bear responsibility for the well being of their own citizens, even beyond individual state borders, was the embedding of the principles of R2P-like intervention in the African Union Constitutive Act (2002). Article 4(h) affirms:

> the right of the Union to intervene in a Member State pursuant to a decision of the Assembly in respect of grave circumstances, namely: war crimes, genocide and crimes against humanity.

Article 7(e), of the AU Protocol of the Peace and Security Council reinforces and gives responsibility for implementation to the Council:

> recommend to the Assembly of Heads of State intervention, on behalf of the Union, in a Member State in respect of grave circumstances, namely war crimes, genocide and crimes against humanity, as defined in relevant international conventions and instruments.

The AU commitment explicitly to R2P was reiterated prior to the September 2005 World Summit in the March 2005 Ezulwini Consensus:

B. COLLECTIVE SECURITY AND THE USE OF FORCE

i. The Responsibility to Protect
• Authorization for the use of force by the Security Council should be in line with the conditions and criteria proposed by the Panel, but this condition should not undermine the responsibility of the international community to protect.

• Since the General Assembly and the Security Council are often far from the scenes of conflicts and may not be in a position to undertake effectively a proper appreciation of the nature and development of conflict situations, it is imperative that Regional Organisations, in areas of proximity to conflicts, are empowered to take actions in this regard. The African Union agrees with the Panel that the intervention of Regional Organisations should be with the approval of the Security Council; although in certain situations, such approval could be granted 'after the fact' in circumstances requiring urgent action. In such cases, the UN should assume responsibility for financing such operations.

• It is important to reiterate the obligation of states to protect their citizens, but this should not be used as a pretext to undermine the sovereignty, independence and territorial integrity of states.

The African Commission on Human and Peoples' Rights (ACHPR), to which all AU members subscribe, further reinforced in November 2007 the responsibility of states to safeguard their citizens with respect to the principle that gross and widespread violations of human rights give effect to consideration of an R2P intervention:

Recalling the principles under the Constitutive Act of the African Union and the Protocol establishing the Peace and Security Council, which provides that the African Union shall intervene, to prevent, in situation of genocide, war crimes and crimes against humanity, in a Member State of the African Union;

Recalling the report of the International Commission on Intervention and State Sovereignty (ICISS) of 2001, which set the foundation for governmental and civil effort in achieving international consensus on the Responsibility to Protect;

Taking into account the common African position on the proposed reform of the United Nations, otherwise known as the Ezulwini Consensus, where the African Union at its 7th Extraordinary Session of the Executive Council1 of 1–8 March 2005, in Addis Ababa, Ethiopia, adopted the principle of Responsibility to Protect;

Aware of the United Nations Summit Declaration of September 2005, whereby the international community expressed its determination to act where national authorities are unwilling or unable to protect their population from genocide, war crimes, ethnic cleansing and crimes against humanity;

Re-affirming the call made in the September 2005 United Summit Declaration for cooperation between the United Nations and regional organisations, to help protect populations from those grave threats.

It is widely recognized that these commitments mark a very different orientation for the AU from that of its predecessor, the OAU. That there was and remains a large gap between a continent-wide African commitment, and African capacity and willingness to act, is also noted by Mwanasali (2004, p. 26): 'The notion that the AU constitutes a regional security community may strike some with incredulity, considering all the challenges facing the continental organization and its (sometimes unfair) reputation of inefficiency'. This implementation gap also is evident in SADC and ECOWAS, and in IGAD.

To give greater effect to its commitments and provide a means for 'African solutions to African problems', the AU is establishing a peace and security architecture whose centrepiece is the African Standby Force (ASF). Targeted to be ready for deployment by 2010, the ASF is to cooperate with the UN and sub-regional African organizations in conducting peace operations. The ASF plan is to have five sub-regional brigades in the standby force, working with ECOWAS, IGAD, SADC, the Economic Community of Central African States (ECASS), and the Arab Maghreb Union (AMU). In addition to the ASF, other planned parts of the AU peace and security architecture are an early warning system, as well as a Panel of the Wise to assist with preventing the outbreak or escalation of conflict (Puley 2005, pp. 10–11).

The Peace and Security Council of the AU in 2005 gave IGAD the job of coordinating the states of East Africa, the Indian Ocean, and Rwanda for the Eastern Africa Standby Brigade (EASBRIG), the purpose of which is 'to carry out in a timely manner the functions of maintenance of peace and security as mandated by the Peace and Security Council of the African Union in accordance with the Constitutive Act of the African Union' (Eastern Africa Region 2005, Article 3). However, this decision was subsequently revisited in 2008 as the projected 2010 readiness of EASBRIG approached. Due to IGAD's limited membership of seven states, the much broader cast of participating states in EASBRIG opted to have this coordinating task lie elsewhere. EASBRIG headquarters currently is in Addis Ababa (as is the AU's headquarters), with the planning and training functions in Kenya (Cilliers and Malan 2005, pp. 10–12). At a recent EASBRIG Coordination Mechanism workshop in Kigali, it was announced that a standby police force, known as the Formed Police Unit, should be ready by 2010. While a military wing is also in the plans, implementation is being delayed by 'the different languages used within the region and lack of resources,' according to the training officer attached to EASBRIG in Nairobi (Kwizera 2009).

Whatever the stated objections of Sudan (or other IGAD members) may be to R2P, all IGAD member states are party to these explicit R2P normative affirmations and security architecture institutions by virtue of their membership in the AU. At minimum a question of consistency arises that will be repeated when looking at regional intergovernmental bodies besides IGAD that have overlapping state membership with the organization.

Other Sub-regional Organizations

The evolving AU security culture of non-indifference and R2P affirmations has its parallels in other African intergovernmental organizations besides IGAD, including some to which IGAD member states also belong. Among these are the East Africa Community (EAC) that embraces the eventual establishment of a political federation (Article 123 of the EAC Treaty) of its member states. The EAC has three long-time members – Kenya, Tanzania, and Uganda – and more recent members Rwanda and Burundi. Only Kenya and Uganda belong to IGAD. In addition to political integration, the EAC (2009) has identified 15 goals in its regional peace and security strategy developed in 2007, with work toward addressing transnational and organized crimes, conflict management, democracy, good governance, and conflicts over natural resources and borders.

Each of these initiatives can be considered contributions to the long-term causes of insecurity, thereby fitting under the 'prevent' pillar of R2P.

The International Conference of the Great Lakes (ICGLR),[4] through its Pact on Security, Stability and Development in the Great Lakes Region (2006), deals with aspects of all three R2P pillars in its 10 Protocols, including the Protocol on Non-Aggression and Mutual Defence, which explicitly acknowledges Member States' responsibility to protect populations from genocide, war crimes, ethnic cleansing, and crimes against humanity. Among the ICGLR's current 11 members are three IGAD member states: Kenya, Sudan, and Uganda.

Intergovernmental organizations such as the EAC and ICGLR represent alternative avenues and even competition for some IGAD member states' limited attention and resources for building sub-regional security. What is important to note is that they are reinforcing an R2P-compatible security culture to which IGAD member states are party, as they are party to the AU. The contradictions apparent in Sudan's R2P commitments through membership in ICGLR match the contradictions between Sudan's objections to R2P, even though it is a member of the AU.

---

4   'Deeply concerned about the endemic conflicts and persistent insecurity in the Great Lakes Region, 11 Heads of State and Government of the Great Lakes Region, met in Dar Es-Salaam, on 19 and 20 November 2004, under the auspices of the United Nations and the African Union. The Presidents of Angola, Burundi, the Central African Republic, Congo, the Democratic Republic of Congo, Kenya, Rwanda, Sudan, Uganda, Tanzania and Zambia declared: their collective determination to transform the Great Lakes Region into a space of sustainable peace and security for States and peoples, political and social stability, shared growth and development, a space of cooperation based on the strategies and policies of convergence within the framework of a common destiny which they are determined to build, in line with the aspirations of their peoples, in conformity also with the AU Vision and Mission, with the full participation of all their peoples, and in partnership with the United Nations, the African Union, and the International Community as a whole.' For more information go to http://www.icglr.org.

Civil Society and R2P in the Horn of Africa

Increasingly intergovernmental organizations have recognized the positive contribution to be made by CSOs in conflict resolution and management and their capacity and knowledge in this area to contribute to policy development. A substantive role for civil society and the promotion and enhancement of the role of women in the processes to address conflicts and build institutions are intended to be key components and not simply add-ons to the IGAD peace and security architecture. The IGAD Secretariat chose to endorse and participate in the previously described APFO project, hosting the first roundtable discussion at its headquarters in Djibouti. It has also chosen to work closely with the ISS.

Other Horn of Africa and East Africa CSOs have sponsored events and made public statements in support of their governments' commitments to R2P. The Institute for Global Policy, a research and policy institute dedicated to the promotion of human security, international justice, the prevention of armed conflict and protection of civilians based in the Hague and New York, worked with the Eastern Africa Civil Society Organizations' Forum (EACSOF), which held its third annual civil society forum in Arusha in March 2009. The event, called 'Strengthening Civil Society in the EAC: Sharing Experiences with other RECs' was organized to support efforts for regional integration to meet the needs of people. Over 90 organizations from all five Partner States attended. Included in the agenda was a panel on the Responsibility to Protect. A communiqué issued at the end of the conference (EACSOF 2009) stated:

> Noting the clear necessity to integrate the Responsibility to Protect norm (RtoP) characterized by the requirement to protect the region against genocide, war crimes, ethnic cleansing and crimes against humanity within the EAC;
>
> [Urging] governments to promote adherence to the RtoP norm and for the EAC Partner States and the continent to accept their responsibility to protect their populations against genocide, crimes against humanity, ethnic cleansing and war crimes and to recognize the role of civil society in the implementation of these principles;
>
> [Undertaking] to fully support the East African chapter of the International Coalition of the Responsibility to Protect (ICRtoP) and the peace and security architectures within the African Union in general and the EAC in particular. (EACSOF 2009)

The East Africa Law Society (2008) issued a communiqué on the peace process in Burundi in July 2008 that stated:

> Promote adherence to the Responsibility to Protect principles and appeal to the government of Burundi to accept its responsibility to protect its population

against genocide, crimes against humanity, ethnic cleansing and war crimes; and to recognize the role of civil society in the implementation of these principles.[5]

The Great Lakes Parliamentary Forum on Peace – AMANI Forum,[6] at its 2009 General Assembly called for:

2. States have a collective responsibility to protect people from gross human rights violations, and where a state is shown to have committed or acquiesced in the commission of human rights violations, the international community ought to intervene;

4. The international community has a duty to react to help protect people in troubled countries, especially where there are gross violations of human rights that are occurring and to help rebuild a troubled state;

6. Parliamentarians have a vital role to play to understand and popularize the concept of Responsibility to Protect (R2P) and to hold governments accountable.

Although these R2P-supportive CSO activities and statements are not directed at IGAD per se, they do engage IGAD member states and their publics in building local constituencies for R2P.

Conclusion

Since the end of the Cold War, concerted collective action to address violent conflicts and increase human security has borne results. According to the Project Ploughshares *Armed Conflict Report* (2009) there has been a 35 per cent decline in the number of violent conflicts across the world since 1998. This downward trend is also apparent in sub-Saharan Africa and, more particularly, the Horn of Africa. New commitment and increased funding and personnel for peacemaking and post-conflict reconstruction through the United Nations is a major part of this story (Human Security Report Project 2008). Regional organizations such as the Africa Union and sub-regional organizations like ECOWAS, SADC, and IGAD, along with CSOs, are also making important contributions to this positive momentum.

Even without R2P-specific statements or commitments by IGAD, it is participating, however modestly in light of the severe Horn of Africa security

5   http://www.responsibilitytoprotect.org/index.php/document-archive/civil-society?view=fjrelated&id=2411.

6   http://www.responsibilitytoprotect.org/index.php/former-r2pcs-project/reports-and-statements/1674-perspectives-from-east-africa-and-the-horn-april-17-18-kampala-uganda, p. 6.

dynamics and capacity challenges, in the evolving African security culture that has placed R2P commitments at its core. Continuing international support for IGAD's current efforts to build an effective peace and security architecture can only contribute to what the world hopes will be a sustained, longer-term trend of declining violent conflicts and an associated decline in the number of deaths and displacements in violent conflicts in the Horn of Africa.

References

African Commission on Human and Peoples' Rights. 2007. ACHPR/Res.117 (XXXXII) 07: Resolution on Strengthening the Responsibility to Protect in Africa. November. http://www.responsibilitytoprotect.org/index.php/africa.

African Union. 2002. Constitutive Act of the African Union. http://www.au2002. gov.za/docs/key_oau/au_act.htm.

African Union. 2005. The Ezulwini Consensus. http://www.responsibilitytoprotect. org/index.php/africa.

Brunnee, Jutta and Toope, Stephen J. 2006. Norms, Institutions and UN Reform: The Responsibility to Protect. *Behind the Headlines* 63: 3.

CEWARN. 2009. History. http://www.cewarn.org/index_files/Page355. htm#mechanism.

Cilliers, Jakkie and Malan, Mark. 2005. Progress with the African Standby Force. ISS Paper 98. May. http://www.iss.co.za/AF/RegOrg/unity_to_union/ auresearch.htm.

Deng, F. et al. 1996. *Sovereignty as Responsibility: Conflict Management in Africa.* Washington, DC: The Brookings Institution.

East Africa Community. 2009. Press Release: Conference To Popularise EAC Peace and Security Programme. 14 September. http://www.eac.int/component/ content/304.html?task=view.

East Africa Law Society. 2008. http://www.responsibilitytoprotect.org/index.php/ component/content/article/2231.

Eastern Africa Civil Society Organizations' Forum. 2009. In International Coalition for The Responsibility to Protect. ICRtoP participates in Eastern Africa Civil Society Forum (EACSOF), RtoP included in final communiqué. http:// www.responsibilitytoprotect.org/index.php/component/content/article/129- africa/2309-icrtop-participates-in-eastern-africa-civil-society-forum-eacsof- rtop-included-in-final-communique-.

Eastern Africa Region. 2005. Memorandum of Understanding on the Establishment of the Eastern Africa Standby Brigade (EASBRIG). Addis Ababa, 11 April. http://www.easbrig.org/docs/mouapr05.pdf.

Evans, Gareth. 2006. The Responsibility to Protect: From an Idea to an International Norm. Keynote Opening Address by Gareth Evans, President of International Crisis Group and Co-Chair of International Commission on Intervention and State Sovereignty, to the Chicago Council on Global Affairs et al. Conference on *The Responsibility to Protect*: Engaging America, Chicago, 15 November, International Crisis Group.

Great Lakes Parliamentary Forum on Peace – AMANI Forum. 2008. Global Consultative Roundtables on the Responsibility to Protect: Perspectives from East Africa and the Horn. Civil Society Consultation Conference Report: Discussion Draft, 17–18 April, Metropole Hotel, Kampala, Uganda. http://www.responsibilitytoprotect.org/index.php/former-r2pcs-project/reports-and-statements/1674-perspectives-from-east-africa-and-the-horn-april-17-18-kampala-uganda.

Helly, Damien. 2009. 'Africa, the EU and R2P: Towards Pragmatic International Subsidiarity?' IPG 1/2009. http://library.fes.de/pdf-files/ipg/ipg-2009-1/05_a_helly_us.pdf.

Human Security Report Project. 2008. *Human Security Brief 2007.* Simon Fraser University. http://www.humansecuritybrief.info/HSRP_Brief_2007.pdf.

IGAD. 1996. *Agreement Establishing the Inter-Governmental Authority on Development (IGAD)*. http://www.igad.org/etc/agreement_establishing_igad.pdf.

IGAD. 2006. Terms of Reference, Development of an IGAD Peace and Security Strategy.

IGAD. 2007. Peace and Security.http://www.igad.org/index.php?option=com_content&task=blogcategory&sectionid=1&id=24&Itemid=65.

IGAD. 2009a. About IGAD. http://www.igad.org/index.php?option=com_content&task=view&id=43&Itemid=53.

IGAD. 2009b. IGAD and ISS reaffirm their cooperation. August. http://www.igad.org/index.php?option=com_content&task=view&id=276&Itemid=92.

IGAD Capacity Building Programme Against Terrorism (ICPAT). 2009. About us. http://www.icpat.org/index.php/about-us-mainmenu-110.

IGAD News. 2008. Addressing migration challenges in Eastern Africa. March-April. http://www.igad.org/index.php?option=com_docman&task=cat_view&gid=44&Itemid=61.

International Commission on Intervention and State Sovereignty (ICISS). 2001. *The Responsibility to Protect.* IDRC: Ottawa. http://www.idrc.ca/en/ev-9436-201-1-DO_TOPIC.html.

IDRC. 2009. Projects in Sub-Saharan Africa. http://www.idrc.ca/en/ev-122025-201_103402-1-IDRC_ADM_INFO.html.

International Conference of the Great Lakes. 2006. Pact on Security, Stability and Development in the Great Lakes Region. 14 and 15 December. http://www.icglr.org/icglr-pacte.php.

Kaldor, Mary and Salmon, Andrew. 2006. Military Force and European Strategy. *Survival* 49: 1, pp. 19–34.

Kenya, Government of. 2009. Statement by Mw. Grace W. Cerere, Charge D'affaires, AI of Kenya Mission to the United Nations at the General Assembly Plenary Meeting on 'Implementing The Responsibility To Protect'. 28 July. http://www.responsibilitytoprotect.org/Kenya_ENG.pdf.

Kwizera, Charles. 2009. Rwanda: Regional police ready next year. allAfrica.com, 24 August. http://allafrica.com/stories/200908250128.html.

Mwagiru, Makumi, ed. 2008. *Human Security: Setting the Agenda for the Horn of Africa*. Africa Peace Forum, Nairobi, Kenya.

Mwanasali, Musifiky. 2004. *Emerging Security Architecture in Africa*. Centre for Policy Studies, Johannesburg, February.

Mwanasali, Musifiky. 2006. Africa's Responsibility to Protect. Adekeye Adebajo and Helen Scanlon, eds. *A Dialogue of the Deaf: Essays on Africa and the United Nations*. The Centre for Conflict Resolution, South Africa.

Opande, Gen. Daniel. 2004. Reality Check. The Fund for Peace, Number 8, February.

Prendergast, John and Thomas-Jensen, Colin. 2007. Blowing the Horn. *Foreign Affairs* 86: 2, pp. 59–74.

Project Ploughshares. 2009. *Armed Conflicts Report 2009*. http://www.ploughshares.ca/libraries/ACRText/ACR-TitlePage.html.

Puley, Greg. 2005. *The Responsibility to Protect: East, West, and Southern African Perspectives on Preventing and Responding to Humanitarian Crises*. Project Ploughshares Working Paper 05–5. Prepared for Africa Peace Forum, African Women's Development and Communication Network, Africa Institute of South Africa, and Project Ploughshares, September. http://www.ploughshares.ca/libraries/WorkingPapers/wp055.pdf.

Rafael, Monica Juma, Velásquez, García and Kesselman, Brittany, eds. 2006. Compendium of Key Documents Relating to Peace and Security in Africa. Pretoria University Law Press (PULP). A joint publication of SaferAfrica and UPeace. http://www.chr.up.ac.za/pulp/peace_security/Complete%20book.pdf.

Regehr, Ernie. 2009. Revisiting and Reviving the R2P. *Embassy Magazine*, 22 July.

Sahnoun, Mohamed. 2009. Africa: Uphold Continent's Contribution to Human Rights, Urges Top Diplomat. allAfrica.com, 21 July.

Sudan, Government of. 2009. Responsibility to Protect. 29 July. http://www.responsibilitytoprotect.org/Sudan_ENG.pdf.

Terlinden, Ulf. 2004. IGAD – Paper Tiger facing Gigantic Tasks. Berlin, February. Kurzberichte aus der internationalen Entwicklungszusammenarbeit Afrika.

Weiss, Thomas G. and Hubert, Don. 2001. *ICISS, The Responsibility to Protect: Research, Bibliography, Background*. IDRC: Ottawa. http://www.idrc.ca/en/ev-9439-201-1-DO_TOPIC.html.

Chapter 7

Complementary Approaches to Peacekeeping? The African Union and United Nations in Burundi

Devon Curtis and Gilbert Nibigirwe

On 1 June 2004, troops from the African Union (AU) peace operation, the African Union Mission in Burundi (AMIB) were re-hatted to become United Nations (UN) peacekeepers in the United Nations Operation in Burundi (ONUB). AMIB, which deployed from April 2003–May 2004, was the first ever AU peace operation, and the experiences of this first mission provide insights into the possibilities and constraints for peacekeeping missions elsewhere in Africa.[1]

Most observers view AMIB as a qualified success that heralds the launch of a new era of peacekeeping in Africa. At a time when the UN is unwilling or unable to launch peacekeeping missions in certain contexts, AU missions are increasingly viewed as a potential short-term alternative. The underlying idea is that an AU mission is not intended to be a replacement for the UN, but rather, an AU force can create space and momentum at a key volatile time, in order to set the groundwork for a more comprehensive UN mission later. Therefore, according to many analysts, the missions in Burundi were examples of a new trend in peacekeeping, where the United Nations is no longer the dominant or exclusive external peacekeeping actor.[2] In Burundi the UN played an important supporting and legitimizing role, but the AU sent a peacekeeping force in the earlier more volatile period, when the UN was unwilling to act. Following from this view, the AMIB-ONUB handover

---

1   This chapter draws extensively from Devon Curtis, 'The Problems with Building Peace: Power-sharing Governance, Peacekeeping and the State in Burundi' forthcoming 2010.

2   See for instance, Isobelle Jaques, 'International Peace Operations: How Can the Capacity Challenges be Met?', *Report on Wilton Park Conference WP844*, 4–7 June 2007. Jaques writes that 'Some suggest the AU's advantage in peacekeeping could be to provide short-term, holding-pattern operations, with a robust mandate if possible, as a complement to long-term multidimensional UN operations.' (para. 14). See also Alex J. Bellamy and Paul D. Williams (2005), 'Who's Keeping the Peace? Regionalization and Contemporary Peace Operations,' *International Security*, vol. 29, no. 4; and Bruce Jones with Feryal Cherif (2003), *Evolving Models of Peacekeeping*, New York: UN Department of Peacekeeping Operations.

was a success, since it reflected an initial AU readiness and commitment to act, combined with the longer term peacebuilding expertise and resources of the UN.

However, even among supporters, the experiences of AMIB and ONUB have generated mild criticism, often framed in terms of lessons learned, best practices, or challenges for future hybrid operations. These challenges are largely technical in nature, and tend to include, first and foremost the need for better coordination and delineation of responsibilities among various peacekeepers and third party intervenors. Other potential problems frequently cited with this 'Burundian model' include the chronic problem of under-funding, and operational difficulties such as lack of capacity. Political challenges are also sometimes addressed in the literature, but usually in terms of a 'lack of political will' on the part of troop-contributing countries or donors.[3]

This chapter argues that while it is important to highlight these technical problems, they tend to obscure the larger political problems inherent in the peacebuilding enterprise – problems that are common to both the AU and the UN. The organizations face fundamental dilemmas and contradictions, which are central to any third party involvement in conflict, since they have to do with the logic of peacekeeping itself. By their very nature, peacekeeping operations alter the political landscape of a country, but the perceived costs and benefits of using violence depend on a number of factors largely beyond the reach of these kinds of peacekeeping missions. These include the nature of state institutions, regional dynamics and the availability of the means of violence. This chapter therefore argues that AU and UN approaches to the conflict in Burundi have followed well-established peacekeeping logics, which inevitably have mixed results.

The chapter begins by explaining how AU–UN cooperation came about in Burundi. It briefly outlines past UN and OAU/AU involvement, before explaining how and why the AMIB and ONUB missions were established, and the mandates and core principles underpinning the two missions. It then discusses the success of these operations in effectively reaching their mandates. Next it explores the consequences of AU and UN involvement in Burundi in terms of the political configurations in Burundi, including how external involvement may have influenced calculations about the use of violence. Rather than being a watershed moment in African peacekeeping, the chapter shows how AU–UN involvement in Burundi faced typical challenges and trade-offs and that in order to explain political outcomes in Burundi, we must understand these peacekeeping missions in the context of other events in the Great Lakes region. The chapter therefore shows that the 'success' now seen in Burundi is much more precarious than it appears, and depends on a number of inter-related structures and events.

---

3   See for instance, Emma Svensson (2008), 'The African Mission in Burundi: Lessons Learned from the African Union's First Peace Operation', *Defence Analysis* (Sweden: Swedish Defence Research Agency, pp. 18–20; Paul D. Williams (2006), 'The African Union: Prospects for Regional Peacekeeping after Burundi and Sudan', *Review of African Political Economy*, vol. 33, no. 108, pp. 352–7.

UN and AU Involvement in Burundi before the Arusha Process

Burundi has experienced several rounds of violence as a result of colonial and post-colonial structures and practices.[4] The Arusha Peace Process began in 1998 and eventually led to the deployment of AMIB and ONUB (from June 2004– December 2006), but as detailed below, both the UN and the AU/OAU had previously been involved in Burundi. The latest violence in Burundi was sparked by the assassination of the democratically elected President Melchior Ndadaye in October 1993, along with other senior members of his predominantly Hutu political party, the *Front pour la démocratie au Burundi* (FRODEBU). Widespread ethnic violence ensued as some of Ndadaye's mainly Hutu supporters attacked their Tutsi neighbours, and the predominantly Tutsi army launched harsh reprisals against Hutu civilians.[5] Faced with this outburst of violence, the United Nations established a small political office, the United Nations Office in Burundi (UNOB), with Ahmedou Ould-Abdallah as the UN Special Representative of the Secretary-General.[6]

Due in part to commitments elsewhere and the reluctance to launch another peacekeeping mission in Africa, the United Nations did not send an intervention force to Burundi to guarantee the democratic institutions, despite requests from FRODEBU.[7] Instead, Ould-Abdallah played a strong diplomatic role, brokering a deal between the main Burundian political actors, which culminated in a power-sharing agreement in September 1994, called the Convention of Government.[8] Crucially, this agreement did not include the reform of the (predominantly Tutsi)

---

4   For a history of violent conflict in Burundi see: Rene Lemarchand (1994), *Burundi: Ethnic Conflict and Genocide*, Cambridge: Cambridge University Press.

5   The Burundian conflict is sometimes characterized as a conflict between the majority Hutu and the minority Tutsi, where the Hutu are more numerous but historically disadvantaged. While ethnicity has certainly been a crucial issue in the conflict, this view is an oversimplification of politics and conflict in Burundi. Rather, conflict in Burundi has ethnic, regional and social dimensions, rooted in Burundi's particular historical circumstances and its position as a small resource poor country where the capture of the state is virtually the sole source of power and resources.

6   See Ahmedou Ould-Abdallah, *Burundi on the Brink 1993–1995: A UN Special Envoy Reflects on Preventive Diplomacy*, Washington: United States Institute of Peace, 2000.

7   International donors and diplomats had put heavy pressure on the Burundian government to hold multi-party elections, but they did not want to send a peacekeeping force to protect those fledgling institutions.

8   Following the assassination of President Ndadaye, Cyprien Ntaryamira became President. On 6 April 1994 following a summit in Arusha to discuss the implementation of the peace agreement between the Government of Rwanda and the RPF rebel group, Ntaryamira was killed in the plane crash that also killed Rwandan President Juvenal Habyarimana. This event sparking the genocide in Rwanda. Sylvestre Ntibatunganya of FRODEBU became President of Burundi.

military. Some members of FRODEBU, led by Leonard Nyangoma, split from the party to form the rebel group *Conseil national pour la défense de la démocratie* (CNDD).[9] They complained about the lack of army reform, and vowed to bring FRODEBU back to power, if necessary by force.

The OAU was also active in this period. In November 1993, following a request from the Government of Burundi, the OAU decided to send an observer mission to help build confidence and promote dialogue. This was the beginning of extensive regional involvement in the conflict in Burundi. The Observer Mission of OAU in Burundi (OMIB) lasted from 1993 until 1996. It initially had 47 observers but the number was later increased to 67.[10]

The situation in Burundi remained highly unstable, leading some analysts to call the 1993 assassinations and its aftermath part of a 'creeping coup'.[11] President Sylvestre Ntibantunganya did not have the support of the predominantly Tutsi army, and he was unable to control the country. Tutsi militia groups launched a series of strikes in the capital city Bujumbura (*villes mortes*) and after the signing of the Convention of Government, the number of rural insurgency attacks and army reprisal campaigns increased, as the conflict spread to other parts of the country. The two predominantly Hutu rebel movements (the CNDD-FDD and the Palipehutu-FNL) continued to attract support.

As the political and security situation in Burundi deteriorated and the Convention of Government became increasingly unworkable, the region remained very active.[12] In 1994, the OAU called on former Tanzanian President Julius Nyerere to be the mediator in the crisis in Burundi. In November 1995, the Presidents of Burundi, Rwanda, Uganda and Zaire announced the creation of a Regional Peace Initiative on Burundi. These were gatherings of regional leaders to discuss the Burundi crisis and to assist the people of Burundi in finding means to achieve

---

9   Leonard Nyangoma was a Hutu from Bururi province who had been Minister for Public Service in the FRODEBU government led by President Ndadaye. Along with many other FRODEBU politicians, Nyangoma wanted FRODEBU to return to power after the assassination of President Ndadaye, and wanted the military to be reformed. Immediately after the assassination, Nyangoma worked closely with other FRODEBU members. However, after trips to Congo and Tanzania he decided to form the CNDD, for reasons related to personal ambition and politics. He believed that the only way that they could win back power was through the use of force. In 1998, the CNDD split into two factions. Nyangoma continued to lead the CNDD, whereas Jean-Bosco Ndayikengurukiye led the CNDD-FDD (*Forces pour la défense de la démocratie* (FDD)). Most fighters remained with the CNDD-FDD.

10   United Nations General Assembly. Report of the Secretary-General, 'The Situation in Burundi'. Agenda items 20(b) and 26, A/50/541, 11 October 1995.

11   Allison des Forges, 'Burundi: A Failed or a Creeping Coup?' *Current History*, vol. 93 no. 583, May 1994.

12   The Convention of Government signed in September 1994 gave 45 per cent of cabinet positions to Tutsi opposition parties. A prime minister chosen by the opposition parties had to countersign all presidential decisions.

peace, stability and reconciliation. Uganda would be the chair, and Nyerere of Tanzania would continue his role as Special Envoy of the region to Burundi.[13]

In July 1996, former President Pierre Buyoya of the *Union pour le progrès national* (Union for National Progress), UPRONA, launched a coup, citing the increased violence and instability in the country as his motivation.[14] The region reacted strongly and negatively to this development, and the Regional Initiative adopted sanctions against Burundi, in an attempt to punish Buyoya and to put pressure on him to negotiate with Burundian opposition parties and movements.

The period between 1993 and 1998 therefore brings into focus several key points that have a bearing on future UN and AU involvement. First, the United Nations was unwilling to take on anything more than a diplomatic and confidence-building role. It refused to commit to sending troops and to take robust action to sustain Burundi's democratic institutions and enforce security.

Second, this period shows increased involvement by regional diplomats. Even though Burundi was a small country, regional leaders recognized its importance in the wider Great Lakes context. Yet the region was by no means unified. Divisions existed both between the countries of the region, and between the region and other (equally fragmented) third party actors. For instance, the regional sanctions against Buyoya's regime were highly controversial, with some Western diplomats saying that they were counterproductive and/or unnecessary. Attitudes and approaches towards the two Hutu rebel movements, the CNDD-FDD and the Palipehutu-FNL (*Parti pour la libération du people Hutu-Front nationales de libération*/Party for the Liberation of the Hutu People – National Forces of Liberation), were also quite divided. For instance, some Burundian Tutsi accused Tanzania of being complicit in the recruitment, training and arming of the Hutu rebellions. Since 1972, Tanzania had been home to hundreds of thousands Burundian Hutu refugees.

Third, this period shows a rise in the number of third party actors, including mediators, facilitators, special envoys and so on, that were involved in Burundi, especially after the 1994 genocide in neighbouring Rwanda. While these different mediators had a range of reasons for being involved, there were two important consequences. Burundian leaders and groups were often able to play different mediators off of one another. If one mediator seemed unfavourable, they could

---

13   It is important to keep in mind that it was not inevitable that the region would play such a prominent role. The former President of Mali, Amadou Toure and former US President Jimmy Carter were both considered as Special Envoys, instead of Nyerere. Nyerere was chosen on the basis of his moral stature and his knowledge of Burundian politics. The fact that Nyerere was chosen and the region became so intricately involved at this earlier stage, had important consequences later.

14   Pierre Buyoya was a Tutsi from Bururi who had become President of Burundi through a military coup in 1987. Under pressure from international donors after massacres in Ntega and Marangara in 1988, Buyoya had implemented a number of democratic reforms. These culminating in multi-party democratic elections in 1993, which Buyoya erroneously believed that he would win.

find another, more sympathetic third party actor as an interlocutor, leading to overall coordination problems in the international effort.[15] Secondly, Burundi became a 'laboratory' of dominant conflict resolution techniques and approaches by international actors. Since it was perceived as a small, relatively manageable country, international NGOs and other organizations saw it as a site to try their preferred approaches. If these approaches could not work in Burundi, went the rationale, how could they work in larger countries such as the Democratic Republic of the Congo, Sudan, or Somalia?[16]

Arusha and the AU and UN Peace Missions: Mandates and Principles

In June 1998, Nyerere convened further negotiations with Burundian delegates in Arusha, which eventually led to the signing of the Arusha Peace and Reconciliation Agreement in August 2000. The negotiations were designed to be comprehensive in both participation and substance. The two main political parties, UPRONA and FRODEBU, attended along with a number of smaller parties. Five commissions chaired by foreign facilitators were established to negotiate different aspects of the agreement.[17] The Arusha negotiations however, triggered further splits within some of the Burundian movements. In particular, the two predominantly Hutu rebel movements, the CNDD-FDD and the Palipehutu-FNL did not participate, which was a notable weakness in the peace process. These two groups continued their armed struggle throughout the negotiations process, and claimed that the only way to restore democracy in Burundi and to achieve military reform was through armed struggle.

Nyerere died in 1999 and was replaced as facilitator by former South African President Nelson Mandela. Mandela was initially quite reticent to accept the role

---

15   For instance, the main approach by the UN in this period was to try to support moderates in UPRONA and FRODEBU, and then to implement the Convention of Government. Other organizations however, thought that it was important to engage with hardliners to stop them from spoiling an agreement. Fabienne Hara shows how the 'multiplicity of initiatives – some aiming to marginalize the extremes, as Ould-Abdallah wishes, and others seeking to include them – meant that neither strategy could be pursued consistently'. Michael Lund, Barnett Rubin and Fabienne Hara, 'Learning from Burundi's Failed Democratic Transition 1993–1996', in Barnett Rubin (ed.), *Cases and Strategies for Preventive Action*, New York: Council on Foreign Relations, Century Foundation, 1998.

16   See Fabienne Hara, 'La diplomatie parallèle ou la politique de la non-indifférence: le cas du Burundi', *Politique Africaine*, no. 68, December 1997.

17   The commissions were: 1) The nature of the Burundian conflict, the problems of genocide and exclusion and their solutions; 2) Democracy and good governance; 3) Peace and security for all; 4) Economic reconstruction and development; and 5) Guarantees for the implementation of the agreement. Each commission included a representative from each of the Burundian negotiating parties. The fifth commission on guarantees and implementation only met in the later stages of the negotiations.

of facilitator. He was told, however, that the negotiations were well advanced, and that it would only take three months to finalize a deal. Once Mandela became facilitator, he adopted a heavy-handed approach to the Burundian negotiations. Under significant pressure from Mandela, the 19 negotiating parties signed the Arusha Agreement in August 2000, but six Tutsi parties signed with reservations. The two Hutu rebel movements did not sign and remained outside the process.[18]

The Arusha agreement was a broad-based agreement touching on many different aspects of Burundian life. It set out the principles for specific political power-sharing provisions, and also addressed the legal, social and economic aspects of conflict and peacebuilding. It outlined provisions for the reform of key political institutions in Burundi during a three-year transitional period, in which power would be shared between Hutu and Tutsi. It did not, however, contain a cease-fire agreement since the CNDD-FDD and Palipehutu-FNL did not participate. Instead, the Arusha agreement outlined the principles of army reform, which stated that no ethnic group could exceed 50 per cent of army positions for a period of time determined by the Senate, but left the cease-fire to be negotiated later.

By 2000 therefore, there was a peace agreement in Burundi, but no peace. The United Nations congratulated the facilitation team and Burundians on their agreement, but refused to send peacekeeping troops in the absence of a viable peace, even though the Arusha Agreement envisaged a request to the UN for a peacekeeping force.[19] A 29-member Implementation and Monitoring Committee (IMC) was established to monitor the implementation of the agreement, but the chair of the IMC, the UN Special Representative of the Secretary-General, Berhanu Dinka took more than a year to transfer his office to Burundi. The OAU was not in a position to assume a leadership role, since it was preoccupied with its internal organizational dynamics and its transformation into the African Union (AU), which was ongoing at the time.[20]

Once again, South Africa played a critical role in keeping the Burundian peace process on track. Many key questions, including the question of who would lead the transitional period in Burundi, were not yet resolved. Mandela facilitated an agreement over transitional leadership and also put pressure on the South African government to send a protection force for Burundian politicians who were returning from exile to take part in the transitional institutions. The South Africa

18   The 19 parties that signed the agreement included the government, the National Assembly, and 17 political parties, as well as a number of observers.

19   Protocol 5, Article 8.

20   The African Union took over from its predecessor, the Organization of African Unity (OAU) in July 2002. For an analysis of the limitations of the OAU Mechanism for Conflict Prevention, Management and Resolution, see: Monde Muyangwa and Margaret Vogt, *An Assessment of the OAU Mechanism for Conflict Prevention, Management and Resolution, 1993–2000*, New York: International Peace Academy, November 2000.

Protection Support Detachment (SAPSD) deployed 700 troops in October 2001, thus allowing the transitional institutions to be established.[21]

The SAPSD was supposed to help in the establishment and training of a Burundian Protection Unit to take over the protection of politicians, but this did not happen due to political stalemates. Under continued South African facilitation, cease-fire agreements were reached with a small faction of the CNDD-FDD (led by Jean-Bosco Ndayikengurukiye), a small faction of the Palipehutu-FNL (led by Alain Mugabarabona) and the larger faction of the CNDD-FDD (led by Pierre Nkurunziza).[22] The UN remained unwilling to commit to a peacekeeping force, as long as some rebel movements were still actively fighting. This incomplete peace was therefore the backdrop for AMIB's deployment. Under the October 2002 cease-fire agreement between the transitional government and the armed movements and factions, the cease-fires would be verified by either a UN or AU-mandated mission, following the establishment of joint liaison teams. The December 2002 cease-fire agreement said that an 'African mission' would verify and control the agreement.[23] South Africa, which had played a large role in the establishment of the African Union, pushed for an AU force. The deployment of AMIB was therefore approved by the Central Organ of the Mechanism for Conflict Prevention, Management and Resolution at the AU in February 2003, and mandated in April 2003.[24]

AMIB's objectives included overseeing the implementation of the cease-fire agreements, supporting DDR, striving towards favourable conditions for the establishment of a UN peacekeeping mission, and contributing to political and economic stability in Burundi.[25] It was an AU mandated force, but the leadership, mandate, and capacities depended heavily on South Africa. In April 2003, SAPSD was integrated into AMIB so South African troops were re-hatted to become AU

---

21   'South Africa's peacekeeping role in Burundi: Challenges and opportunities for future peace missions' ACCORD Occasional Paper Series (vol. 2, no. 2, 2007), p. 28.

22   However, implementation with the larger CNDD-FDD faction (led by Nkurunziza) was stalled and the larger Palipehutu-FNL faction, led by Agathon Rwasa, would not sign a cease-fire.

23   Article 3.

24   The Peace and Security Council (PSC) of the AU is now responsible for AU peace operations, but this was not created until May 2004, after the AMIB mission. For an early assessment of the PSC, see Delphine Lecoutre, 'Le conseil de paix et de sécurité de l'Union africaine, clef d'une nouvelle architecture de stabilité en Afrique?' *Afrique contemporaine*, vol. 4 (212), 2004.

25   AMIB's mandate included: 1) establishing and maintaining liaison between parties; 2) monitoring and verifying implementation of the cease-fire agreements; 3) facilitating activities of Joint Ceasefire Commission and Technical Committees for establishment and restructuring of national defence and police forces; 4) securing assembly and disengagement areas; 5) facilitating safe passage; 6) facilitating and providing technical assistance for disarmament, demobilization and reintegration (DDR) processes; 7) facilitating the delivery of humanitarian assistance; 8) coordinating mission activities with United Nations; 9) providing VIP protection for returning leaders. Svensson, 2008, p. 12.

troops, which formed the backbone of the force. The other troop contributing countries, Mozambique and Ethiopia, delayed deployment for technical reasons until September/October 2003.[26] Meanwhile, UNOB was mandated to provide AMIB with technical assistance and advice.

The AMIB mission did not significantly deviate from other UN peacekeeping missions. Its mandate was fairly typical, and it was perhaps more important as a symbol of AU commitment, rather than as a symbol of a new peacekeeping vision for Burundi. It was always intended to be a stop-gap force until a UN mission could be authorized. The rules of engagement for the mission were based on self-defence, but force could also be used to secure the freedom of movement of AMIB personnel and to 'protect civilians under imminent threat of physical violence.'[27] Negotiations with the main rebel factions continued, and in November 2003 an agreement was reached on cease-fire implementation with the largest remaining rebel movement, the CNDD-FDD (Nkurunziza). This development encouraged UN officials to reconsider the question of establishing a UN peacekeeping operation. In December 2003 in an address to the UN Security Council, South African Deputy President Jacob Zuma said that conditions were now conducive for the UN to take over from the AU mission.[28]

In May 2004, the UN Security Council authorized ONUB, which replaced AMIB.[29] It was mandated to have up to 5,650 troops, operating under a Chapter VII mandate. ONUB's immediate task was to take over and build upon the work of AMIB, and on 1 June 2004, AMIB's 2,612 troops were re-hatted to serve under the UN.[30] Initially, these were the only troops to serve in the new UN mission.

ONUB's mandate included monitoring and ensuring the implementation of the various ceasefire agreements, contributing to security conditions for humanitarian assistance, facilitating the return of refugees and internally displaced persons, co-operating with the government in the extension of state authority and administration throughout the territory, and assisting in the electoral process by ensuring a secure environment for the holding of free, transparent elections. There was a series of elections, starting with the referendum on the new Constitution in February 2005,

---

26   The AMIB force was composed of 1600 troops from South Africa, 980 from Ethiopia, 280 from Mozambique. South African Major-General Binda was the force commander and Ethiopian Brigadier-General Ayele was deputy force commander. AMIB also included military observers from Burkina Faso, Gabon, Mali, Togo, and Tunisia, and various civilian components. See Boshoff and Francis, 2003.

27   See Boshoff and Francis, 2003.

28   For more details on this process, see Stephen Jackson, 'The United Nations Operation in Burundi (ONUB) Political and Strategic Lessons Learned,' Independent External Study for UN DPKO, July 2006.

29   See United Nations Security Council resolution 1545. See also Henri Boshoff, 'The United Nations Mission in Burundi: An Overview', *Africa Security Review*, Vol. 13, No. 3, 2004.

30   'Transfer of Mandate from AMIB to ONUB: UN Peacekeeping Mission Launched in Burundi' ONUB-MIAB Press Release 1 June 2004, ONUB/PIO/PR/01/2004.

and culminating with the election of the former rebel leader of the CNDD-FDD Pierre Nkurunziza as President in August 2005.[31]

In 2007, ONUB was replaced by the United Nations Integrated Office in Burundi (BINUB).[32] BINUB was mandated to assist the Government of Burundi on peacebuilding priorities including: peace consolidation and democratic governance; disarmament, demobilization, reinsertion and reform of the security sector; promotion and protection of human rights; and communications and development. It was also intended to assist the Government of Burundi in the transition to development programming, and to coordinate international assistance. It played a supporting role in the negotiations between the Government of Burundi and the Palipehutu-FNL, facilitated by the South Africans. In September 2006, the Government and the Palipehutu-FNL rebel group signed a cease-fire agreement, but cease-fire violations continued to occur. In December 2008, the Palipehutu-FNL agreed to change its name to FNL, thus removing its ethnic identification. This paved the way to its recognition as a political party. In April 2009, following a meeting of the Political Directorate of the Facilitation in South Africa, it was agreed that 3,500 ex-FNL combatants would be integrated in the army, and 5,000 others would be demobilized.[33] The FNL has therefore been recognized as a political party in time for the 2010 elections.

Effectiveness of the Peacekeeping Missions

The problem of how to evaluate peacekeeping effectiveness has been extensively discussed in the literature.[34] Should missions be judged according to whether or not they succeed in their mandate? Or, should they be assessed according to a particular human security benchmark, or another basket of goods? By most measures, AMIB and ONUB are judged to have been more 'successful' than previous interventions by the OAU/AU and UN. The sustained involvement of the AU, the UN and other actors in Burundi is in marked contrast to the non-involvement and disinterest of the world when genocide occurred in Burundi in 1972, and the fragmented and sometimes counterproductive international and regional approaches to the crisis from 1993–98.

Both AMIB and ONUB had mixed success in reaching their aims. AMIB did build confidence and was able to stabilize the situation so that the UN operation in Burundi (ONUB) could take over in June 2004. The biggest success for AMIB was getting the CNDD to join the peace process, and providing security for Burundian

---

31   The CNDD-FDD won nearly 59 per cent of the popular vote. IFES election guide, http://www.electionguide.org, accessed on 21 September 2009.

32   BINUB was established through SC Resolution 1719, in October 2006.

33   For details of the negotiations and agreement with the FNL, see International Crisis Group, 2009.

34   See for instance Stedman, Rothchild and Cousens, 2002; Paris, 2004.

leaders returning from exile through its special protection unit.[35] It also may have sent a powerful signal to elements in the former Burundian army that had been in favour of a coup in 1993.[36] It succeeded in its objective of facilitating the delivery of humanitarian assistance. AMIB established a Civil Military Coordination Centre to consult with humanitarian agencies on operational requirements.

For ONUB, the greatest success was the relatively peaceful electoral process. There was some violence provoked mainly by the FNL, but on the whole there was less intimidation, less violence and a higher turnout than many observers had predicted.

Nonetheless, on disarmament, demobilization and reintegration (DDR), AMIB had only limited success. It reached an agreement with the government on a first preassembly and disarmament area for former combatants, at Muyange, a town in northwest Burundi in the Kayanza province. It also succeeded in repelling an attack on Muyange in July 2003.[37] AMIB also identified sites for demobilization centres and assembly areas. Overall, however, AMIB never fulfilled its DDR objectives. In the first cantonment site, which was established in June 2003, AMIB was only able to accommodate 200 ex-combatants due to a lack of funding and lack of troops to protect cantonment areas.[38] Eventually the EU funded food supplies for these 200 ex-combatants, but resources were limited. In addition, AMIB initially lacked clear criteria for combatant verification, so it was difficult to assess who was a combatant and who was not. A second cantonment site opened only in May 2004.

In terms of overall coordination of peacekeeping efforts, the two missions constituted an improvement compared to earlier efforts. From the Arusha period onwards, there were four key external players and better coordination between them. There was the UN (ONUB and then BINUB), the AU (AMIB and then the African Union Special Task Force), the Facilitation (led by Julius Nyerere, then Nelson Mandela, then Jacob Zuma and then Charles Nqakula), and the Regional Initiative (chaired by Ugandan President Yoweri Museveni).

Yet while coordination improved, there were still some challenges and rivalries between these actors. Throughout the period, there was a quiet rivalry between South Africa and the Regional Initiative, especially between South Africa and Tanzania. Some members of the Tanzanian facilitation team felt that they were sidelined by the South Africans. And while there were contacts between the AU and UN during the AMIB mission both within Burundi and with the mission in

35 This unit had 260 special forces troops. See Agoagye, 2004, p. 12.

36 Filip Reyntjens, 'Chronique politique du Rwanda et du Burundi, 2003–2005', *In L'Afrique des Grands Lacs annuaire 2004–2005*. Stefaan Marysse and Filip Reyntjens (eds) L'Harmattan, 2005.

37 It is unclear who perpetrated this attack. After this incident, there were no further attacks on AMIB. Vrey, 2003–2004.

38 AMIB was supposed to disarm approximately 20,000 combatants, at a daily rate of 300. Agoagye, 2004, p. 11.

neighbouring Congo,[39] Festus Agoagye writes that the first lesson to be learned from AMIB's experience is that there should be a formal division of responsibility between regional forces and the UN.[40]

In the course of the negotiations with the CNDD-FDD and the FNL, other mediators, including, for instance, the Government of Gabon and an Italian NGO called the Community of Sant' Egidio, also became involved. It was sometimes difficult for the mediation to adopt a unified approach. In 2007, the FNL claimed that South Africa was biased towards the CNDD-FDD government, and wanted Tanzania to play a larger facilitation role. This sparked a series of meetings between various special envoys to Burundi to re-launch facilitation (under the leadership of South African Charles Nqakula)[41] and to present a coordinated, coherent front. A Political Directorate based in Burundi was established to provide assistance to the South African facilitation.[42] Indeed, BINUB emphasized strategic planning and coordination. In March 2007, the Government of Burundi and the United Nations agreed upon a United Nations Integrated Peacebuilding support strategy, which defines crucial peacebuilding priorities for Burundi and a strategic peacebuilding framework.[43]

The biggest impediment for AMIB and ONUB was the continued violence in the country. The cease-fires were not comprehensive, and several factions refused to participate in DDR. It was impossible for AMIB (and later for ONUB) to deter all potential spoilers and both missions faced difficulties because there were so many different cease-fires with various parties, rather than one cease-fire that encompassed all the former armed groups.[44] Throughout the AMIB and ONUB

---

39   The UN Mission in the Democratic Republic of the Congo (MONUC) also provided capacity support to AMIB and ONUB.

40   Agoagye, 2004, p. 14.

41   Charles Nqakula was South African Minister for Safety and Security from May 2002–September 2008, and Minister of Defence from September 2008 until May 2009. From May 2009, he has served as one of South African President Jacob Zuma's political advisers.

42   This Political Directorate included the Ambassadors of Uganda, South Africa and Tanzania as well as representatives of the UN, AU, EU, the facilitation, the Government of Burundi and the FNL.

43   See United Nations Peacebuilding Commission PBC/1/BDI/4, 22 June 2007. The objectives included: promoting good governance, completing the cease-fire agreement between the Government and Palipehutu-FNL, continuing security sector reform and disarmament, ensuring equitable access to justice and promoting human rights, finding solutions to the land issue and socio-economic recovery, mainstreaming gender (p. 7).

44   Waldemar Vrey, a DDR officer in ONUB and Henri Boshoff said that the separate ceasefire agreements led to animosity between the parties, and delays in the negotiations process. See Waldemar Vrey and Henri Boshoff, 'Burundi's DDR and the Consolidation of the Peace', *Africa Watch*, South Africa: Institute for Security Studies, vol. 14, no. 4, 2005. However, there is an inevitable trade-off between reaching a cease-fire with one party and

missions, the FNL continued to fight, finding support in the refugee camps in Tanzania and within some communities in Burundi.[45]

Financing was another problem that hindered the effectiveness of the AMIB mission in particular. The total budget for AMIB was US$134 million, with pledges from donors amounting to only $50 million.[46] The AU said that troop contributing countries had to be self-sustained for the first two months of deployment. Ethiopian and Mozambican deployment was delayed in part because of these financial constraints. Their troops would not have been able to deploy at all without outside funding. The US contributed $6.1 million to Ethiopia's costs, and the United Kingdom contributed $6 million to the Mozambican contingent.[47] Still, financial constraints affected other parts of the AMIB mission. The limits of the mission could be seen when the FNL launched a big attack on the capital Bujumbura in July 2003. The attack lasted almost a week, despite the presence of AMIB. Donor funding coordination was also a problem for the AU, since the Union did not always know what was given to the troop contributing countries.[48]

Were the two missions effective at contributing towards larger peacebuilding goals, such as the protection of civilians and reinvigorating the economy? There were no provisions to protect civilians in the AMIB mission, although the rules of engagement said that force could be used to protect civilians in imminent danger. Yet to intervene on behalf of citizens would require effective and immediate intelligence, and this capacity was underdeveloped in AMIB. Even in ONUB, civilian positions in the Joint Mission Analysis Cell took a very long time to be filled.[49] ONUB's mandate allowed it to protect civilians under imminent threat of physical violence, without prejudice to the responsibility of the transitional government of Burundi, but there was still significant violence throughout this period according to Amnesty and Human Rights Watch reports. More ambitious ONUB goals, such as the re-launching of the economy, were also not successful. As in other missions, the usual market distortions of aid were seen in Burundi,

---

waiting for a more comprehensive agreement with multiple or all parties (with the latter being perhaps an impossible objective).

45   As mentioned previously, it is only in December 2008, that the FNL agreed to change its name to eliminate the reference to ethnicity, so that it could participate in the 2010 elections.

46   Only approximately $10 million (excluding in-kind contributions from the UK and US for the Mozambican and Ethiopian deployments) were actually given to the AMIB trust fund. The most important donors were the USA, UK, Italy, the EU and South Africa. For a detailed account of donations and funding constraints, see Agoagye, 2004, p. 13 and fn 5.

47   Agoagye, 2004, p. 13.

48   Svensson 2008, p. 17.

49   Jackson, 2006, p. 15.

such as the high price for renting accommodation, the rise in prices for goods, and the demand for jobs as drivers and security agents for the aid community.[50]

Politics and Peacekeeping

The above assessment describes both the difficulties and the successes attributed to the AMIB and ONUB peacekeeping missions. Despite the challenges, the security situation had improved, and elections had been held relatively peacefully leading to a veritable change in regime as the former CNDD-FDD rebels took up government office.

Yet the missions also confronted the same political issues that affect all peacekeeping efforts, whether they are carried out by the UN or by another third party actor. Outside peacekeeping affects political calculations and the domestic balance of power. Yet when combined with existing institutions, power structures and regional dynamics, these changes can have unintended consequences. This manifested itself in several different ways in Burundi.

First, and perhaps most importantly, peacekeeping missions change calculations about the use of violence. The idea behind peacekeeping missions is to guarantee a political and security agreement signed by former belligerents, and thus to ensure that the price of violence is raised and remains high. During the deployment of AMIB and ONUB, the price of violence was raised, but the benefits of violence for some Burundian parties also remained quite high. When peacekeepers leave, the price of violence often falls again, and leaders may resort to force because it is effective and often decisive. In Burundi, reports from the peacekeeping missions say that 95 per cent of the country was stabilized.[51] But what does this mean over the longer term, when peacekeepers have left, governance has been militarized and the benefits of violence remain very high?

In Burundi, the CNDD-FDD electoral victory highlighted that the capacity for violence is a useful political tool. Indeed, the electoral disappointment of the CNDD faction (under the leadership of Leonard Nyangoma) that had renounced violence and participated in Arusha negotiations served as a lesson to some parties (including the FNL) that violence and the threat of violence is an effective electoral tool. The timing of the FNL transformation into a political party and its intransigence in giving up the capacity for violence ahead of the 2010 elections, show that calculations about violence are still very much part of the political landscape in Burundi. The ruling party, the CNDD-FDD, has ruled in an authoritarian manner, and has not hesitated to use force unlawfully in the lead up to the elections. For instance, Human Rights Watch reports that since the end of 2008, CNDD-FDD youth groups have been mobilized in quasi-military ways, and that their illegal behaviour was 'encouraged or tolerated by government and party officials'.[52] Between June and April 2009, over 100 individuals associated with opposition parties were arrested.[53] These include people such as Alexis Sinduhije, the leader of the Movement for Solidarity and Democracy (MSD) party, and the former President Domitien Ndayizeye of FRODEBU.

These calculations about violence affect other aspects of the peace agreements as well. For instance, while peacekeepers may think of disarmament and demobilization as intrinsically important, the parties to the conflict may make strategic calculations regarding these programmes. There is some evidence that after the latest cease-fire agreement between the FNL and the Government of Burundi, the FNL continued to recruit soldiers, mostly unemployed youth, using the promise of demobilization packages. This helped the FNL bolster their ranks during negotiations, although the exact number of combatants continued to be disputed.

Second, peacekeeping missions legitimize some Burundian actors over others. The Arusha negotiations were elite driven, and it was difficult for the peace missions to know which elites to accommodate, and which ones to marginalize. The fragmentation of rebel groups and political parties contributed to the confusion on the part of regional and international peacekeepers. One conclusion that can be drawn is that better intelligence and more local knowledge are required for peace missions, so that the Burundian divisions and factions can be better understood. The problem is that the fragmentation of political groups is a result of political incentives. It is a political issue, not a technical one, and it does not necessarily follow that more knowledge would have led to improved results.

The Burundian elections provide a useful illustration of this. After the 2005 elections, there was considerable friction between the CNDD-FDD victors and ONUB. In UN circles, this was interpreted as a result of the UN's misjudgement about who the likely election winners would be. UN staff had become accustomed to dealing with the traditional Arusha partners, in particular FRODEBU and UPRONA, and they had ties with leaders of these political parties. The UN did not anticipate, until a very late stage, that the CNDD-FDD was likely to win. According to this view, the UN had not cultivated relationships with senior CNDD-FDD officials, and these CNDD-FDD officials felt that ONUB was biased towards FRODEBU and UPRONA. This led to post-election frictions, with the CNDD-FDD government requesting that the UN mission withdraw, soon after it had taken power.[54] Yet an alternative view would suggest that the relationship between the UN and the CNDD-FDD was bound to be tense. The government felt

52   Human Rights Watch, *Pursuit of Power: Political Violence and Repression in Burundi* (May 2009), p. 64.
53   Human Rights Watch, 2009, p. 59.
54   Jackson takes this view in his evaluation of ONUB. See Jackson, 2006.

that it had won the elections fairly, and wanted to assert its sovereignty. It saw ONUB as a principal rival, and preferred that international diplomats and donors focus on development assistance, rather than on governance issues. ONUB, on the other hand, felt that the new government was inexperienced and that withdrawal was premature, since a number of Arusha tasks had not been completed. In particular, the security situation was still tenuous, since the Palipehutu-FNL were still active.[55]

Third, the two missions affected the domestic political landscape through the creation of high expectations, which was bound to lead to a certain degree of popular disillusionment. As the Arusha process wore on and security did not dramatically improve, many Burundians felt that the peace process was of very little relevance to their lives.[56] The victory of the CNDD-FDD in the elections showed that the majority of the population was disillusioned by the Arusha process and the parties associated with Arusha, and were receptive to the CNDD-FDD message of security and change.[57] In the legislative elections, the CNDD-FDD won 58.5 per cent of the vote.[58]

In general, however, popular support for the two peacekeeping missions was high. When, the AU announced plans for AMIB, most, though not all, Burundians were welcoming. Most of the G7 Arusha parties were positive about the force.[59] Many of these parties had called for an external intervention in 1993 following the assassination of President Ndadaye and were pleased to see a force that would help provide security in the transitional period. The G10, on the other hand, had always viewed any intervention force as an occupation force, and some groups had called for public demonstrations against AMIB.[60] However, the calls from some

55   The Government of Burundi may also have wanted ONUB to leave so that they would not report on its human rights abuses in operations against the Palipehutu-FNL.

56   See Mariam Bibi Jooma, 'We Can't Eat the Constitution: Transformation and the Socio-economic Reconstruction of Burundi' ISS Paper 106, May 2005.

57   Stephen Jackson says that a considerable number of Tutsi voted for the CNDD-FDD, which shows how disillusioned they had become with the Arusha parties. See Jackson, 2006, fn 13.

58   Voter turnout for the constitutional referendum on 28 February 2005 was high (93 per cent of registered voters) and the constitutional was approved by 92 per cent of those who voted. In the legislative elections of 5 July 2005, voter turn-out was 77.2 per cent of registered voters. IFES election guide, http://www.electionguide.org, accessed on 21 September 2009.

59   During the Arusha negotiations, the parties split into two groupings. The G7 parties were the predominantly Hutu parties including FRODEBU, the CNDD, the RPB, PP, PL, Frolina, Palipehutu. The G10 were the predominantly Tutsi parties including PARENA, PRP, ABASA, ANADDE, PSD, Inkinzo, Av-Intwari, PIT, and later UPRONA, the government and the National Assembly.

60   For instance, Charles Mukasi, the leader of one of the wings of UPRONA, said that the South African military were coming to occupy Burundi. See Charles Mukasi, 'Appel pour une mobilisation générale contre l'invasion du Burundi par les troupes militaires

members of the G10 against AMIB did not resonate within the army or Burundian population, and the threats were not borne out. Relations between Burundian civilians and the 'sousa'[61] were generally positive.

In 2006, the UN Department of Peacekeeping Operations commissioned a public opinion survey of ONUB's work in Burundi.[62] This survey showed mixed attitudes about the peacekeeping mission. Only 37 per cent of respondents said ONUB had done a good or very good job at making them feel safe, and there were many complaints about the sexual behaviour of peacekeepers.[63] On the other hand, 87% of respondents said that the UN had done a good or very good job in ensuring the 2005 elections were free and fair. So while the perception of the UN mission was fairly positive with respect to the electoral process, Burundians' views were not as favourable when asked about the issues that they perceived to be the biggest challenges, such as security, poverty, hunger and development.

Conclusions

Burundi is a safer place in 2009 than it was at the beginning of the Arusha process in 1998, or at the time of the AMIB and ONUB deployments in 2003 and 2004 respectively. As a sign of its recognition of Burundi's progress, the World Bank and the International Monetary Fund reached an agreement with the Government of Burundi in January 2009 to cancel over 90 per cent of Burundi's debt, worth an estimated US$1.4 billion.[64] There are other positive signs. Competition in Burundi is no longer predominantly organized along ethnic lines, successful elections were held in 2005, and further elections are planned for 2010. While there have been setbacks in the DDR process, for every step back there seem to have been two steps forward. Peace in Burundi has not followed a linear route, but politics in Burundi is more peaceful than before the Arusha process and the peace missions

---

sud-africaines', *Declaration n.29/10/2001* of the UPRONA party, Bujumbura, posted on Burundinet, http://www.netpress.bi/Ago/uprona11.htm.

61   This was the nickname given to the South Africans, due to the difficulty Burundians had in pronouncing the word 'south'.

62   Krasno, 2006.

63   In the survey, many respondents expressed anger about the reported sexual abuse by United Nations peacekeepers. *Ibid.*, p. 6. In July 2005, two UN peacekeepers were dismissed for having sex with prostitutes and minors in Burundi while off-duty. See http://news.bbc.co.uk/1/hi/world/africa/4697465.stm.

64   IMF Press Release No. 09/18, 'IMF and World Bank Support Burundi's Completion Point Under Enhanced HIPC Initiative and Approve Debt Relief under the Multilateral Debt Relief Initiative', 29 January 2009. See also Iacovos Ioannou and Bernardin Akitoby, 'Burundi's Debt Relief Savings to go to Food, Health, Schools', *IMF Survey Magazine*, 5 February 2009.

that accompanied it. This had led some authors to say that the AU and UN missions were indispensible for peace.[65]

This chapter has taken a slightly different view. While it is undeniable that Burundi is more peaceful today than in the 1990s, and that the AU and UN missions helped contribute to these changes, the chapter has argued that the two peacekeeping missions encountered the same contradictions and difficulties that affect peacekeeping missions everywhere. These contradictions go beyond technical difficulties with coordination, funding and logistics.

So what can we learn from the Burundian case? First, that peacekeeping alters politics, but not always in predictable ways. Peacekeeping missions often set out to ensure security, help build states, and refashion societies in non-violent, market-friendly ways. But the questions of why and how this happens in some contexts and not others are still poorly understood. In short-term peacekeeping missions such as AMIB and ONUB, it is impossible for the missions themselves to fulfil all these tasks. Much depends on how the infusion of an external peacekeeping mission will interact with existing domestic politics. Indeed while strategic plans and coordinated external action may be laudable, a certain degree of flexibility needs to be maintained, so that third party actors can change course if necessary.

Second, in the Burundian case, South African involvement was absolutely critical, but this involvement was not inevitable and therefore may not be easily replicated. South African interest was due to a confluence of factors, including the choice of Mandela as the replacement for Nyerere. Mandela had enormous influence by virtue of his personal stature. It was his personal intervention that convinced the South African government to send the SAPSD protection force, despite the reluctance of the chief of staff of the South African army who was aware of the high risks involved in such an operation.[66] Mandela tended to misinterpret the Burundian conflict, often seeing false parallels between the South African conflict and the Burundian one.[67] Yet he convinced key decision-makers around the world of the importance of Burundi; for instance, he persuaded US President Bill Clinton to attend the signing of the Arusha agreement. Without South African involvement, it is highly unlikely that the Burundi peace process

---

65   See for instance, Tim Murithi, 'The African Union's Evolving Role in Peace Operations: The African Union Mission in Burundi, the African Union Mission in Sudan and the African Union Mission in Somalia', *African Security Review*, 17, 1, March 2008. Murithi says that 'In the absence of the AU Mission Burundi would have been left to its own devices, which probably would have resulted in an escalation of violent conflict' (p. 75).

66   Reyntjens, 2005.

67   Even after Mandela's time as Facilitator, some of the parallels drawn between South Africa and Burundi were rather stretched. For instance, when South Africa facilitated the negotiations between the Transitional Government of Burundi and the CNDD-FDD, some observers claimed that there were natural affinities between the CNDD-FDD and South Africa. The CNDD-FDD called itself a 'liberation movement' thus making parallels to South Africa's own experience.

would have evolved as it did. From the time that Mandela took over the facilitation of Arusha, right through to ONUB and BINUB, South Africa was a pivotal state, providing leadership, commitment, finances, and most of the logistics behind the missions.[68]

Third, if peacekeeping missions seek to influence calculations about the use of violence, they must be aware that calculations about violence are made within the context of particular sets of state institutions and regional dynamics. Within both the AU and UN, there is the recognition that state-building and the strengthening of political institutions, are keys to peacebuilding, so institution-building must be part of multifaceted peacekeeping missions. Unfortunately however, given the Burundian state, it is unlikely that governance will be fully demilitarized. While efforts to make the Burundian state more inclusive are laudable, the fact remains that Burundi is a small, resource-poor state in a difficult Great Lakes neighbourhood, where politics and privilege depends on patrimonial relations. Violence is likely to remain a useful political resource, yet the capacity for violence, and the cost of violence depend greatly on regional politics.[69] That is why the commitment of Burundi's neighbours, and the politics of bordering regions, is so critical to political outcomes in Burundi.

The Arusha process and the subsequent AMIB and ONUB missions certainly affected politics in Burundi, but the capacity of these kinds of missions – short of extensive long-term external presence – is necessarily limited. Decisions about the use of violence and the modalities of governance in Burundi have not been settled conclusively, so in the lead up to the 2010 elections all those with an interest in Burundi must avoid complacency.

---

68   Kristina Bentley and Roger Southall, *An African Peace Process: Mandela, South Africa and Burundi*, Cape Town: Human Sciences Research Council, 2005.

69   For instance, the availability of arms in the region, the possibilities for rear bases and recruitment in neighbouring countries, and funding opportunities are all ways in which the region contributes to the cost of violence.

Chapter 8

Partnerships for Peacebuilding in Burundi: Some Lessons Learned

Youssef Mahmoud[1]

Introduction

The aim of the chapter is to discuss the cooperation/partnerships of the United Nations with the African Union, and the South African Facilitation in Burundi to help the parties implement the last phase of the peace process. The chapter also discusses mechanisms within the UN system for greater integration and for enhancing the impact and efficiency of UN support to Burundi. Finally, the chapter offers some lessons learned and observations on the challenges facing the integration of the United Nations system in its efforts to support post-conflict peacebuilding.

Background/Context

The assassination of the first democratically elected Hutu President of Burundi, Melchior Ndadaye in October 1993, set in motion the latest cycle of political, ethnic and regional conflicts which lasted more than a decade. Unsuccessful internal mediation with Burundian conflicting parties led to the designation in 1996 by the Great Lakes Regional Peace Initiative on Burundi[2] of late President Julius Nyerere of Tanzania as Facilitator of negotiations between the Government of Burundi, other national stakeholders, and the various armed political movements. In 1998, following the death of President Nyerere, President Nelson Mandela of South Africa was designated by the Regional Peace Initiative as Facilitator of the negotiation process. His sustained efforts and the relentless pressure of regional

---

1   Youssef Mahmoud is the Special Representative of the United Nations Secretary-General and Head of the United Nations Mission in Central African Republic and Chad (MINURCAT). He previously served for three years in Burundi as Executive Representative of the Secretary-General and Head of the United Nations Integrated Office (BINUB). This chapter reflects the personal views of its author and not necessarily those of the United Nations.

2   The Great Lakes Regional Peace Initiative on Burundi was established after 1993 and is composed of the countries of the Great Lakes region, the Horn of Africa and East Africa.

leaders and the international community culminated in the signing in August 2000 of the Arusha Agreement for Peace and Reconciliation by 19 negotiating parties, including the Presidents of the Burundian National Assembly and Senate, and political parties.

The Arusha Agreement[3] identified the nature of the conflict as twofold: a fundamentally political conflict with 'extremely important ethnic dimensions' and resulting from the fight to acquire and maintain power at all cost, including through marginalizing substantial segments of the population and manipulating ethnic differences. To overcome this sad legacy, the Agreement set out a new political, economic, social, cultural and judicial order inspired by democratic standards and specific/genuine compromises on power-sharing arrangements. It envisaged a series of reforms of key institutions (parliament, legal system, defence and security forces, etc.) to be undertaken during a 36-month transitional period and established the principle of joint administration of the country through political and ethnic balance between the main ethnic Hutu and Tutsi groups. The Agreement generally stipulated that the transitional government should promote ethnic balance. It stated that not more than 50 per cent of the national defence and security forces should be drawn from any one ethnic group. Specific ethnic quotas in the legislative and executive as well as administration were subsequently defined in the Constitution that was adopted in 2005.

However, the Agreement suffered from several weaknesses. It lacked the support of the two principal armed groups, the *Conseil national pour la défence de la démocratie-Force nationale pour la démocratie* (CNDD-FDD) of Pierre Nkurunziza and the *Palipehutu-Forces nationales pour la libération* (Palipehutu-FNL) of Agathon Rwasa, who were absent from the Arusha negotiations, and several signatory parties recorded formal reservations. In the view of these parties, the Agreement was also silent on the key issue of who would lead the transitional government and how security sector reform would be implemented. A compromise solution was later found to address the former issue. National stakeholders eventually agreed to divide the transition in two periods of 18-months each. The first period was presided by UPRONA's President, Pierre Buyoya, with a vice-Minister from the Hutu ethnic group and the second by FRODEBU's President, Domitien Ndayizeye, with a vice-Minister from the Tutsi ethnic group. Furthermore, the Agreement did not include a ceasefire agreement, although its basic principles were adopted by the signatories.

In November 2003, the CNDD-FDD agreed to a ceasefire agreement and to participate in the transitional government. The ceasefire agreement called for the deployment of an African Union Peacekeeping mission in Burundi. Despite

---

3   The Agreement's provisions are set forth in five protocols: I. Nature of the conflict, problems of genocide and exclusion and their solutions; II. Democracy and good governance; III. Peace and security for all; IV. Reconstruction and development; and V. Guarantee on the implementation of the Agreement.

regional and international pressure, the other armed political movement, the Palipehutu-FNL, remained for several years outside of the Arusha process.

Following the assassination of President Melchior Ndadaye on 21 October 1993, the Secretary-General, at the request of the Security Council, dispatched a Special Envoy on a good offices mission to facilitate the return of the country to constitutional rule and appointed a Special Representative for Burundi, who subsequently established the United Nations Office in Burundi (UNOB) as a confidence-building presence.[4] In November 1993, at the request of the Government of Burundi, the then Organisation of African Unity (OAU) also established a mission in Burundi, with United Nations support through the establishment of a voluntary fund. The OAU mission aimed at contributing to confidence building; promoting dialogue between the government and the other components of the Burundian society (political, military, civil society, etc.); and facilitating the national reconciliation process, in close collaboration with UNOB.[5]

As provided for by the November 2003 ceasefire agreement with the CNDD-FDD, the OAU mission was transformed into a peacekeeping operation, becoming the African Mission in Burundi (AMIB), the first of its kind on the African continent. Its mandate was to: oversee the implementation of the ceasefire agreements; support disarmament and demobilization initiatives and advise on reintegration of combatants; strive to create conditions favourable for the establishment of a United Nations peacekeeping mission; and contribute to political and economic stability in Burundi.[6] UNOB was tasked in 2003 to provide AMIB with technical assistance and advice and acquired further responsibilities with regard to the establishment of ceasefire agreement implementation mechanisms.[7]

In June 2004, the UN Security Council established the United Nations Operation in Burundi (ONUB), thus replacing UNOB and integrating AMIB troops. ONUB's mandate included contributing to the creation of the necessary security conditions for the provision of humanitarian assistance, and facilitating the voluntary return of refugees and internally displaced persons, as well as contributing to the successful completion of the electoral process stipulated in the Arusha Agreement, by ensuring a secure environment for free, transparent and peaceful elections[8].

The adoption via referendum in March 2005 of a new Constitution, which was substantially inspired by and included many of the provisions of the Arusha

4   S/26757, Note by the President of the Security Council, 16 November 1993.

5   See Central Organ at the ministerial level, 17–19 November 1993; Headquarters Agreement between the Government of Burundi and the OAU, 8 April 1994.

6   See Central Organ at ambassadorial level, 14 January 2003; Central Organ at the level of heads of State and Government, 3 February 2003; Central Organ at ambassadorial level, 2 April 2003.

7   See Secretary-General's report on the situation of Burundi of 4 December 2003, S/2003/1146.

8   Security Council resolution 1545 (2004) of 21 May 2004.

Agreement, paved the way for the subsequent general election process, which culminated in the nomination by Parliament of Pierre Nkurunziza, leader of the CNDD-FDD, as President in August 2005, thus bringing the transitional period to an end. The presence of ONUB throughout the transitional period was instrumental in the preparation and smooth conduct of the elections.

As in many post-conflict countries, the new government faced multiple challenges of equal urgency and importance. These included improving the security and human rights situation, fighting impunity, including sexual violence, reducing corruption and improving governance, restoring trust and promoting reconciliation, facilitating the safe return of refugees and their reintegration in the communities, and ensuring equitable access to the basic socio-economic needs of a deeply impoverished population. The Human Development Index (HDI) for Burundi was estimated for 2005 to be at 0.413, which ranked Burundi at 167 out of 177 countries with data.[9] For 2006, the HDI was estimated at 0.382 with a rank of 172 out of 179 countries with data.[10] In addition, one of the most immediate challenges was to bring the last rebel group (the Palipehutu-FNL) to the negotiating table in order to consolidate peace.

To help address these challenges, the international community remained strongly engaged in Burundi. The South African Facilitation mandated by the Regional Peace Initiative pursued its mission towards the resumption of negotiations between the government and this last armed political movement in Tanzania with the support of the African Union and the United Nations. Ultimately, in 2006, the government of President Nkurunziza and the leader of the movement, Agathon Rwasa, signed in Dar es Salaam the Agreement of Principles towards lasting Peace, Security and Stability in Burundi in June and a Comprehensive Ceasefire Agreement in September of that year.

In December 2006, the International Conference on the Great Lakes Region, which is composed of 11 members,[11] signed the Pact on Security, Stability and Development in the Great Lakes Region that became effective in June 2008. The Pact is composed of 10 protocols and four regional programmes of action: peace and security; democracy and good governance; economic development and integration; and humanitarian and social issues. The Pact also foresees a regional follow-up mechanism and a Special Fund for reconstruction and development.[12] Burundi currently hosts the Executive Secretariat of the Conference. Burundi also became a full member of the East African Community in July 2008.

---

9   Human Development Report (HDR) of 2007/2008, UNDP.

10   Update 2008, Burundi factsheet, HDR, UNDP.

11   Angola, Burundi, Central African Republic, Congo, Democratic Republic of Congo, Kenya, Rwanda, Sudan, Tanzania, Uganda and Zambia.

12   For more information, see www.icglr.org.

The Role of the United Nations in the Post-transition Phase

In November 2005, the democratically elected government demanded a reduction of UNOB, on the grounds that Burundi was fully equipped to handle the residual peacekeeping challenges without the mission. This demand for withdrawal was perceived by the United Nations and the international community in general as rather premature. Within the partners in Burundi, there was a strong consensus on the need for a subsequent United Nations presence or structure that could continue to help the country address its human rights, transitional justice needs, security sector reform, and peace and governance transformation necessary to consolidate peace and spur reconstruction.[13] Following informal but intense discussions, the government and the United Nations attained a basic common ground on the way forward. On 24 May 2006, an agreement was reached with the government stipulating that an integrated office would be established following the end of ONUB's mandate. The agreed priority areas requiring United Nations assistance were: (a) peace and democratic governance; (b) security sector reform and civilian disarmament; (c) human rights, judicial sector reform and transitional justice; (d) information and communications; and (e) reconstruction and socio-economic development.[14]

On the basis of the above agreement and following the recommendation of the Secretary-General, the Security Council established in October 2006 through resolution 1719, the United Nations Integrated Office in Burundi (BINUB) which became operational in January 2007. The Council mandated BINUB to harness the collective capacities of the United Nations system in an integrated and coherent manner to help Burundi address the above peacebuilding priorities and thus usher in a transition from peacekeeping towards a development-focused engagement by the United Nations. To facilitate this task, the Council directed that the Executive Representative of the Secretary-General (ERSG) and head of the mission also act as the Resident Coordinator of the UN operational activities in the country and as the Resident Representative of the UN Development Programme (UNDP). The Council also tasked BINUB to facilitate a partnership between the government and international donors and strengthen the former's capacity to coordinate international assistance for development. The government-led Partners Coordination Group which was established in the first half of 2008 is now functional and has become a viable forum for dialogue between the Government of Burundi and its partners.

Subsequently, in resolutions 1791 (2007) and 1858 (2008), the Security Council requested the Secretary-General, including through BINUB, to play a 'robust political role' in support of the peace process being led by the South African Facilitation and aiming at the full implementation of the Comprehensive

---

13   See seventh report of the Secretary-General on the United Nations Operations in Burundi of 14 August 2006, S/2006/429.

14   Seventh report of the Secretary-General on the United Nations Operations in Burundi, Addendum, of 14 August 2006, S/2006/429/Add.1.

Ceasefire Agreement between the government and the Palipehutu-FNL, which had dragged on for far too long, since its signature in September 2006.[15]

BINUB's support to Burundi was further guided by the need to ensure that all United Nations actions were implemented within the national plans for development and peace consolidation, notably the Poverty Reduction Strategy Paper and the Strategic Framework for Peacebuilding in Burundi, and by the principle that the government bore the primary responsibility and ownership for sustaining peace and laying the foundation for economic recovery. The Poverty Reduction Strategy Paper was developed in September 2006 with the government in the lead with the active participation of national and international partners. Peace and governance, the private sector and other economic growth sectors were among its priorities. As to the Strategic Framework for Peacebuilding, it was developed in June 2007, between the government and the Peacebuilding Commission, as a means for guiding the concerted engagement and dialogue between the Government of Burundi and its national and international partners around a shared set of peacebuilding priorities, including the promotion of good governance, the implementation of the Comprehensive Ceasefire Agreement between the government and the Palipehutu-FNL, security sector, justice and the promotion of human rights, the land issue and socio-economic recovery.

Furthermore, the ERSG as head of mission and UN Resident Coordinator (RC) was also guided by the United Nations Peacekeeping Operations Principles and Guidelines of 2008 which stipulates that

> an integrated mission is one in which there is a shared vision among all UN actors as to the strategic objective of the UN presence at country level. This strategic objective could reflect a shared understanding of the operating environment and agreement on how to maximize the effectiveness, efficiency and impact of the overall response. This approach should be based on a common strategic plan and a shared understanding of the priorities and types of programme interventions that need to be undertaken. Structural or programmatic intervention between UN actors should be driven by an assessment of whether or not it will add real value and improve the impact of the UN's engagement.[16]

In June 2008, a Directive by the Secretary-General further refined integration as means for maximizing the impact of the collective and individual response of the United Nations on the ground by focusing on those activities that consolidate peace.

Taking into account these nationally-owned frameworks and the above UN policy guidance, BINUB and the rest of the UN system endeavoured to organize themselves at the strategic, programmatic and operational levels, in such a way so as to avoid fragmentation and enhance the impact of their actions. In March

---

15   See Secretary-General's report on Burundi of 23 November 2007, S/2007/682.
16   United Nations Peacekeeping Operations Principles and Guidelines (2008).

2007, the government and the United Nations system in Burundi endorsed the United Nations Integrated Peacebuilding support strategy which integrated the peace consolidation goals mandated by the Security Council with socio-economic recovery goals that have an added value for peace consolidation. These include the promotion of local private sector and the socio-economic reintegration of returnees and ex-combatants. At the programmatic level, BINUB adopted three core integrated programmes. These are the peacebuilding and governance programme; security sector reform and small arms programme; and human rights, justice and fight against impunity programme. Given that addressing socio-economic/ humanitarians needs were also at the core of peace consolidation, the ERSG in his capacity as United Nations Resident Coordinator (UNRC) helped the rest of the UN system identify and pursue joint programmes in the areas of democratic governance and community recovery, which in addition to their intrinsic value, would explicitly contribute to peacebuilding and reconciliation by insuring *inter alia* that these programmes are inclusive and do not unwittingly exacerbate conflict. Finally, there was an attempt to integrate the various UN presences at the level of leadership and supporting structures. Among these structures is the United Nations Integrated Management Team (UNIMT) which brings together BINUB sections chiefs and the heads of agencies. This structure serves as a forum for joint decision-making and for reducing the compartmentalisation of the United Nations' work in Burundi.

In January 2007, on the basis of a priority plan jointly developed by the government and the United Nations, in collaboration with civil society and international partners, the Secretary-General of the United Nations approved an allocation of US$35 million from the UN Peacebuilding Fund (PBF) he had established to support critical peacebuilding projects in Burundi.[17] The role of the PBF is to establish a bridge between conflict and recovery at a time when other funding mechanisms may not yet be available. In helping addressing the most immediate out of the multiple challenges facing post-conflict countries, the PBF also aims at stabilising and strengthening national institutions in order to enhance their capacity to sustain the peace process. In essence, the role of the PBF is catalytic.

A Joint Steering Committee composed of representatives of the government, the United Nations, international partners and civil society was established in early 2007 to approve and follow-up on the implementation of the 18 projects[18] that had been developed in accordance with the priority areas submitted to the Peacebuilding Commission[19] (PBC) in December 2006. These areas are: (a) good

---

17 The Secretary-General formally announced the allocation of US$35 million in his address to the African Union Summit in Addis Ababa, Ethiopia, on 29 January 2007.

18 For details of the project, see http://www.unpbf.org/burundi/burundi-projects. shtml.

19 The Peacebuilding Commission was established by the General Assembly and the Security Council on 20 December 2005 through resolutions 60/180 and 1645 (2005).

governance; (b) strengthening of rule of law within the defence and security forces; (c) strengthening of justice, promotion of human rights, reconciliation and fight against impunity; (d) the contentious of land scarcity and the conflicts surrounding it, particularly the return of refugees from neighbouring countries. The main criteria for approval of these projects as alluded to in the previous paragraph were the direct and visible impact their execution would have on the population and the added value in strengthening the human and institutional capacities of Burundians so they can self-sustain the short-term results of these peacebuilding interventions.

A joint evaluation by those donors who have contributed to the PBF was conducted to assess the effectiveness of the structures and modalities for accessing and disbursing the peacebuilding funds and the initial results achieved by these projects.[20]

The above efforts, commendable as they were, continued to be overshadowed by slow progress in the implementation of the Comprehensive Ceasefire Agreement between the government and the Palipehutu-FNL and by the sense of insecurity that this unfinished last phase of the peace process created among the population. In July 2007 after a hopeful start two months earlier, the process of the implementation of the Comprehensive Ceasefire Agreement stalled and the Palipehutu-FNL left the country, dissatisfied that its political grievances were not being properly addressed.

In order to help overcome the stalemate, the Facilitator, South African Minister of Safety and Security, Charles Nqakula, who later became Minister of Defence, established a Burundi-based mechanism, called the 'Political Directorate', to: (i) address political obstacles arising in the course of the implementation of the comprehensive ceasefire agreement; (ii) serve as a 'listening forum'; (iii) facilitate dialogue between the two parties, including on political arrangements aimed at the inclusion of FNL into the national institutions within the framework of the Constitution; and (iv) monitor and assist the parties in implementing these arrangements.[21] The Political Directorate is composed of the representatives of South Africa, Tanzania, Uganda, the African Union, the European Union and the United Nations, as well as representatives of the government and the Palipehutu-FNL. At the request of the Facilitator, the Special Envoys for the Great Lakes

---

It is composed of 31 Member States for renewable terms of two years, as applicable. The PBC has been tasked, among other things, to bring together all relevant actors to marshal resources and to advise on the proposed integrated strategies for post-conflict peacebuilding and recovery.

20   See Review of the Peacebuilding Fund by Nicole Ball and Mariska van Beijnum, 4 June 2009, at http://www.unpbf.org/docs/PBF_Review.pdf.

21   The mandate of the Political Directorate is outlined in the Programme of Action of the Facilitator adopted by the Group of Special Envoys for the Great Lakes Region on 22–23 February 2008 in Cape Town, South Africa. See Secretary-General report on Burundi of 15 May 2008, S/2008/330.

Region formed themselves into a support group to review progress in the Burundi peace process and agree on how best to support the efforts of the South African Facilitation.

It is within the Political Directorate, that BINUB exercised 'the robust role' entrusted to it by the Security Council. This was done mainly through the provision to the Facilitation of political advice as well as substantive and technical support, using as needed BINUB's logistical assets and conference facilities.

Concerted and sustained efforts as well as pressure from the leaders of the Regional Peace Initiative, the Facilitator, the Political Directorate and the international partners resulted in the return of the Palipehutu-FNL leadership in May 2008 and the resumption of the implementation of the Comprehensive Ceasefire Agreement. The Regional Initiative leaders and the Facilitator set 31 March 2009 as the deadline for completing the Disarmament, Demobilization and the Reintegration (DDR) component of the Agreement and the subsequent transformation of the FNL into a political party. Given the slow pace of implementation, the above tasks could not be completed by the stated deadline. However, a decisive step forward was taken in April as the FNL formally disarmed and was registered as a political party. At a landmark meeting of the Political Directorate in Pretoria on 8 April 2009, chaired by the South African Facilitation, the government and the FNL agreed on a roadmap for the integration of the FNL into civil and military institutions and the demobilisation of its combatants, with special considerations afforded to women.

The South African Facilitation ended its mission on 31 May 2009 and handed over the residual tasks of the DDR process to the government. The African Union, with the support of BINUB, took over the responsibility to oversee the process. A new mechanism called the Partnership for Peace in Burundi (PPB) was launched by South Africa on 27 May 2009 to monitor the implementation of the residual elements of the peace process, including the release of political and war prisoners and the separation of children associated with the FNL, and provide early warning to the Regional Initiative leaders. It is composed of the Political Directorate, the Executive Secretariat of the International Conference for the Great Lakes Region and BINUB. BINUB serves as its Secretariat. The UN Peacebuilding Commission and the Group of Special Envoys for the Great Lakes Region act as a support network for the PPB.

Subsequently, senior FNL members were appointed to civil service posts, combatants were either integrated into the security and defence forces or demobilised. In addition, as a special measure, a total of 11,000 adults associated with FNL combatants, including 1,000 women, were provided with return assistance to their communities.

The first half of 2009 was thus characterized by significant advances in the peace process. At the time of writing, there remained few outstanding issues, such as the appointment of the remaining FNL members to civil posts and the release of the remaining political prisoners, which fall under the purview of the Political Directorate.

Conclusions and Observations

A number of conclusions and lessons learned can be drawn from the partnerships between the African Union, the United Nations, the Regional Peace Initiative and the Facilitation, which contributed to the peacemaking, peacekeeping and peacebuilding in Burundi.

First, while the situation is still fragile in Burundi, the undeniable progress that has been achieved since the Arusha Agreement is largely due to the steadfast engagement of the Regional Initiative leaders, the South African Facilitator and the African Union. If the process looks increasingly less reversible it is largely due to the African efforts, with the United Nations playing a supportive, albeit important role, particularly during the peacekeeping and peacebuilding phases of its engagement.

Second, peacemaking and peacekeeping are largely exogenously-driven processes. The former (e.g. the Arusha peace process) aims at helping conflicting parties move from violence to politics through various forms of mediation processes culminating in a peace agreement. The latter (e.g. AMIB, ONUB) endeavours to help create a secure and stable environment for the implementation of that agreement. Peacebuilding on the other hand is fundamentally an endogenous process. To succeed, it must be internally driven and owned, however weak, divided or unwilling the national partners may be. It is the above observation and this fundamental principle that has guided the design and functioning of BINUB. A conscious and consistent effort was made to shift at the outset the onus of sustaining peace to national stakeholders while ensuring continued engagement of regional and international actors in support of these stakeholders. This explains the importance given to building and enhancing national, human and institutional capacities as an integral part of our peacebuilding interventions.

This however, has been a challenging endeavour for the peace partners in Burundi for a number of reasons. The first were the difficulties they encountered in weaning national actors from communicating/working with each other through proxies because of the deep distrust between these actors largely as a result of four decades of cyclical violence that wracked Burundi. Hence, the imperative need that was felt to help restore trust and restructure broken relations among these actors as a priority. The Peacebuilding Fund project on national dialogue launched in early 2008 was aimed at creating a safe environment for Burundians at all levels to listen to each other and jointly formulate strategies for addressing peace and development challenges, and in so doing help build trust among them.

Another reason is that building national ownership takes time, patience and requires humility. National actors, because of lack of capacity or political will or both invariably, shy away from assuming responsibility. On the other hand, international partners, including the United Nations are still struggling to strike a balance between the need for quick results that their funding processes require and the medium- to long-term nature of building a nationally owned sustainable peace.[22]

Third, building peace has to be part of a larger process. It is undeniable that the priorities outlined in the various Security Council resolutions are fundamental to prevent the return of conflict and consolidate peace whether these relate to building legitimate and capable institutions, promoting good governance, transforming leadership or fighting impunity. However, pursued alone these priority endeavours are not sufficient in a post-conflict context. They must be combined with efforts that aim at meeting the basic socio-economic needs of people, particularly the most vulnerable among them, the returnees, women and children. Restoring/building elementary health and sanitation services, educating women and children are at the core of peacebuilding, albeit they take time. In this regard, the decision of the President of Burundi to provide free schooling for children under five and free healthcare for pregnant women were steps in the right direction.

The fourth observation relates to the integration of UN efforts on the ground as mandated by the United Nations Secretary-General in his June 2008 Directive. These efforts, as outlined above, aim at ensuring that the political, security and socio-economic priorities of Burundi are pursued simultaneously as one agenda, despite diverse, overlapping mandates and multiple sources of funding. The designation of the head of BINUB as UNRC among other functions was designed to help achieve that common strategic vision and translate it into integrated actions.

This also proved to be a difficult task, despite notable progress in certain areas, namely in the integration of efforts at the strategic, programmatic and operational levels.[23] The main reasons are that the local representatives of the various UN agencies, funds and programmes tend to be more beholden to their respective central and regional structures, including the various Headquarter-based Executive Boards, rather than to the lead official on the ground, mandated by the Secretary-General and the Security Council to coordinate UN responses. A related impediment is the concern that integration may lead to the loss of the visibility of individual agencies which is essential for resource mobilization and individual career advancement.

The strategic, programmatic instruments and structures set up by BINUB under the leadership of the ERSG/UNRC were designed to help temper this upward accountability by empowering these various UN entities to be accountable for the peacebuilding impact of their actions on the ground without jeopardizing the execution of their respective mandates. This endeavour will remain rather tenuous – personality driven in the absence of performance incentives that rewards integration.

---

22   See Secretary-General's report on peacebuilding in the immediate aftermath of conflict of 11 June 2009, A/63/881 – S/2009/304.

23   See UN integration in Burundi in the context of a peacebuilding office BINUB, Lessons learned from June 2006 to October 2007, BINUB, Bujumbura, February 2008.

BINUB's core objective is to support Burundians develop their capacities to self-sustain peace and to lay the foundation for economic recovery. In implementing its mandated tasks, BINUB, despite the challenges outlined above, is not only contributing to this goal, but also establishing good practices for UN integration. Its experience has also provided lessons for how to transit from a UN peacekeeping-oriented presence to a development-oriented engagement.[24]

BINUB represents an intermediate phase in which a strong political mandate is retained in order to better address the residual challenges of the peace process after the withdrawal of a peacekeeping operation. This intermediate phase had been missing in past peacekeeping operations and, in some cases, such as Haiti and Timor Leste, a premature political and security disengagement unwittingly brought about a rapid deterioration of the situation and compelled the international community to redeploy peacekeepers.

Much is therefore at stake as we continue our efforts in support of Burundian and regional actors. While helping consolidate peace is at the core of our actions, the lessons learned from our experience could have a longer-term impact on future UN engagement in post-conflict situations in other regions.

Background Documents

Agreements between Parties in Conflict in Burundi

Arusha Agreement for Peace and Reconciliation in Burundi, Arusha, 28 August 2000.

Comprehensive Ceasefire Agreement between the Government of transition of Burundi and the *Mouvement conseil national pour la défense de la démocratie – Forces pour la défense de la démocratie* (CNDD-FDD), Dar es Salaam, 16 November 2003.

Dar es Salaam Agreement of Principles towards lasting Peace, Security and Stability in Burundi, Dar es Salaam, 18 June 2006.

Comprehensive Ceasefire Agreement between the Government of Burundi and the Palipehutu-FNL, Dar es Salaam, 7 September 2006.

Official Documents

Poverty Reduction Strategy Paper for Burundi, September 2006.

Strategic Framework for Peacebuilding in Burundi, PBC/1/BDI/4*, 22 June 2007.

Security Council resolution 1719 (2006), S/RES/1719 (2006), 25 October 2006.

Security Council resolution 1791 (2007), S/RES/1791 (2007), 19 December 2007.

---

24   *Ibid.*

Security Council resolution 1858 (2008), S/RES/1858 (2008), 22 December 2008.

UN Integration in Burundi in the context of the peacebuilding office BINUB, 'Taking Stock and Lessons Learned from June 2006 to November 2007', BINUB, Bujumbura, February 2008.

United Nations Peacekeeping Operations Principles and Guidelines, 2008.

Articles/Books

René Lemarchand, 'Burundi: Ethnic Conflict and Genocide', 1996, Washington DC, Woodrow Wilson Center Press.

Youssef Mahmoud, 'Post Conflict Peace building: Reflections on the Experience of the United Nations in Guinea-Bissau', 2001, Negotios Estrangeiros, Lisbon.

Howard Wolpe, 'Burundi: Facilitation in a regionally Sponsored Peace Process', 2003. Unpublished manuscript prepared for a United States Institute of Peace conference on best facilitation practices.

Howard Wolpe et al., 'Rebuilding Peace and State Capacity in War-torn Burundi', 2004, The Roundtable, Vol. 93, No. 375, pp. 457–67.

Chapter 9

The DDRR and SSR Process in Liberia: Prospects and Challenges

Thomas Jaye[1] and John Mark Pokoo[2]

Introduction

Liberia was declared independent on 26 July 1847 by African-Americans who were returned to the West Coast of Africa after long years of enduring slavery in North America. Liberia therefore became the first republic in Africa. Like Ethiopia, it was never colonized. One of the challenges facing Liberia from the very beginning was the issue of internal administration which manifested itself in the coexistence of the modern Liberian state with traditional forms of governance. Like other African countries, the West African state also suffered long years of authoritarian rule (including a decade of military rule); political repression and exclusion; economic mismanagement including corruption; and social deprivation for the vast majority of the people. A combination of these factors led to 14 years of war and mayhem.

After 14 years of armed conflict (from 1990–2003) which resulted in the killings of more than 250,000 people and displaced 1.3 million people (including those who fled the country)[3] out of a population of approximately 3.5 million, Liberia needed a disarmament, demobilization and reintegration (DDR) programme to address the trauma of ex-combatants and reintegrate them back into the larger society as part of a comprehensive security sector reform (SSR) process, which seeks to inject efficiency, coordination and coherence in the undertakings of security institutions in the country and transfer the oversight responsibilities over the sector to a democratic and accountable leadership.

The war was caused by multiple factors mainly rooted in ethnic and historical cleavages as well as persistent bad governance with poor social and economic

---

1   Dr Thomas Jaye is a Senior Research Fellow at the Kofi Annan International Peacekeeping Training Centre (KAIPTC) in Accra, Ghana.

2   John Mark Pokoo Project Coordinator of the Small Arms and Light Weapons Project at the KAIPTC.

3   US Agency for International Development (USAID), Overview of Activities in Liberia, 4 May 2004, cited in Sean McFate, 'Outsourcing the Making of Militaries: DynCorp International As Sovereign Agent', *Review of African Political Economy*, No. 118, 2008, p. 645.

indicators. For example, one of the ethnically-based explanations indicates that the Americo-Liberians established an oligarchy that excluded and oppressed the indigenous inhabitants, despite constituting 5 per cent of the population for more than 130 years.[4] Americo-Liberian is the word generically used to refer to the blacks who were freed from slavery and repatriated from North America in the early 1820s. They set for themselves the mission of 'civilizing' and 'Christianizing' the people they met on the shores of Africa. The state which emerged in the early nineteenth century enveloped much more than the meeting of two cultures.[5] The settlers imposed a central administration on diverse ethnic communities, a problem which over a century later most post-colonial Third World states would face at birth. In these states, according to Caroline Thomas, a modern western-style state system was imposed on areas where society remained predominantly traditional and where loyalties flowed to traditional centres of authority.[6] These stresses and strains were bound to impact upon future developments in Liberia, and affect its secure development, good governance and the rule of law.

Even though Liberia was established because of the 'love of liberty', the history of this country has been characterized by different and ugly experiences: political repression, lack of rule of law, social exclusion and deprivation, economic mismanagement, and poor governance. All of these factors conspired to produce the 14-year armed conflict in Liberia.[7]

Other explanations conclude that Liberia was faced with problems of political repression, economic mismanagement, and lack of access to scarce resources, to health care, education, and lack of broader political participation. Although there are no available figures, many people in the country were unemployed and poverty was pervasive.[8]

These factors thus created opportunities for war mobilization and led to the emergence of several armed factions, which complicated the conflict and the subsequent implementation of DDR and SSR in the country. These were seen as stabilizing measures towards the implementation of more comprehensive and integrated security and justice sector reforms.[9] All the factions in the conflict

---

4   Adekeye Adebayo, *Liberia's Civil War. Nigeria, ECOMOG and Regional Security in West Africa* (Boulder and London: Lynne Rienner, 2002) p. 45.

5   D. Elwood Dunn, 'Liberia's Internal Responses to ECOMOG's Interventionist Efforts' in Karl P. Maygar and Earl Conteh-Morgan (eds) *Peacekeeping in Africa. ECOMOG in Liberia* (New York: St Martin's Press, Inc., 1998) p. 78.

6   Caroline Thomas, *In Search of Security. The Third World in International Relations* (Hemel Hempstead, Hertfordshire: Harvester Wheatsheaf, 1987) p. 16.

7   See Thomas Jaye, 'Liberia: Setting Priorities for Post-Conflict Reconstruction' *Journal of Security Sector Management*, Vol. 1 No. 3, December 2003.

8   Jaye, 2000: 157.

9   The armed factions that emerged after the war included: the National Patriotic Front of Liberia (NPFL), the Independent National Patriotic Front of Liberia (INPFL), United Movement for the Liberation of Liberia (ULIMO), which split into ULIMO (J) and ULIMO (K), Liberia Peace Council (LPC), the Black Berets, Liberians United for

were guilty of gross abuses – i.e. killing of innocent people, rape, recruiting child soldiers, looting of the national economy, and the destruction of properties among other forms of abuse.

Thus the threats to the security of the country came from disaffected groups such as the demobilized personnel of the Armed Forces of Liberia (AFL) who were not satisfied with their severance payment and pension benefits. After the war, the new administration carried out measures aimed at downsizing the army. As a result thereof, about 9,400 'war conscripts' (1990 to 1997) and Regular Service personnel who joined the army prior to the outbreak of war in 1989 were duly discharged from the army. A total of 13,673 people were deactivated from the army.

Reintegrating these people into the larger society has constituted a major challenge for the new administration. One of the difficulties facing the government is that, regrettably, many of the ex-soldiers and veterans do not have the skills required to be reintegrated into the larger society immediately. Thus, the issue of ex-soldiers and veterans raises not just security but also development issues.

In the case of ex-combatants, many of them illegally occupied rubber plantations throughout Liberia in the immediate post-conflict period but were persuaded out of their actions by the United Nations Mission in Liberia (UNMIL) and the new administration of the country through dialogue; former members of the ATU who are demanding inclusion into the armed forces demobilization programme maybe because they were seen as a non-statutory group organized for President Taylor; ex-fighters who are yet to benefit from the reintegration programme and those who have been trained but are unemployed. There are also deactivated personnel of the Special Security Service (SSS) and the Liberia National Police (LNP).[10]

In October 2005 the first post-conflict and violent free elections in Liberia produced the new administration of Ellen Sirleaf Johnson. One of the challenges of this government is to overturn the legacy of bad governance and lack of rule of law, the increasing rates of crime and to devise an effective strategy of restoring a functioning security sector for the country including the formation of a national army and civil police for the people of Liberia without creating disaffection in the population.

This chapter argues that the DDR process in Liberia was incomplete because many parts of the country were not covered due to impassibility; and because some of the genuine ex-combatants did not benefit from the scheme. This occurred because the so-called commanders responsible for verifying members of their factions substituted the real fighters with their own relatives for economic benefits. Nevertheless, the process did contribute to the relative peace and security enjoyed prior to the elections of October 2005. It also argues that the SSR process has been conducted without proper coordination among donors as well as among Liberian

---

Reconciliation and Democracy (LURD), Lofa Defence Force (LDF), and the Movement for Democracy in Liberia (MODEL). The Armed Forces of Liberia (AFL), the national army, also transformed itself into a sort of warring faction.

10   Eleventh Progress Report, 2006: 3.

actors or between the Liberian actors and donors. It has been skewed in favour of the army and police.

Background to DDR in Liberia

During the 14 years of armed conflict, Liberia underwent two different DDR processes. The first took place from November 1994 to 6 April 1996 after the signing of the Cotonou Agreement on 25 July 1993 by Liberian stakeholders. The Cotonou Agreement provided for disarmament, encampment and demobilization of the fighters of the armed factions under the supervision of ECOMOG but to be monitored and verified by the UN observer mission.[11] Subsequently it was reinforced by the Akosombo Accord of 12 September 1994 signed by Charles Taylor[12] (NPFL), Alhaji Kromah[13] (ULIMO-K) and others. The second took place after the signing of the Comprehensive Peace Agreement from December 2003 to 30 October 2004. It provided for the cantonment, disarmament, demobilization, reintegration and rehabilitation of the ex-fighters. Under this Agreement, it was agreed that a National Commission on Disarmament, Demobilization, Reintegration and Rehabilitation (NCDDR) would be established comprising agencies of the National Transitional Government of Liberia (NTGL), representatives of GoL,[14] LURD, MODEL, ECOWAS, the UN, AU and the International Contact Group on Liberia (ICGL). The body was charged with the responsibility to oversee and coordinate the entire process until it was closed down in July 2009. There were roughly five interim governments starting with the Interim Government of National Unity (IGNU) led by Amos Sawyer[15] and ending with the National Transitional Government of Liberia (NTGL) led by Charles Gyude Bryant.[16]

---

11   See Cotonou Agreement, 25 July 1993, Cotonou, Benin.

12   Charles Taylor was leader of the NPFL which started the armed incursion against the regime of Samuel Doe. He was later elected President of Liberia during the elections of 1997 but resigned after being indicated by the Special Court in Sierra Leone. Later in 2006, he was transferred to the International Criminal Court in The Hague, Netherlands, where he stands trial for war crimes.

13   Alhaji G.V. Kromah was leader of the ULIMO (K) faction which opposed Taylor during the war years. He later served on the Council of State in 1996 and is among recommended by the TRC of Liberia for war crimes.

14   GoL means Government of Liberia. This is how the representatives of the Taylor forces were referred to.

15   Prof. Amos Sawyer is former President of the Interim Government of National Unity (IGNU). Previously, he served as Dean of Liberia College, University of Liberia and has been involved with the radical Liberian group, the Movement for Justice in Africa (MOJA). He is a Liberian academic who now heads the Governance Commission of Liberia.

16   Charles Gyude Bryant was elected as Chair of the National Transitional Government of Liberia (NTGL), which governed Liberia before the elections of 2005 that

The Process and Challenges

The first DDR programme started on 22 November 1994 but was aborted by the violence of 6 April 1996 erupted between ULIMO (J) and forces loyal to Taylor and Kromah. It erupted because of an attempt by Taylor and Kromah to remove D. Roosevelt Johnson (ULIMO)[17] from the Council of State (COS) because they accused him of murder and Roosevelt refused to be arrested. This eroded trust among the warring factions and intensified the struggle for power among them and the consequent unwillingness to disarm.[18] However, the disarmament process was re-started after the April 1996 violence for three months even though weapons turned in were unserviceable neither did the subsequent victory of Taylor in the 1997 elections provide the enabling environment for a comprehensive and successful reform of the army.

Nevertheless, the first DDR programme was implemented in various stages. The first stage involved disarming, registration, interviewing and counselling of ex-fighters; stage two involved participation in empowering programmes,[19] which included work and training programmes in formal and vocational education[20] that would enhance their skills and productivity. The final stage involved reintegration, a longer-term process such as preparing them for reinsertion into the larger society. This would require formal education and vocation training, and pre-discharge orientation.[21] Here the assistance package for the ex-fighters included food and tools for work. At the cantonment site, they were fed three times daily and after five days of processing and career counselling, they were given a fixed ration comprising food and non-food items such as blankets, clothes, footwear and $150 to enable them return to their communities ahead of the RR phase.[22] These were followed by reintegration coupons or food rations to the demobilized fighters who were transported to their final destinations.[23]

Under the RR phase, they benefited from programmes supported by the EC and the USAID while the Trust Fund was managed by the UNDP. Under a Parallel Programme funded by the EC and USAID, they were provided with meals while in training for nine months and toolkits after the training was completed as a start up

---

brought President Ellen Johnson to power. He was elected at the Accra peace talks but before then, he is believed to have run his own small-scale business.

17   D. Roosevelt Johnson subsequently led part of the ULIMO into a separate faction under his leadership.

18   Informal discussion with ULIMO (J) and LURD members, August, 2006.

19   What was called bridging activities in 1995 was termed rehabilitation in the second DDR process (2003–2005).

20   Formal Education: university, college, secondary school, and computer studies; Vocational: agriculture, plumbing, carpentry, masonry, electronic, electricity, auto-mechanic, cosmetology, tailoring and others.

21   Twentieth Progress Report, 1996: 6.

22   Email exchange with a former staff of NCDDRR, October 2009.

23   Twenty-First Progress Report, 1997: 4.

package for reintegration.[24] Whereas under the Trust Fund programme, they were given $30 per month as allowance for attending classes, in the formal education sector, they received $30 per month for the first year; $15 per month for year two and nothing for the final year.[25]

By the end of the process on 9 February 1997, about 24,500 of the estimated 33,000 fighters (74 per cent) had been disarmed and demobilized. These included 4,306 child soldiers and 250 adult female fighters. More than 9,570 weapons and 1.2 million rounds of ammunition were also surrendered, and ECOMOG's cordon-and-search operations yielded another 917 weapons and 122,162 rounds of ammunition.[26] Although the process was incomplete because some fighters did not go through it due to the impassability of many areas, the number of arms and ammunition collected, and the number of people who participated in this process illustrated that positive achievements were made under this programme.

The second DDR process in Liberia was marked by the signing of a Comprehensive Peace Agreement (CPA) by the armed factions and other stakeholders on 18 August 2003, in Accra, Ghana. Among others, the CPA included agreements on Disarmament, Demobilization and Reintegration (DDR) and Security Sector Reform (SSR). In the CPA, the overall aim of the Disarmament Demobilization Rehabilitation and Reintegration (DDRR) programme was to sustain the implementation of its mandate to disarm the armed factions to the conflict.[27] To this end, the programme comprised two major components: the disarmament and demobilization component, which involved the collection and cantonment of weapons and ammunition; as well as the disengagement of disarmed fighters from their command structures. The second component, rehabilitation and reintegration, involved providing reintegration support to ex-fighters to enhance their skills and make them productive. This second component rested on three pillars namely: formal education, vocational training and social reintegration.[28]

A National Commission on Disarmament, Demobilization, Rehabilitation and Reintegration (NCDDRR) was established in December 2003 as an interdisciplinary and interdepartmental body to coordinate the DDR programme.[29] However, an ad hoc task force was established earlier during the same year to work as a transitional mechanism while the NCDDRR was being established. Incidentally, it was this task force, mainly constituted by multilateral donors, UNDP and UNMIL, which developed the actual DDRR programme of Liberia.[30] The task force was

---

24 Email exchange with former staff of the NCDDRR, October 2009.
25 Email exchange with former staff of the NCDDRR, October 2009.
26   Adebayo, 2002: 208–9.
27 Comprehensive Peace Agreement between the Government of Liberia, The Liberians United for Reconciliation, Democracy (LURD) and the Movement for Democracy in Liberia (MODEL) and Political Parties, Accra, Ghana, 18 August 2003.
28 UNDP Liberia, DDRR, 29/06/2006.
29 CPA, 2003.
30 Liberia DDRR Programme Framework, 31 October 2003: 7, 17 and 24.

effectively abolished when the NCDDRR was fully constituted in 2004. When the DDRR started on 7 December 2003, much of the UN staff was redeployed from the mission in Sierra Leone.

Disarmament and Demobilization

The 2003 DDRR programme went through three stages of development. The first phase started on 7 December 2003 with UNMIL troops disarming 13,490 fighters and collecting 8,679 weapons and 2,650 unexploded ordnance and 2,717,668 rounds of ammunition at the Camp Scheffelin near Monrovia.[31] The precarious security situation prompted an early start to the programme even though not much preparation had occurred. At the time, the command and control structures of the factions were in place; fighters were still holding to their weapons; and there was a general state of insecurity. Given the massive turn out of the ex-fighters for the disarmament phase, the process was aborted on 15 December 2003. This was caused by the lack of preparedness to disarm and demobilize the number of fighters arriving on the first day; and inadequate security, while the situation degenerated into violence and looting at the Cantonment sites.[32]

The false start to the programme was also caused by the fact that political and military leaders were marginalized in the planning and implementation of the programme.[33] Why they were marginalized could not be established. Importantly, instead of following the policy guidelines that stipulated that the disarmament process should start simultaneously with all three factions, the UN personnel decided to start with the GOL fighters. On hearing this, other fighters from the remaining two factions – LURD and MODEL, decided to participate. Perhaps they thought that they would be left out of the process, but their readiness to disarm could also indicate their readiness to end the war. It could also be construed that this prompted faster implementation of the programme that resulted in a relatively successful disarmament on the part of the authorities.

Based upon the above experiences and after rethinking and careful planning, the UN initiated stage two on 15 April 2004 at the Gbarnga site, north east of Monrovia. Three other cantonment sites were set up in April in Buchanan, Tubmanburg, and VOA in Monrovia. The third set of cantonment sites was set up from early July through September in Zwedru (South East), in Ganta/Kpein (North Central), Voinjama (North), and Harper (South East).[34]

One major lesson from the false start of the programme is that in order for such a programme to become successful, there must be 'adequate in-house expertise,

---

31   UNMIL, DDRR. http://www.unmil.org/content.asp?cat=ddrr. 08/08/2006.

32   UNDPKO, Peacekeeping Best Practice Unit, *Lessons Learned Study on the Start-Up Phase of the United Nations Mission in Liberia*, April 2004: 16.

33   NCDDRR, *Briefing Notes on Status of the DDRR Process*, Office of the Executive Director, January 2006: 1.

34   UNMIL, DDRR. http://www.unmil.org/content.asp?cat=ddrr. 08/08/2006.

preparation and consultation with national, UN and non-governmental organization (NGO) partners, and the commitment of the parties to the peace agreement'.[35] Above all, local ownership is crucial if such programmes are to succeed. The UN mistake was its attempt to do the usual 'quick fix' and uncritical 'cut and paste', and 'one size fits all' approach. For example, maybe they made the initial false start in Liberia because they failed to consult the armed factions properly but assumed that they could do because of previous knowledge of DDR from elsewhere.

Unlike the case of the first DDR programme that did not provide any adequate resettlement package for the ex-combatants, the new programme offered multiple insertion packages including money and materials before the demobilized ex-combatants left for their communities. The insertion package was divided into two parts: At D2, they were given $150 with the understanding that the remaining $150 would be given to them after three months.[36] Basic things like bedclothing and household utensils were also provided.[37]

Rehabilitation and Reintegration

The rehabilitation and reintegration of ex-fighters constitute different aspects or elements of the overall DDRR programme. Rehabilitation involves psychosocial and trauma counselling, vocational, and formal educational training with the objective to prepare the ex-fighters to be reintegrated into the society. Reintegration involves reinsertion into society with families, relatives or within communities. But within the Liberian context, these two aspects were never been differentiated and this caused some confusion. While formal education was part of the rehabilitation process, it could have been an integral part of the reintegration process. The data on the RR phase does not disaggregate both aspects of the programme. As indicated in some of the reports, the distribution of ex-fighters by eligibility to RR opportunities illustrates that 98 per cent of the 103,019 persons disarmed were qualified for rehabilitation and reintegration training. However, initially only 65 per cent of the 101,874 qualified ex-combatants accessed the RR programme.[38] The remaining 35 per cent eligible ex-fighters accessed the RR opportunities only in June 2007 because of lack of resources.[39] Unless this conceptual confusion is dealt with, it will be difficult to easily assess the successful implementation of the RR aspect of the programme.

However, based on the available literature on the programme, this chapter attempts to differentiate between the two integral aspects of the programme.

---

35   UNDPKO, Peacekeeping Best Practice Unit, *Lessons Learned Study on the Start-Up Phase of the United Nations Mission in Liberia*, April 2004: 16.
36   Interview with Moses Jarbo, Executive Director of the NCDDRR 28 September 2006.
37   DDRR Framework Document, October 2003, p. 30.
38   DDRR Summary Reintegration Briefs, 8 May 2006.
39   Eleventh Progress Report, 9 June 2006: 4.

Rehabilitation

The rehabilitation component of the DDRR programme in Liberia consists of training opportunities that are sub-divided into three principal categories: formal education at primary, secondary and university levels; vocational training programmes; and apprenticeship. The vocational skills training programme included but not limited to agriculture, auto-mechanics, pastry, tailoring, tie-dye, etc. The ex-fighters were given an opportunity to choose or identify their training preferences. As a result thereof, about 40 per cent chose formal education, 14 per cent auto mechanics, 11 per cent generic skills training, 7 per cent driving, 7 per cent tailoring, 4 per cent agriculture and 3 per cent masonry.[40] By 15 February 2005 the Joint Implementation Unit (JIU) had approved 15 rehabilitation and reintegration projects offering ex-fighters vocational skills. Other programmes were sponsored by the USAID and the EU in different parts of the country. Currently, about 66,000 out of the total of 101,874 demobilized fighters have completed or are participating in training and educational programmes funded under the UNDP-managed Trust Fund and through bilateral arrangements. However, this aspect of the programme lacks psycho-social counselling for ex-fighters because it was not given a priority for reasons best known to the designers and planners of the programme.[41] Consequently, even though there was evidence that ex-fighters including child soldiers were forced to take marijuana and other drugs during the war years, very little was done to address this as part of the rehabilitation process.

Reintegration

Several ex-fighters have returned to their respective communities with some moving back in with their parents or close relatives. Out of the 15 counties in Liberia, the reintegration of ex-fighters by county of interest shows that the majority preferred Montserrado (44.4 per cent). Counties like Nimba (11.7 per cent) and Bong (10.4 per cent) were also preferred by a high number of ex-fighters for reintegration[42] as a result of their proximity to Monrovia, capital of Liberia, and also because many fighters originated from these areas.

However reintegration has not been an easy affair for some ex-fighters who feel stigmatized and marginalized. Some have organized into self-help groups such as the National Ex-Combatants Peace Building Initiatives, INC. (NEPI). In 2006 it was involved in psychosocial and peacebuilding programmes in Zorzor, Lofa County in the north.[43] Both residents of the city and ex-combatants were given short-term training in basic psychosocial trauma counselling and peacebuilding

---

40   UNMIL, DDRR, 08/08/2006.
41   Interview with Moses Jarbo, Executive Director of the NCDDRR 28 September 2006.
42   Eleventh Progress Report, 9 June 2006: 4.
43   RECEIVE, Traditional Forms of Reconciliation. Unpublished Report, 2005.

issues before working within the communities. The psychosocial element involved how to deal with traumatic stress; identifying traumatized persons and victims; and the peacebuilding element dealt with the issue of conflict circle, perceptions and reconciliation. It was after this training that they began to work in the community.

SSR in Liberia

Liberia's on-going security sector reform is underlined by the provisions of the Comprehensive Peace Agreement (CPA) signed on 18 August 2003 in Accra, Ghana, which guided that country from 14 years of protracted violent armed conflict into a new phase of transitional democracy. Subsequent to the signing of the CPA, Charles Taylor, then President of Liberia who was also seen as a key factor in the sustenance of the conflict, resigned and went into exile; a National Transitional Government of Liberia (NTGL) was installed into office; and President Ellen Johnson-Sirleaf's administration was elected in 2005 to lead on the difficult, convoluted and politically sensitive process of post-war reconstruction process in the country.

As a process, SSR is about reforming or at best transforming the security sector so that it can become efficient, coordinated, and coherent in undertaking its responsibilities and functions with oversight responsibilities for that sector vested in a democratic leadership. Additionally, reforming the security sector is presented in this chapter as inclusive of DDRR and integral to the national reconstruction process. Development and security are inextricably and indissolubly linked; therefore, any SSR process should be conceived as a governance process that seeks to ensure that the way in which the security agencies carry out their work is highly consistent with overall democratic principles and norms of governance including the rule of law. This transformative process is important in post-conflict societies because of the nature or state of security. But the SSR process should not be limited to post-conflict experiences; countries that are relatively stable should also undertake this exercise because it contributes immensely to political stability and development.

Contexts for SSR in Liberia

There are two dimensions to the context of SSR in Liberia- the internal and external contexts. However, these dimensions combine to inform the on-going reforms in that country. The internal context for SSR includes long years of single party and authoritarian rule, which led to cronyism and over-centralization of power in an 'imperial' presidency. This led to defective and poor security sector governance because of a weak legislature that could not exercise its oversight responsibilities. Additionally, SSR in Liberia follows 14 years of war during which the entire security sector became bloated both in sheer size and the budget it consumed. It also became factionalized and dysfunctional; lacked discipline and professionalism; and because of the state of the country's security legislation, the agencies performed overlapping functions.

The external security environment is marked by uncertain political conditions in neighbouring countries including the lingering crisis in Côte d'Ivoire and recurring political riots in Guinea. Within West Africa, there is rising youth unemployment, economic growth without development, and decline in basic social services – education and health service as evidenced by the lack of educational and health infrastructure. For example, because of classroom spaces most students, including university students, wait in classrooms for more than 30 minutes in order to have a seat for lectures. This is common story across the sub-region. There is also high rate of transborder crimes such as drugs smuggling, money laundering, and human trafficking, and also the problem of small arms proliferation. These have direct implications for SSR in Liberia.

Legal Frameworks for SSR in Liberia

The other significant factor that must be factored into any discussion of the SSR process in Liberia is the legal frameworks within which it is taking place. There are three key legal instruments that provide the framework for reforming the country's security sector and these include: the Constitution of Liberia (1985); the Comprehensive Peace Agreement (2003); and the UNSC Resolution 1509 of 19 September 2003.

Under Article 54 of the Constitution, the President is the Commander-in-Chief and has powers to make all security appointments but with the consent of the Senate. Article 34 (b&c) provides legal authority for the Legislature of Liberia to provide for the security of the country.

One of the issues included in the Accra peace agreement was security sector reform. Although the emphasis was placed on professional efficiency at the expense of security sector governance perhaps because the framers of the document saw SSR as purely a technical exercise, under Part Four, Articles VII and VIII, the signatories to the CPA called for reform of the security sector. In this light, they called for a restructured Armed Forces of Liberia (AFL) under a new command; and that recruits should be drawn from the ranks of the GOL, LURD, MODEL and civilians with appropriate background and experience. It specifically requested the United States to play a leading role in the restructuring and training of the army with support from ECOWAS, AU and the International Contact Group on Liberia (ICGL).[44] Even before the issue of defence reform could be debated in Liberia, the agreement also identified the mission of the new army: defend 'national sovereignty and in extremis, respond to natural disasters'. In fulfilment thereof, the US government contracted two of its private military companies, namely DynCorp International, and the Pacific Architects Engineers (PAE), to train and

---

44   See the Comprehensive Peace Agreement (CPA).

restructure the army. On their part, ECOWAS, AU and ICGL do participate in the meetings of the Security Pillar, one of the four pillars identified by President Sirleaf as priority areas, but there is no evidence to suggest that they are providing direct training to the security forces. However, individual member countries of these bodies have made contributions to the process. For example, the Chief of Staff of the new Liberian army is a Nigerian; Nigeria is also providing training to batch of the new army; Ghana is scheduled to provide training to a cohort of Immigration officers.

Article VIII, Section 2 called for the disarmament and disbanding of the following agencies: ATU, SOD of the Police, and paramilitary bodies such as the National Port Authority (NPA), Liberia Telecommunication Corporation (LTC), Liberia Petroleum Refining Corporation (LPRC), and Roberts International Airport (RIA). These are state agencies that run their security bodies. The existence of these groups raises questions about their relationship to the core security agencies in the country. In one incidence in 2008, there was a clash between the Freeport Police and the Liberia National Police (LNP) over jurisdictional matters. As far as the process in Liberia is concerned, there is a huge deficit in relation to the implementation of the terms and conditions of the CPA regarding these agencies. These agencies have not been reviewed nor has there been an attempt to disband them as required under the CPA. This clearly verifies the assumption that there has been too much focus on the army and the Police at the expense of the other security services.

Finally, the UNSC Resolution 1509 mandated UNMIL to support the 'transitional government of Liberia in monitoring and restructuring the police force of Liberia, consistent with democratic policing, to develop a civilian police training programme, and to otherwise assist in the training of civilian police, in cooperation with ECOWAS, international organizations and interested states'. On the basis of this mandate, UNMIL has continued to play a leading role in training the new Liberia National Police (LNP) with support from individual countries such as the United States which has contracted DynCorp to help with the training of the police. DynCorp is specifically providing training for the Emergency Response Unit (ERU), an elite squad within the LNP, which is supposed to comprise 500 officers. While all of this is going on, with the exception of the army for which a Defence Act was adopted by parliament in 2008, there are corresponding changes in the obsolete legislative acts that govern the security bodies in the country.

Thus, the existing legal frameworks constitute important entry points for carrying out SSR in Liberia.

SSR Process in Liberia

Security Sector Reform is not an event; it is a process that is politically sensitive. In Liberia, there were donors and securocrats who thought that it is a one-off event. But many are now realizing that this is a long process that requires human and material resources in order to be successful. It has its own politics and requires making compromises with different actors as the process unfolds. The second point to make is that very often, when there is discussion about the SSR process in Liberia, there is the tendency to think that this process started with the CPA and the NTGL. This is only partially true because historically the first discussion about SSR started with demand by the Inter-Faith Mediation Committee (IFMC) to restructure the army and other security agencies in 1990. The IFMC comprised a mixed of Christian and Islamic groups that took upon them the responsibility of intervening in the conflict. Subsequently, this theme was included in other peace agreements but the real efforts towards SSR in Liberia began with the Abuja Agreement of 1996 which mandated ECOMOG to restructure and train the Liberian army. At the time President Charles Taylor invoked Liberian sovereignty and prematurely terminated the services of ECOMOG to undertake this exercise.

The current process started after the signing of the CPA and it involved two different sets of activities: promoting efficiency and professionalism through training; and a national dialogue on security sector governance. The former was undertaken by state actors, and the second by civil society institutions in close collaboration with the Governance Commission. More specifically, the CSDG, ASSN and DCAF played a critical role in this respect.

After the NTGL was installed into office in 2005, the SSR process started with broader discussions about the reforming of the security sector. Through the initiatives of UNMIL, the re-documentation of the personnel of the LNP, SSS, BIN, and Seaport Police was carried out. About 6,300 police officers, SSS and BIN were re-documented and the average 'age of serving personnel was 38.5 years of age'.[45] Less than 10 per cent had university education and less than 20 per cent had undergone regimented training. Similarly, of the 13,650 AFL personnel re-documented, about 65 per cent were conscripts with junior high school education and limited regimented military training.[46] The average age was 39.5 years of age and many had served from 14 years to almost half a century.[47]

AFL soldiers were paid demobilization packages, severance, retirement, and pension payments before the restructuring process started.[48] Currently, more than 1,000 troops have been trained by DynCorp and PAE whereas UNMIL has provided training for the Police. Although agencies within the sector have benefited from the SSR process, it remains extremely skewed in favour of the army and police. Disturbingly, the entire SSR process has not included the paramilitary bodies at the LPRC, RIA, Freeport, LTC, Forestry Development Authority (FDA) and others. Under the CPA, these were supposed to be disbanded but on the contrary,

---

45   Brownie Samukai, 'Peace and Security in Liberia – Drawing Interim Balance Sheet' in Tobias von Gienanth, Thomas Jaye et al. (eds), *Post Conflict Peacebuilding in Liberia: Much Remains to be Done, Report of the Third ZIF/KAIPTC Seminar*, 1–3 November 2007, pp. 18–19.

46   *Ibid.*

47   *Ibid.*

48   *Ibid.*, p. 19.

this has not happened because the SSR process is currently skewed in favour of the police and defence; they may not be priority areas for work. The other groups left out of the SSR debates are private security companies, which continue to increasingly play a role in providing physical security to the elites that live in 'gated communities', commercial houses, foreign embassies, and perhaps public buildings. Finally, the role of 'traditional' security institutions in the rural areas has not been factored into the overall SSR debate in the country largely because there is focus on the core security agencies that have a presence in the capital. The other factor could be that those in charge of the process are not fully aware of the need to include this sector into the overall SSR debate because they provide security where there is weak statutory security presence.

So far, the most decisive entry point was the appointment of Amos Sawyer as Chairman of the Governance Commission and his willingness to collaborate with the Africa Security Sector Network (ASSN) in conducting policy seminars on understanding SSR and related oversight issues for Liberian parliamentarians. Since 2005, the ASSN has conducted no fewer than five seminars for Liberian parliamentarians, personnel of the security agencies, civil society, and international actors.

The participatory approach of the Governance Commission (GC)[49] is underlined by its nationwide consultation on SSR issues that involved a cross-section of people including local officials, chiefs, civil society, judges, women and security personnel in the counties. These were useful in completing the national security strategy that was agreed upon by the President and the National Security Council in January 2008. The security pillar, which comprises state officials, foreign embassy officials, UNMIL, ECOWAS, AU and others, played a role in discussing the document that is on the verge of being printed for public consumption. Therefore, the document enjoys legitimacy but implementing it will require political will and commitment from the government; and support from the donor community and civil society.

In order to address the issue of the lack of local ownership and provide the basis for coordination among the different stakeholders, a national task force on SSR was formed in 2007 to support the GC in its policy debates and formulation. This body comprised all the critical stakeholders involved in the SSR process. Once again, civil society groups, state officials, members of parliament, UNMIL, UNDP, ECOWAS and others were part of this body. It agreed to the policy statement, and outline for the national security strategy.

---

49   Mandated to lead on governance reforms in the country. It has worked on the Anti-Corruption Strategy; led on the land reform isssues; developed the national security strategy; and is leading on decentralization, public sector reform and others.

Challenges of SSR in Liberia

Against the backdrop of the above, some of the challenges of the SSR process in Liberia include:

- ensuring local ownership so that when the international actors depart from Liberia the State will be in the position to shoulder the responsibility of providing its own security;
- ensuring that local expertise on SSR is developed in order to reduce the excessive reliance on foreign experts. However, it is important to recognize the fact that foreign experts can transfer and develop skills for local people;
- ensuring that the country generates its own resources for SSR work in order to reduce the over reliance on donor funding for SSR work. Unfortunately, it has not been able to do so and therefore, process depends entirely on external actors;
- dealing with the politics of SSR: making compromises and building alliances in order to identify and deal with spoilers and drivers of change;
- ensuring that there is continued political will and commitment for SSR work;
- mainstreaming gender issues in the overall SSR process in the country.

Conclusion: Future outlook for the Peacebuilding Process in Liberia

There are serious difficulties in determining the impact of the DDRR and SSR processes on the overall peacebuilding exercise in Liberia because of the limited amount of assessment and monitoring that was conducted. In June 2006, an independent mid-term assessment of the DDRR programme was started in order to determine the way forward but at the time of completing this essay, this was not available yet. However, the available literature says very little or nothing about the impact of the process on peacebuilding. That said it is worth noting that a DDR process minimizes the risks of relapse to violence, but it does not remove all threats to the security of the people and the state. The socio-economic and political situation in post-conflict Liberia will also impact on the reintegration and rehabilitation of ex-fighters. The relatives or parents with whom many of the ex-fighters are being reunited are surviving on less than $1 per day. Under conditions of such extreme poverty, it is also difficult for these families to cope with the burden of an extra person into their homes. In Liberia, the infrastructure (including social infrastructure) was badly damaged. The dislocation of the economy led to an unemployment rate of 85 per cent. Forty per cent of the ex-fighters are choosing to acquire formal education, but there are few jobs for them at higher education levels. It is argued that while a successful DDRR can impact on peacebuilding, its successful implementation also depends on the socio-economic and political climate in which it is taking place; both factors are therefore linked and reinforce each other.

One of the lessons learned from the DDR process in Liberia was manifested in the weaknesses of the first phase of the process. During the first phase, there was emphasis and focus on 'gun-carrying combatants', which usually excluded women and children; the failure to restructure the national army; and the lack of commitment in the leadership of the country. Child combatants aged 17 and under were the primary combatants in the Liberian conflict. Since the coming into office of the Sirleaf administration, some measures have been taken to correct some of these errors. For example, a new national army of 2,000 soldiers has been trained.

Finally, the SSR process can only impact on the society if it is pursued as a comprehensive process. In as much as the training of the LNP and AFL is laudable and commendable, it is also evident that the two institutions do not have the capacity to deal with the multiple security challenges facing the country. There must be corresponding attention paid to the remaining institutions, particularly those involved in border security and management, and intelligence work. It is the lack of effective intelligence that makes it difficult to deal with the increasing crime rate even with the presence of UNMIL in the country. The borders are not only porous but the agencies in charge of them are extremely weak, lacking logistics and infrastructure to perform their duties.

However, it is important to use the existing mechanism at the borders to promote cooperation between border security agencies in the four Mano River Union countries such as Liberia, Sierra Leone, Guinea and Côte d'Ivoire. Currently, they hold regular monthly meetings to share information and exchange intelligence on broader security issues. Such meetings can serve as the basis for a sub-regional approach to SSR in the MRU countries.

Chapter 10

The Darfur Conflict and the Responsibility to Protect: Towards a Sustainable Peace

Ayesha Kajee[1]

Introduction

Although a small number of responsible political analysts have sincerely tried to de-mythologize the often naïve and overly simplistic readings of the Darfur conflict in the mass media, many persist in defining the war in Sudan's Darfur region as primarily an ethnic cleansing of Africans by Arab government-backed militias, the so-called *Janjaweed*[2] (literally translated as: 'evil spirits on horseback'). Several commentators have even erroneously conflated the Darfur crisis with the North-South Sudanese civil war that was concluded with the signing of the Comprehensive Peace Agreement (CPA)[3] in January 2005. Unless such misconceptions are exposed and the complex realities of Darfur are grappled

---

1   Ayesha Kajee is Program Director of the International Human Rights Exchange at the University of the Witwatersrand, South Africa and former Head of the Democracy and Political Party Systems Project at the South African Institute for International Affairs. Her areas of expertise include the International Criminal Court and her focus countries include Sudan and Chad.
2   The Janjaweed are mostly natives of Darfur, belonging to so-called 'Arab' tribes, mainly nomadic pastoralists, such as the Baggara and the Bahhara tribes of the region. Since the 1960s these 'Arab' tribes have been wooed as a political and military allies by domestic political factions as well as by regional players such as Libya, who have pursued a policy of Arabization in the region. During the North-South civil war, and more recently in Darfur, the government has armed 'People's Defence Forces' as proxies to fight alongside or in support of Sudanese army troops. (see Flint, J. 2009. *Beyond Janjaweed: Understanding the Militias of Darfur.* Geneva: Small Arms Survey).

3   The CPA, signed between the National Islamic Front (NIF) government and the Sudan Peoples' Liberation Movement (SPLM) is predicated on three main elements: power-sharing in national government between North and South until a referendum is held to determine whether the South will secede; wealth-sharing of oil revenues from southern oilfields; and reciprocal movement of northern Army troops out of southern areas and SPLM troops out of northern areas (see: *Comprehensive Peace Agreement Between the Government of the Republic of Sudan and the Sudan Peoples' Liberation Movement,* 9 January 2005. Available at: http://unmis.unmissions.org/Portals/UNMIS/Documents/General/cpa-en.pdf).

with, our collective responsibility to protect the civilians of the region will remain unfulfilled, with little prospect of an enduring peace.

The North-South war and the Darfur conflict *are different but interlinked.* Many of the root causes are the same and none of the Sudanese conflicts can be totally separated. For example, the global media focus on Darfur in recent years has sometimes been blamed by the southern Sudanese for the slow pace of CPA implementation. This will probably continue, since the March 2009 indictment of Sudanese President Omar-al-Bashir by the International Criminal Court (ICC)[4] will keep global attention focused squarely on this westernmost region of Africa's largest country.

The Darfur crisis has regularly been labelled 'state-sponsored genocide' by some media pundits, a host of show-business celebrities, and even by officials of several governments. While the conflict indubitably contains genocidal elements, the genocide label is problematic; both in terms of the legal ramifications and in terms of its effect on public opinion. In this case, it has catalyzed protests and demands for action around the world on a hitherto unprecedented level. The large body of research undertaken to assess whether or not the Darfur conflict constitutes a genocide has involved attempts at quantifying the casualties and displaced persons, and various reflections on the organized nature of conflict and the intent to cause harm on the part of government forces. Given the ICC indictment, it is evident that war crimes and crimes against humanity have definitely occurred; thus, we should refer to the situation in Darfur in these terms, avoiding the emotive effects of the 'genocide' label that has already hampered peace-brokering attempts.

Various respected Sudan analysts, such as Alex de Waal, David Hoile, Julie Flint and Gerard Prunier,[5] now agree that the Sudanese government's actions in Darfur, while undoubtedly heinous and criminally irresponsible, began as a scorched-earth type counter-insurgency aimed at suppressing various armed rebel groups in the region. The government attempted to do this via its *Janjaweed* proxies, mainly 'Arabs' from the camel-herding *Baggara* tribes in Darfur and Chadians

---

4   The ICC Indictment is based on the court's findings that there are reasonable grounds to believe that, as President of Sudan and Commander-in-Chief of the Sudanese Armed Forces between 2003 and 2008, Bashir was an indirect perpetrator of attacks against civilians, of pillage as a war crime and of crimes against humanity including rape, murder, extermination, forcible transfer and torture (see International Criminal Court. *Warrant of Arrest for Omar Hassan Ahmad al Bashir.* 4 March 2009. The Hague: ICC).

5   Collectively, these analysts combine an intimate knowledge of the region and its history with a wealth of experience in genocide-related work. They have based their findings on research involving all the actors in Darfur, and careful analysis of the often contradictory reports that emanate from the area (see: Flint, J. and de Waal, A. 2005. *Darfur: A Short History of a Long War* and 2008. *Darfur: A New History of a Long War.* London: Zed Books; Hoile, D. 2005. *Darfur in Perspective.* London: European-Sudanese Public Affairs Council; Prunier, G. 2005. *Darfur: The Ambiguous Genocide*' New York: Cornell University Press; and de Waal, A. 2004. 'Counter-Insurgency on the Cheap'. *Review of African Political Economy*, Vol. 31(102)).

with territorial ambitions. Such scorched earth policy had served the Sudanese government well in its protracted battle with the SPLM in southern Sudan, and was escalated in Darfur after the April 2003 targeting of government bases in the capital city, el-Fashr. The government believed that by ravaging civilian villages, support for the insurgency would wane. This strategy ultimately backfired as the conflict grew well beyond the government's capacity to control it, with genocidal behaviour on the part of various belligerents, including Sudanese Army Forces. Further, the complex historical, ethnic, regional and tribal dimensions to the Darfur conflict contextualize this war, but have received cursory treatment in most analyses.[6]

Attempts at peacekeeping on both the regional and international levels have met with limited success, and recent attempts to impose global justice mechanisms have further exacerbated the already complex environment in which this conflict is located. The contextual elements, the peacekeeping efforts thus far, and the sometimes contradictory imperatives of peace and justice, are the main subject of this analysis; which ultimately returns to the issue of whether or not the various initiatives currently underway strengthen or impede the overarching responsibility of the international community to protect civilians.

Key Contextual Issues

The past and current peacekeeping efforts and other interventions in Darfur cannot be analysed without some appreciation of the political and historical context in which the various Sudanese conflicts have developed. My expanded version of Emily Wax's '5 Truths about Darfur'[7] is a useful aid in this respect:

1. *a root cause* of most Sudanese conflicts is *historical under-development* of the peripheral areas of the country; exacerbated in Darfur by *seasonal droughts* which heightened tribal tensions between nomadic herders and agrarian pastoralists;

---

6   Journalists have generally ignored complexities involved, as they do not make for riveting headlines; and many policy analysts have either been too lazy or tainted by bias to make serious attempts at unpacking the labyrinthine convolutions of historic ethnic and tribal allegiances in the region (see: Prunier 2005. pp. 4–8 and 148–58; and: de Waal, A. 2005 'Who are the Darfurians? Arab and African identities, violence and external engagement'. *African Affairs*. Vol. 104(415)).

7   Wax, E. '5 Truths About Darfur'. *Washington Post*. 23 April 2006. pp. B3. Emily Wax is a *Washington Post* correspondent formerly based in Nairobi, who has travelled in Darfur and has first-hand knowledge of the region. Given the *Washington Post*'s large and politically-conscious readership, and its leadership stature amongst print media organs globally; Ms Wax's writing has wide reach and influence, including amongst policy-makers around the world. (see: The Medill Medal for Courage in Journalism, http://www.medill. northwestern.edu/about/sponsoredawards.aspx?id=58387).

2. everyone in Darfur is black – of African appearance;[8]
3. nearly everyone in Darfur is Sunni Muslim;
4. it's all about *(domestic and regional) politics*. Darfuris comprise a significant voter base in domestic elections, and a potential manpower resource for regional manipulation;[9]
5. *international actors and access to resources* (at local and global levels) must be factored in to this conflict;
6. the 'genocide' label[10] (possibly) made it worse;
7. no party to this conflict is totally innocent of wrongdoing.[11]

-----

8   There are between 40 and 150 tribes and sub-tribes among the inhabitants of Darfur. The Fur, Marsalit and Zeghawa are among the most important 'African' identities in Darfur; while the Baggara (cattle-herders) and Bahhara (camel-herders) are amongst the better-known broad 'Arab' designations. Genetic study of Fellata nomads, a sub-group of the Baggara Arabs in southern Darfur, reveals a mix of Arab characteristics from North-Eastern ancestors and West African genetic markers, giving credence to the assertion that all Darfuris are black and that 'Arab' and 'African' are not racial designators in this context (see: Kajee, A. 2006. 'Darfur Stereotyping Fraught with Danger' *Africa Report No. 81.* Institute for War and Peace Reporting; de Waal. 2005; and: Weiss, J. et al. 2009 *The Social Structure of Darfur.* Report to Andrew Natsios, US Special Presidential Envoy to Sudan).

9   Since the 1960s, Darfuri voters, based on their Muslim identity, have been wooed by various Sudanese Islamist parties in Khartoum during domestic elections. From the Mahdist elements to the followers of Hassan-al-Turabi, their religious affiliation has been used to bind Darfuris to the Khartoum political elites. In recent decades, ethnic and tribal overtones have entered this mix, with so-called 'Arabs' being armed and provisioned as military proxies. Regionally, this is a tactic that has long been employed by the Libyans and the Chadians in particular, using pan-Arabist or pan-African identity as a spur to supporting specific regional agendas such as the overthrow of former Chadian leader Hassan Habre (see: Prunier 2005, pp. 42–7).

10   First described officially as a genocide by former US Secretary of State Colin Powell in 2004, this label attracted widespread and controversial critiques. On the one hand, it allowed for the rapid global conscientization of the crisis and brought valuable international aid flows to the region. On the other, the concentrated media attention, combined with irresponsible inflation of numbers in some cases, made the peace-brokering process extremely difficult. Key facilitators at Abuja have confided that the extravagant and avaricious demands of some of the warring parties were a direct result of the public pressures to reach an agreement. The unprecedented publicity arising from the genocide label has also factored into the fracturing of the main rebel groups into splinter movements, which has further impeded peace attempts (see de Waal, A. 'Deaths in Darfur: Keeping ourselves Honest' *Sudan Tribune*, 18 August 2007; and Hoile 2005, pp. 64–73).

11   While there has been perpetration of war crimes by all the major belligerents, there is little doubt that the considerable resources of the government and its proxies has skewed the playing field. But the tendency of media commentators, analysts and respected human rights watchdogs to place most of the blame on one side, has certainly been detrimental to efforts at a peaceful resolution of the conflict (see: Hoile 2005, pp. 162–72).

Marginalization

In Darfur, as in other areas of Sudan, the ultimate root cause of the conflict can be traced to historical marginalization of the peripheral areas of Sudan. From the colonial period through to the present, the far-flung outer reaches of the country were ignored in favour of development of the capital, Khartoum, and its surrounds. Thus, for decades, Darfur has suffered underdevelopment and poor social service delivery.[12] It was virtually forgotten except during election periods. This underdevelopment was exacerbated by successively worse seasonal drought cycles over the past four decades, which led to competition for land resources between the settled agrarian population and the nomadic cattle- and camel-herders in the region; sparking tribal clashes between and within the nomadic and pastoralist groups that had hitherto coexisted fairly peacefully.

Political Manipulation

These tribal clashes have been deliberately and cynically exploited. On the one hand by domestic political elites who, since the late 1960s, deliberately 'ethnicized' these conflicts in order to mobilize voter support from either 'Arabs' or 'Africans' in the region. From the Nimeiry administration (1969–85) to the Mahdist Party, through Hassen al-Turabi's flirtation with and subsequent estrangement from the current National Islamic Front regime, Darfur has been a pawn on the domestic political chessboard.[13] The Darfur voting bloc is numerically important to Khartoum's power-brokers and may be a determining factor in the 2010 Sudanese elections (if they take place on schedule).[14] The outcome will also impact on the 2011 referendum in South Sudan to decide on secession or unity. Many Darfuris were also drawn into the lengthy civil war between North and South Sudan; on both sides of the divide.

On the other hand, Sudan's peripheral regions have long been vulnerable to manipulation by those intent on resource extraction or consolidating regional

---

12   According to the World Health Organization (WHO), in 2003 the three Darfur states had 2.5 physicians per 100,000 people, compared with the average for the Northern Sudanese state of 18.4 and the Khartoum average of 48.9. South Darfur had 22.7 hospital beds per 100,000 compared with 240 in Northern State and an average of 73.5 for the North of Sudan. In 2000, UNICEF reported that infant (under-5) mortality in the region was 8.5 per 10,000 per day, an appalling statistic when one considers that the 'emergency' threshold for children under 5 is generally held to be two per 20,000 per day (see: Phillips, D. 2008. *Darfur Early Recovery and Development Dossier.* New York: Columbia University Center for Human Rights).

13   See Prunier 2005. pp. 34–6. Also de Waal, A. 2006. 'I Will Not Sign' *London Review of Books* Vol. 28(23) pp. 17–20.

14   Given that Darfuris currently comprise almost 19 per cent of Sudan's population, their value as a domestic voting bloc in upcoming elections cannot be ignored (see: Phillips 2008, pp. 13).

power. Sudan has lengthy and porous borders with various countries that are resource-rich or conflict-prone or both. Among these are Chad, the Congo, Central African Republic, Ethiopia and Uganda. Libya, for example, as part of Qaddafi's pan-Arabization plan for North Africa, has traditionally used Darfur as a launching pad for various attempts at 'regime change' in neighbouring Chad.[15] The Libyans used the tribal tensions already extant in the region by recruiting 'Darfuri Arabs' to fight their various proxy wars in Chad throughout the 1970s and 1980s.[16] Both the domestic polity and regional political agendas have thus contributed to the ethnicization of Darfur into 'Arabs' and 'Africans'.

While less significant in the Darfur context, Egypt, Eritrea and Ethiopia have all at different times, played a role in Sudan's various internal conflicts[17]. Conflicts in the region, combined with easily traversed borders, have contributed to the proliferation of small arms available to the belligerents in Darfur.[18] Additionally, the Sudanese government's alleged sponsorship of rebel movements in neighbouring states such as Chad;[19] further complicates the Darfur map.

---

15   Brewer, W. 1982. 'The Libyan-Sudanese "Crisis" of 1981: Danger for Darfur and Dilemma for the United States'. *Middle East Journal* Vol. 36(2).

16   From 1973 onward, Libyan forces occupied parts of northern Chad, and between 1980 and 1982, Libya supported President Goukouni Oueddei against the French-backed forces of Hassen Habré, who had previously had Libyan support Even after Habre's government in Chad (1982–90) was recognized by the Organization of African Unity, Libya continued to support resistance to Habre; including the arming and deployment of 'Arab' Darfuris as military proxies (see: Brewer 1982; Burr, M. and Collins, R. 1999. *Africa's Thirty Years War: Libya, Chad and the Sudan*. Boulder: Westview Press).

17   For example, the Sudan-Eritrea border was closed in 2002, when Khartoum accused Asmara of supporting a rebel offensive near Kassala in eastern Sudan. Full diplomatic ties were only resumed in 2006 (see: Rankhumise, P. 2006. *Civilian (In)Security in the Darfur Region of Sudan*. Pretoria: Institute for Security Studies Occasional Paper 123).

18   A survey commissioned in 2000 by the Norwegian Initiative on Small Arms Transfers found that 'Darfur by its geographical boundaries to Libya, Chad, CAR and southern Sudan lies in an area amenable to small arms proliferation', and estimated that a total of over 132,000 small arms circulated in Darfur at that time. Annual small arms surveys (see: smallarmssurvey.org) between 2000 and 2009 indicate that this is a continuing pattern that flows from regional conflicts, and cyclically contributes to new conflicts in the region.

19   Since the early 2000s, Khartoum has actively supported Chadian rebel groups with links in Darfur. The Dar Sila region in south-eastern Chad has been regularly raided by Janjaweed militias, allegedly armed by Khartoum. In 2006, the Khartoum-supported Chadian rebel group, the *Front uni pour le changement démocratique* (FUCD), attacked the Chadian capital, N'Djamena. The attack was circumvented at the eleventh hour via French support for the Chadian government (BBC News 2006. 'Chad Cuts Sudan Ties After Attack' *BBCNEWS*. 14 April 2006).

Ethnicity and Religion

The simple truth is that everyone in Darfur is black, i.e. of African physiognomy. Indeed, one often finds that so-called 'Arabs' are darker-skinned than those who are designated 'African'. These terms are really indicative of livelihood rather than race. Traditionally, most nomadic and animal-herding tribes were designated 'Arab'; while more settled agrarian farmers were designated 'African'. Historically, it was not uncommon for someone who gave up crop farming to become a herder to change identity from 'African' to 'Arab' within a few years, and vice versa.[20]

Furthermore, whereas the North-South civil war was between the Muslim Northerners and the largely-Christian or Animist Southerners; nearly everyone in Darfur is Sunni Muslim, a fact that is often overlooked by international commentators. Indeed several of them compound their error by conflating the North-South war with the one in Darfur.

International Factors: Geopolitics and Resources

Lastly, in contextualizing the Darfur conflict it is impossible to ignore the international dimension and the geopolitical interests that characterize this conflict. Western powers, including France and the United States, have a history in Darfur that dates back to the use of Darfur airstrips by the American CIA during and after World War II.[21] Today, the vast natural resources of Sudan generally, and of Darfur particularly; and the strategic geographic position of Darfur; cannot be discounted in the current global context of emerging economic giants in Asia and their rising demand for energy and industrial raw materials. These issues impact on the manner in which Darfur's war is portrayed in mainstream international media; and they particularly affect energy policy in a climate of economic recession. Geological survey reports indicate there are potential oil, copper, uranium and other mineral resources in various parts of Darfur.[22] Even discounting the alleged unexploited oil reserves in South Darfur,[23] it is indisputable that the simplest cost-effective conduit for oil from Chad (where there is extensive Western stake-holding) would be through Darfur to the Red Sea.[24]

---

20   Prunier 2005.

21   *Ibid.*, p. 48.

22   Snow, K. 2007. 'America's War in Darfur' *Global Research.* 25 November, 2007.

23   Gidley, R. 'Oil Discovery Adds New Twist to Darfur Tragedy'. *Reuters Alertnet.* 15 June 2005 (available at http://www.alertnet.org/thefacts/reliefresources/111885496661. htm; accessed 16 May 2008).

24   Given current overland transport costs, the projected long-term savings of a direct route through Darfur would be in the order of at least 20–30 per cent. (This estimate is based on conversations with a political risk analyst specializing in East Africa.)

An additional dimension in the geopolitical arena is the substantive investment of China and Malaysia (and more recently India), in the infrastructure for extracting and transporting oil from the southern Sudanese oilfields to the Red Sea. Given China's military cooperation with Khartoum since 2002,[25] and allegations that Chinese armaments are used by Sudan's army in the Darfur war,[26] China has played a surprisingly constructive role in negotiations to expand the original African Union peacekeeping Mission in Darfur (AMIS) to the current hybrid UN/AU force (UNAMID).[27]

The procrastination in US and UN circles during the height of the Darfur war (2003–05) and the global haggling over the type and composition of international intervention have brought into question the international community's commitment to its responsibility to protect civilians. An extra complication in the global context is the ICC's March 2009 indictment of President Bashir for war crimes in Darfur (the first time an incumbent head of state has been charged in such a manner). While the move is a welcome indicator that impunity on the part of leaders is no longer tolerated; the *timing* of the indictment is problematic; given the looming Sudanese elections in 2010, the failure of the Darfur Peace Agreement (DPA)[28] and the slow progress in implementing the CPA. These issues were highlighted by

---

25   A 2009 study by Mike Lewis for the small arms survey indicates that while China's supply of heavy weaponry to the Sudanese state is invisible within the UN voluntary reporting system, it is evidenced by photographs and military parades. Chinese military hardware supplied to Sudan includes battle tanks, armoured vehicles and combat jet trainers; as well as a vast array of small arms and ammunition manufactured between 2003 and 2007. In return, China protects its huge (40 per cent) stake in the Sudanese oil pipeline and ensures its continuing source of energy from the southern Sudanese oilfields. Lewis, M. 2009. Skirting the Law: Post-CPA Arms Flows to Sudan, *Sudan Working Papers* Number 18, September 2009.

26   Andersson, H. 2008. 'China is Fuelling War in Darfur'. BBC News, 13 July 2008.

27   Large, D. 2008. 'Sudan's Foreign Relations with Asia, China, and the Politics of "Looking East"'. ISS Paper 158. Pretoria: Institute for Security Studies.

28   The DPA, signed in May 2006 between the Government of Sudan and one of the major rebel groups in Darfur (SLA-Minnawi), has been observed more in the breach than in its implementation. Given that two of the three numerically significant rebel factions were not signatories, the agreement was flawed from the start and compromised the perceived neutrality of the African Union peacekeepers, as the enforcers of the agreement. In particular, the absence of Abdel Wahid, commander of another SLA faction, and one of the original founders of the Darfur rebellion, was seen by many civilians as having excluded 'their' representative. Also, the agreement, developed along similar lines to the CPA between North and South Sudan, failed to consider the key differences of the Darfur conflict and omitted to incorporate broad-based consultation at grassroots and community levels (see: Van der Lijn, J. 2008. *To Paint the Nile Blue: Factors for Success and Failure of UNMIS and UNAMID*. The Hague: Clingendael Institute).

senior members of the southern Sudanese government on a February 2009 visit to South Africa.[29]

Peacekeeping and Other International Interventions: Joint Responsibility in Action or Hollow Political Construct?

AMIS

The numerically small and poorly-resourced African Union Mission in Sudan (AMIS), while a laudable and decisive action by the AU at a time when the rest of the international community seemed unwilling to act, could not, in view of its size (about 2,350 in May 2005[30]) and limited mandate, adequately fulfil the responsibility to protect Darfuris. Even when upgraded to 7,000-strong in what popularly became known as AMIS II, its mandate was restricted to monitoring compliance with the DPA and to protecting civilians and humanitarian workers.[31] AMIS was equipped mainly with light weaponry and its mandate did not authorize it to use force to, for example, disarm combatants.

Given that not all the belligerent factions were party to the DPA, in practice there was no peace to uphold in many areas of Darfur. AMIS, acting on its mandate, was perceived by non-signatory rebels to be biased in favour of those who had signed the agreement. This was exacerbated by incidents in which leaders of signatory factions, viz. SLA-Minnawi, were seen riding in AMIS vehicles.[32] Another factor that led to distrust of AMIS by civilians and rebels alike, is that the AMIS mandate obliged the peacekeepers to coordinate with the Sudanese government, which itself is a party in the conflict. This severely eroded the principles of neutrality and independence which underpin most multi-lateral peacekeeping missions and compromised perceptions of AMIS among civilians as well as combatants.

Recurrent fragmentation of dissatisfied rebel groups due to infighting in the aftermath of the DPA, also impacted on AMIS via their splinter factions among civilian populations and in camps for internally displaced persons (IDPs). A conflict that, prior to the DPA, was primarily between government and government-supported militias such as the Janjaweed on the one hand, and four or five major rebel groups such as the SLA-Minnawi, the SLA-Abdel Wahid and the Justice and Equality Movement (JEM) on the other; had evolved into a situation where

---

29   Institute for Security Studies (ISS). Seminar: *Developments in South Sudan.* Pretoria. 27 February 2009.

30   United Nations Security Council. *Report of the Secretary General on United Nations Assistance to the African Union Mission in Sudan.* 4 May 2005.

31   Kagwanja, P. and Mutahi, P. 2007. *Protection of Civilians in African Peace Missions: The Case of the African Union Mission in Sudan.* ISS Paper 139. Pretoria: Institute for Security Studies.

32   UN Sudan Bulletin, 17 December 2006.

conflict between rebel groups was increasingly common, as was opportunistic banditry and looting.

A force of 7,000 peacekeepers (including civilians and police) was logistically insufficient to cover the vast terrain of Darfur (over 49,000 square kilometres), with the mission being required to protect over 100 IDP camps and more than 30 bases and sites.[33] Where they were present, AMIS troops did make a significant difference to civilian populations in such ordinary matters as fetching water or getting goods to market without the threat of rape (for women) or death (for men).[34] Where it wasn't able to deploy, the desecration and annihilation of entire communities by the Janjaweed continued (often supported by airstrikes just prior to their arrival[35] and militarized landcruisers in the aftermath)[36]. Also, rebel group infighting and the splintering of rebel militias resulted in the widespread presence of armed factions even within IDP camps.[37] The porous borders between Darfur and neighbouring states, together with the ready availability of small arms, noted above, negated attempts at the demobilization of combatants.[38]

The AU mission's narrow mandate and lack of even basic equipment such as night-flying capability, meant that AMIS was regularly out-strategized by well-equipped and highly-motivated opponents. For example, when AMIS was forced to store its aviation fuel at the government depot in El-Fashr, the fuel was surreptitiously depleted overnight, probably by agents of the Sudanese army, and this severely constrained AMIS capacity to monitor the terrain by air. AMIS was supplied with a limited number of weapons and other equipment, including machine guns, rifles, RPGs, mortars and latterly, armoured personnel carriers (APCs). By comparison, belligerent groups have displayed an astonishing combined arsenal of weapons, including well-armoured off-road vehicles, rifles, machine guns, mortars and even anti-tank equipment.[39] Various groups, including the main factions of the Sudanese Liberation Army (SLA) and the Justice and Equality Movement (JEM) openly display their weapons capacity in areas under their control. In the case

---

33   Dunne, S. 2009. *Darfur: What Hope has UNAMID got in Overcoming Historical Impediments to Peace in the Region?* Peace Operations Training Institute.

34   IRIN News. 2006. 'Sexual Violence Spikes around South Darfur Camp' *IRIN News.* 24 August 2006.

35   Petersen, A.H. and Tullin, L. 2006. *The Scorched Earth of Darfur: Patterns in Death and Destruction Reported by the People of Darfur. January 2001–September 2005.* Copenhagen: Bloodhound.

36   Human Rights Watch. *Darfur Destroyed: Abuses by the Government-Janjaweed in West Darfur.* 6 May 2004.

37   Kahn, C. 2008. *Conflict, Arms and Militarisation: the Dynamics of Darfur's IDP Camps.* HSBA Working Paper 15. Geneva: Small Arms Survey.

38   Grono, N. 2006. 'Briefing-Darfur: The International Community's Failure to Protect'. *African Affairs* Vol. 105(421), pp. 621–31.

39   Some rebel anti-tank equipment is identified as the French-made Milan type, most probably sourced in neighbouring Chad. Other systems of the Israeli type are likely to have come via the SPLM (see: Lewis 2009).

of the Sudanese army or their proxies, visible capacity also included helicopter gunships, APCs and aircraft capable of dropping bombs.[40]

Further, the small personnel numbers spread thinly meant that AMIS was sometimes unable to guarantee its own troop safety, and peacekeepers themselves were vulnerable to attack by combatants from all sides of the conflict. The Haskanita incident on 29–30 September 2007 that left 10 AMIS personnel dead, is a case in point. After weeks of aerial bombardment of rebel positions by the government of Sudan, the AMIS Coy base at Haskanita was attacked, allegedly by around 1000 rebels in more than 30 vehicles, who targeted the communications and artillery centres of the base. About 150 AMIS personnel were at the base, most of them Nigerians. With their single satellite phone disabled, the peacekeepers were unable to request reinforcements from El Daien, 93 kilometres away. They reportedly hid in a ditch once their ammunition ran out, until they were 'rescued' by Sudanese army troops.[41]

The fatal attack might have been prevented or better defended if the transformation of AMIS into a larger and better-resourced joint AU/UN mission, approved in July 2007, had already occurred. The joint mission was delayed by political posturing from the Sudanese government and by the unkept promises of UN members to fund and equip the force.

While the decision to deploy country battalions within AMIS was logistically rational and worked reasonably effectively, the resulting communications gaps hampered the development of a coherent centralized command and control within AMIS. This fragmented its activities and restricted rapid reaction deployment in cases such as Haskanita-Coy.

Lastly, morale among AMIS was adversely affected by the continuing and vocal demands, among Darfuris and within the international community, for a UN mission. AMIS peacekeepers were made to feel they were a 'second-rate' option whose deployment was temporary.[42] Exacerbating the already adverse conditions under which they operated, they had to deal with erratic and often-delayed salary payments.[43]

---

40   Eyewitness accounts documented by organizations such as Amnesty International and Human Rights Watch identify these as modified Russian-made Antonovs and Mi-24 helicopter gunships. See: 'Sudan: Arms Continuing to Fuel Serious Human Rights Violations in Darfur' *Amnesty International, May 2007.*

41   VoANews. 'Africa Union Searches for Motive in Darfur Attack'. 1 October 2007.

42   Confidential interviews conducted with sources in Khartoum, El-Fashr and El-Jeneina.

43   In May 2007 AU Chair Omar Alpha Konare noted that peacekeepers had been waiting three or four months to be paid. Salary payments to AMIS troops were delayed due to AU budgetary shortages and failure by some development partners to meet their promised commitments with regard to funding of the AMIS (see: Lynch, C. 'AU Peacekeeping Mission in Darfur Faces Collapse – officials'. *Sudan Tribune* 14 May 2007).

UNAMID

The mandate of the African Union/United Nations Hybrid Operation in Darfur (UNAMID) is far more robust than that of AMIS. However, ambiguous language in the UN Security Resolution 1769 that approved UNAMID; together with a lack of political will, led to months of delay in its deployment. AMIS was finally converted to UNAMID on 30 December 2007.

Even today, reductionist readings of Resolution 1769, particularly by the Sudanese Government, continue to obstruct UNAMID activity. Under chapter seven of the UN Charter, UNAMID is authorized to take necessary action and deploy its forces to protect civilians and equipment, ensure security, prevent armed attacks, and support implementation of the DPA and subsequent peace agreements. Provision has been made for the deployment of both heavy and light support packages; including communications equipment, helicopters and tactical military staff; all of which will go a long way to addressing basic problems that were faced by the AMIS.

However, lengthy visa and customs processes, for peacekeepers, equipment and even for contractors building the camps in which troops are housed; have continued to decelerate deployment of the full UNAMID force and its equipment. Equipment and personnel delays are further hampered by the failure of some donor nations to fulfil their pledges with regard to funds and equipment. For almost two years, member countries[44] have failed to provide the helicopters that were promised when UNAMID was first mooted; for a region in which air surveillance is often the only viable means of effective intelligence-gathering and rapid transport. UNAMID is authorized for up to 26,000 personnel (including the 7,000 who originally comprised AMIS), and by the end of October 2009,[45] it had deployed over 19,000 uniformed staff in Darfur, including about 14,850 troops and more than 4,200 police officers.

Contrary to initial demands from the Sudanese government that troops be drawn only from African countries, UNAMID has personnel from various Asian, European and Pacific states as well as a large number of African countries. UNAMID differs from previous UN operations that were deployed *parallel* to regional peacekeeping bodies. In those cases, for example in Sierra Leone and Burundi, they worked alongside each other, but independently; whereas both the UNAMID police and military contingents are meant to be integrated hybridized units. Both the UNAMID force commander (General Martin Luther Agwai of Nigeria) and the UNAMID Police Commissioner (Mr Michael Fryer of South Africa), were appointed by the AU in consultation with the UN. Both men report

---

44   The bulk (nearly two thirds) of AMIS' backing was from the EU's African Peace Facility, with Canada, the USA, NATO and Japan also providing significant backing (International Crisis Group. 2005. *The EU/AU Partnership in Darfur: Not Yet a Winning Combination.* Africa Report No. 99, 25 October 2005).

45   See http://www.un.org/en/peacekeeping/missions/unamid/facts.html.

to the Joint Special Representative, Mr Rodolphe Adada, and their appointment is seen as important for continuity (General Agwal was also commander of AMIS).

Multinational coordination of the UNAMID force poses various challenges at the tactical level. The complex nature of UNAMID is evident in that its command and control structure is headquartered at the UN's Department of Peacekeeping Operations in New York, but commanded on the ground by AMIS officers that previously reported to a different structure, and implemented by troops from countries that have a variety of different relationships with the host country. Coordination between battalions from countries speaking different languages and having variegated training, has sometimes resulted in inconsistent interpretations of UNAMID's mandate and operating procedure. Dovetailing from one type of mission (AU) to the other (UN/AU) is difficult enough but issues of whose mandate takes precedence and what that *really* means in international peacekeeping parlance are key here; with a blame-game often the result when incoherent or inconsistent applications of the mandate results in problems. Within the force itself, and within communities on the ground, there is suspicion that UNAMID is really just the UN in another guise.

The hybrid nature of the force, and the perceived disconnect between the experience, skills and capacity of AU and UN personnel respectively; has been problematic. For example, AU peacekeepers have expected the Joint Coordination Support Mechanism[46] to take the lead in decision-making; but UN personnel view its role as liaison and information sharing. Delayed supply of basic equipment has meant that some ex-AMIS forces have tied blue materials over their green AMIS helmets to indicate that they are now part of UNAMID, a small but significant issue. Unfortunately, the force commander's leadership has come under criticism for alleged nepotism in making senior appointments,[47] and also because, as the former AMIS commander, he may already have lost the trust of rebel leaders to whom he had made unfulfilled promises[48].

---

46   The Joint Coordination Support Mechanism, based in Addis Ababa, was set up to ensure seamless communication between the AU and UN parts of UNAMID, and to centralize command and control in order to efficiently fill the mission's mandate (see: UNAMID. 'UN Under-Secretary-General visits Joint Support Coordination Mechanism Office in Addis Ababa'. 31 January 2009; and Peace Operations Monitor. 2007. 'UNAMID Profile' at http://pom.peacebuild.ca/SudanDarfurProfile.shtml).

47   Van der Lijn. 2008. pp. 38.

48   While rebel groups did temporarily cease hostilities in some parts of Darfur after the deployment of AMIS, in the belief that the peacekeepers would succeed in persuading the Sudanese government to call off the Janjaweed and suspend attacks; they felt betrayed when government-supported attacks continued (Abdel Ati, H.A and Din el Tayeb, G. 2009. *Peace in Sudan: So Near ... So Far? Proceedings of the National Civic Forum Dialogue Sessions 2007–2008* Khartoum: National Civic Forum and EDGE for consultancy and research; and Du Toit, F. 'Talking Peace, Making War in Darfur', in: Raftopoulos, B. and K. Alexander. 2006. *Peace in the Balance: The Crisis in Sudan.* Cape Town: IJR, Blue Weaver Press. Chapter 6).

The outright and continuing hostility of the host country government to a UN presence both decreases UNAMID's potential for success and increases the likelihood of attacks on UNAMID troops such as that suffered during July 2008 in North Darfur. In the latter case, which occurred in a Sudanese government-controlled area and was allegedly perpetrated by Janjaweed militias (some of whom were reported to be wearing army uniforms), seven peacekeepers were killed and dozens of others wounded.[49] Such incidents, including the March 2009 and September 2009 attacks at El Jeneina near the Chad border,[50] not only undermine the image and perceived efficacy of UNAMID but also destroy troop morale. Because UNAMID is operating without the goodwill of the host country government; and because other belligerents and civilians may also display hostility to it; paranoia and suspicion are rife and misinformation may be disseminated as fact.

Peacekeeping and Fulfilling the R2P

Various analysts agree that UNAMID is perhaps five years too late, and is now dealing with the fallout from the lack of a robust, well-provisioned peacekeeping mission at the beginning of the Darfur conflict. Between 2003 and 2005 the international community failed in its responsibility to protect the hundreds of thousands of Darfuris who were killed, tortured and displaced. Hamstrung by competing agendas, haunted by the failures of Somalia and other interventions, member states failed to gather sufficient political will to intervene in a timely manner. While Darfur quite literally burned, the government of Sudan lost control of its proxies and belligerent groups on all sides became increasingly lawless and inhumane[51].

Today, it is fairly obvious that, in order to even partially fulfil the responsibility to protect civilians, UNAMID requires an adequate early warning system, including the communications equipment and intelligence ability to receive in a timely fashion the correct information that distinguishes between suspected belligerents and allows for a rapid deployment of troops. UNAMID also needs more active and visible patrolling, as well as greater contact with communities on the ground to build trust and remove suspicion. The latter could be achieved by enhancing its civilian affairs department to actively reach out to key constituencies such as women, children, religious and community leaders. The likelihood of implementing

---

49   Reeves, E. 'Attack on UNAMID Forces in Darfur: The Khartoum Regime is Responsible'. *Sudan Tribune.* 14 July 2008.

50   Reuters. 'FACTBOX: Attacks Targeting UN Staff and Sites in 2009'. *Reuters* 28 October 2009.

51   Julie Flint gives an excellent exposition of the government's loss of control of the Janjaweed and the atrocities committed by various militias in her paper *Beyond Janjaweed: Understanding the Militias of Darfur*, published in 2009 by the Small Arms Survey in Geneva.

both an early warning system and an enhanced patrol and civil affairs capability is largely dependent on political will: on the one hand the political will of the countries that made pledges of support for UNAMID to actually abide by their promises, and on the other the will of the Government of Sudan to cooperate with the mission rather than allowing its proxies (at the very least tacitly) to obstruct and attack UNAMID. Given that the Government of Southern Sudan is in a unity coalition with the National Islamic Front (NIF) incumbents, they may provide an effective avenue for applying pressure on their peers. Members of the SPLM may be able to selectively influence some of their colleagues in Khartoum to change their stance on UNAMID, and begin to cooperate with, rather than hinder, peacekeeping attempts. This is particularly true given that the Government of Sudan's current path would seem to make increasing numbers of senior officials vulnerable to prosecution through the ICC and other bodies.

Sensitivity is required in who is deployed where; given the ethnic, tribal, regional and religious complexities referred to above. Certain nationalities and religions may be more welcome (and consequently more effective) in some parts of the region than in others.[52] This needs to be considered in the deployment of military, police and civilian peacekeepers.

Furthermore, UNAMID still faces challenges in cooperation[53] with the other UN mission in southern Sudan (UNMIS) and with regional missions that essentially address the impacts of the Darfur conflict in neighbouring states, e.g. EUFOR in Chad and MINURCAT (UN Mission in the Central African Republic). This is especially significant in achieving better control of arms in the region; and also to help coordinate the provision of humanitarian assistance to IDPs and refugees where food insecurity and its attendant health hazards are extremely high.

Without a concomitant and urgent political process that produces at the very least a peace agreement which is inclusive of the majority of combatants in Darfur,

---

52   For example, outside mediators might have increased chances of successfully straddling the divides between various factions if they combined Muslim and African identities. Given the history of slavery and colonialism in the region, peacekeepers from the southern parts of the globe might be more effective in fulfilling their mandate than those whose nationality or physiognomy resembles the former slave-masters.

53   Current levels of cooperation, where they exist, are largely limited to information-sharing at irregular intervals. Each mission, given its unique mandate, operates independently, and in the case of non-UN missions, has little contact with UNAMID. The regional dimensions of arms flows and politics, discussed here, can constitute impediments to peacekeeping attempts; thus regular high-level joint briefing and strategy sessions between the various forces could easily be instituted via the use of information and communication technology (see: Lovald, J. 'UN Cooperation with Regional Organisations'. Briefing to UN Security Council by Norwegian Ambassador, 7 October 2009; Van der Lijn. 2008; and Neethling, T. 2009. 'UN Peacekeeping Operations in Africa: Reflections on developments, trends and the way forward' Paper presented at Conference on Strategy: Strategic Theory and Contemporary African Conflicts. 11–12 June 2009. Copenhagen: Forsvaret).

UNAMID will continue to falter in its ability to protect the civilian population.[54] Should this happen, UNAMID, and the international community by extension, will be blamed for ongoing atrocities. Any political intervention must allow for some mechanism to bring the increasingly fractured combatant groups together,[55] so that a secession of hostilities can be effectively upheld by UNAMID. Brokers of such intervention need careful selection, since most of the usual choices are tainted by their associations with major powers or by past failures in the region.

The delays in implementation of the CPA indirectly jeopardize the prospects of peace in Darfur. Not only are the conflicts interlinked, as noted above, but also the procrastination of the Bashir government and its refusal to uphold decisions on boundaries in south Sudan are seen as evidence of bad faith by some of the Darfur rebels[56]. Thus, they are less likely to commit to a peace process with a government that they perceive as untrustworthy and with multilateral organizations that have failed to hold this government to its promises.

Inclusion of the southern Sudanese in the Darfur political process would be logical, given the SPLM's links with the Darfur SLA factions; and can be predicated on renewed multilateral efforts to bring the CPA implementation back on track. However, this type of resolution is unlikely to be welcomed by the Bashir government.

Impacts of the International Criminal Court Case on Prospects for Peace

The UN Security Council decision to refer the case of Darfur to the International Criminal Court (ICC) was problematic in itself, in that key permanent and non-permanent members of the council had conflicting agendas in the matter. Both China and the US are not states parties to the Rome Treaty that birthed the ICC, thus they are inherently opposed to any action that legitimizes the ICC. Further, as noted briefly above, several Western and Eastern countries have extensive energy and other resource interests in Sudan and in the surrounding region.[57] Sudan itself is not a party to the Rome Treaty; thus the ICC referral had to come via the Security

---

54   The Existing Darfur Peace Agreement, as discussed elsewhere in this chapter, has failed; despite various additional protocols being signed.

55   A broad-based consultation, which draws on key civilian constituencies (women, religious leaders, chiefs, etc.) in addition to active belligerents, might be the first step in establishing such a mechanism.

56   The two largest Sudan Liberation Army (SLA) factions respectively led by Abdel Wahid and Minni Minnawi, are particularly important in this regard, given their historical links to the Sudan People's Liberation Movement (SPLM) of south Sudan (see: de Waal).

57   These include extensive investment in the Chadian oil sector by France and the USA, among others, and investment by multinational corporations in the Democratic Republic of Congo for the extraction of resources such as gold, oil, copper, tin-ore and cobalt. Malaysian and Chinese investments in Sudan's oil sector have been highlighted previously (see: International Crisis Group. 2009. 'Chad: Escaping from the oil trap'. *Africa Policy Briefing No. 65*. Brussels: ICG; and Kabel, S. 2004. 'Our Business is People

Council. As in the case of the decision to implement UNAMID, the referral to the ICC was delayed by political wrangling; with the result that the ICC indictment of President Bashir in March 2009 is yet another case of 'too late'.

On a purely human rights basis, practitioners and activists quite rightly welcome the indictment as evidence that impunity on the part of predatory leaders will no longer be tolerated. Had the indictment come two years earlier, most political analysts too would have largely supported it, as the intensity of the conflict was much greater at that time. Also, opinion within the ruling party was divided, in view of the looming spectre of prosecution in an international forum. The interim period and the relative decrease in intensity of the conflict, have allowed Bashir to consolidate support within government. But, aside from the complexities of indicting a sitting head of state (and the concomitant questions of immunity and diplomacy); the timing of this indictment is particularly problematic.

Sudan is due to hold national elections in 2010, and the historical use of Darfur as a political football by competing political factions has already been referenced above. The outcome of the 2010 elections, in the minds of many Northerners at least, will be crucial in the 2011 referendum that decides whether South Sudan will secede from the rest of the country. Combined with the ongoing disputes over oil-rich border areas between North and South, and the delays in CPA implementation, the domestic political environment was fraught well before March 2009. Northerners were already bracing for the potential loss of income from southern oil revenue by as much as 40 per cent.[58] Now, the possibility of maintaining a sufficiently stable political environment in which reasonably fair elections could be held, has been further decreased by the ICC indictment.

In Darfur particularly, the basic humanitarian situation on the ground has been considerably weakened. Hours after the ICC decision was announced, the defiant Government of Sudan expelled 10 humanitarian organizations working in Sudan, including *Medecins Sans Frontieres* (MSF), Oxfam and Save the Children.[59] Several other groups were expelled in the weeks following the indictment. In a context where food is extremely scarce and meningitis has broken out in some parts

---

(Even if it Kills Them): The contribution of multinational enterprises to the conflict in the Democratic Republic of Congo'. *Tulane Journal of International and Comparative Law*).

58   Tellnes, J. 2005. 'Dealing with Petroleum Issues in Civil War Negotiations: The case of Sudan'. Paper presented at the 13th Annual National Political Science Conference at Hurdalssjøen.

59   The expulsion of aid agencies was in retaliation for the ICC indictment, seen as a 'Western plot'. While none of the 13 major organizations who were expelled have been allowed to return, several have returned after registering under a different name, e.g. although Save the Children US was expelled, Save the Children Sweden is allowed to operate in Darfur. Similarly, CARE Switzerland and Mercy Corps Scotland applied to work in Darfur after CARE and Mercy Corps respectively were expelled. Some see this as a cynical divide-and-rule tactic by Sudan's government to use the aid, but limit the aid groups' freedom of action, movement and speech (see: Crilly, R. 2009. 'Aid Groups Return to Darfur – with New Names'. *Christian Science Monitor.* 16 June 2009).

of the country, the expulsion of aid organizations that are often the only recourse available to civilians in conflict-riven areas is dire. In pure human security terms, the loss of life that may result from the lack of health and nutrition support alone, could amount to hundreds of thousands. Aid workers reckon that at least half of the IDPs in Darfur were sustained by the expelled organizations; and the most conservative estimates put total IDP numbers at more than a million people.[60]

While the Bashir government's defiance and retaliatory measures in the face of the ICC indictment may well reflect the desperation of a leader who has been publicly shamed in the international arena; it is equally true that the many states and multilateral organizations have decried the decision and its timing. While national economic interests do play a role in such proclamations, the initiative by the African Union and the Arab League to have the indictment deferred for the period of one year might have been the least harmful option, and one that is provided for in Chapter 16 of the ICC statute.[61] The refusal to defer has been decried by the AU assembly and the ICC has been perceived as targeting Africans, with associated connotations of neo-imperialism. Respected international jurist Justice Richard Goldstone, who participated in the international tribunals for the former Yugoslavia and Rwanda, has cautioned that the ICC needs to counter such perceptions by investigating atrocities in other regions, and where appropriate, indicting perpetrators.[62]

In any event, the ICC will find it extremely difficult to enforce the indictment against Bashir at this time. Usually, the court relies on the national police force to implement the warrant; but in case of a non-state party this is obviously unrealistic. Other countries could be normally be expected to uphold an indictment and arrest the indictee if he or she visits a country which has signed the Rome Treaty. As this is the first indictment of a sitting head of state, however, issues of diplomatic ties between countries and of diplomatic immunity, come into play. It is quite probable, therefore, that many states would take no action.[63] After all, it was only after sustained international pressure that the Nigerian government was persuaded to hand over former Liberian President Charles Taylor to the Special Court for Sierra Leone. Taylor was a former head of state, not an incumbent one, and even then he almost escaped.

A deferral of the ICC mandate could possibly have impacted in an unprecedented manner on Sudan's domestic polity. The current National Islamic

---

60   See www.internal-displacemnent.org which provides estimates by country.

61   The proposed deferral could have provided a window period during which a workable ceasefire could be negotiated, and also an opportunity for peer-to-peer pressure to be applied at head of state level.

62   Goldstone, R. 2009. 'Does the ICC Target Africa?' *Equality of Arms Review Issue 2*. The Hague: International Bar Association.

63   Bashir openly attended the Arab Summit in the Middle East during 2009 without apparent fear of arrest.

Front government is not without its internal fracture lines[64]; and given that elections are looming, Bashir might no longer have been an incumbent head of state in a year's time. Politicians, more than any other grouping, are pragmatists; and leading members of the incumbent ruling elite might have opted to sacrifice one of its members in the hope of ensuring the longer-term survival of the collective.[65] Not insignificantly for the long-term prospects of stability in Sudan as a whole, those same pragmatists may also have been more amenable to implementing the CPA in the hope of retaining Sudanese unity. As a united Sudan was always the aim of deceased southern leader John Garang, it is conceivable that such a scenario would draw the support of several current southern Sudanese leaders too.

Conclusion: Future Alternatives

To date, there have been variety of multi-faceted global responses to the Darfur crisis, yet all have met with very limited success. This can largely attributed to the ambivalence with which major players have reacted – first resist and then agree to refer Darfur to the ICC; lobby for the world's largest peacekeeping operation and then fail to equip it adequately; etc. If it is truly serious about its responsibility to protect Darfuris from further casualties, the international community would be well advised to urgently and decisively take the following actions:

- support a deferral of the ICC indictment in exchange for a return of humanitarian assistance to the region, and an undertaking from the Sudanese government to allow UNAMID to operate freely and without fear;
- provide the necessary funds and equipment to upgrade and provision UNAMID to become maximally effective as envisaged in Resolution 1769;
- initiate a fresh political process towards an inclusive peace agreement for Darfur, incorporating the various elements discussed elsewhere in this chapter;
- actively and visibly support the implementation of the CPA between north and south Sudan (which may include material and logistical support to hold the 2011 referendum);

---

64 Some groupings within the government might have been influenced by fear of being implicated in and prosecuted for atrocities, while others might have had an eye on the potential economic benefits of restored amicable relations with the international community and with the West in particular.

65 That window of opportunity has passed, with a firmer consolidation of power evident among Bashir's allies during 2009. They have done an excellent job of marketing him as a victim of encroaching Western imperialism and intra-party criticism dwindled notably in the run up to the April 2010 elections, which, while flawed, were won by the NCP, thus entrenching Bashir's hold on power.

- utilize China and other Sudan allies to pressure the Sudanese government into implementing its commitments as outlined above.

Some of these measures are, at best, short- or medium-term alternatives. In the longer term, the peace initiative for Darfur will have to be followed through to the actual implementation stage. This implies that UNAMID's stay in Darfur is likely to be extended and that its mandate may be broadened. It also implies that the ICC's existing mandate on Darfur continues to be pursued in as independent a manner as possible, so that perpetrators on all sides of the conflict who are guilty of heinous crimes are brought to justice in a visible and even-handed manner.

Chapter 11

Steady but Uneven Progress: The Operationalization of the African Standby Force

Benedikt Franke

Almost a dozen attempts at establishing some sort of Pan-African military force preceded the creation of the African Standby Force (ASF).[1] In fact, the current attempt is very similar to the proposal made by the delegation from Sierra Leone at the 3rd Ordinary Session of the Organization of African Unity (OAU) Defense Commission in 1965. As envisioned over 40 years ago, it does not entail the establishment of a standing multinational force, but is built around a standby arrangement whereby states earmark and train specific units for joint operations and then keep these units ready for rapid deployment at appropriate notice.[2] This chapter seeks to detail the current state of this force.

The Concept and Structure of the ASF

In July 2002, the Protocol Relating to the Establishment of the Peace and Security Council formally concluded a long process of discussion on the purpose and shape of a continental military force that, in one form or the other, had been ongoing since decolonization.[3] Article 13 of the Protocol provides for the establishment of an African Standby Force 'in order to enable the Peace and Security Council perform its responsibilities with respect to the deployment of peace support missions and intervention pursuant to Article 4(h) and (j) of the Constitutive Act'.[4] While it

---

1   For a detailed history of these attempts see Benedikt Franke, 'A Pan-African Army: The Evolution of an Idea and Its Eventual Realization in the African Standby Force', *African Security Review* 15, no. 4 (2006): 2–16.

2   Cedric de Coning, 'Refining the African Standby Force Concept', *Conflict Trends*, no. 2 (2004): 21.

3   The Peace and Security Council is the AU's 'standing decision-making organ for the prevention, management and resolution of conflicts' (*Protocol Relating to the Establishment of the Peace and Security Council*, Article 2.1).

4   AU, *Protocol Relating to the Establishment of the Peace and Security Council*, 9 July 2002, Durban, Article 13, para. 1.

does specify seven functions for the proposed force (ranging from the conduct of observation and monitoring missions to full-blown humanitarian interventions),[5] the often-cited article provides only very little information about its concept and structure except that it shall be composed of 'standby multidisciplinary contingents, with civilian and military components in their countries of origin and ready for rapid deployment at appropriate notice'.[6] It was only with the adoption of the Policy Framework for the Establishment of the African Standby Force and the Military Staff Committee by the 3rd Meeting of the African Chiefs of Defense Staff (ACDS) in May 2003 and its subsequent approval by the Heads of States in July 2004 that the idea of the envisaged standby arrangement was somewhat clarified.[7]

In its introduction, the Policy Framework refers to the recommendations made by the 2nd Meeting of the ACDS in Harare in 1997 which, amongst others, included the earmarking of five brigade-sized contributions to a common standby force by the continent's most prominent regional organizations, the Arab Mahgreb Union (AMU), the Economic Community of Central African States (ECCAS), the Economic Community of West African States (ECOWAS), the Inter-Governmental Authority on Development (IGAD), and the Southern African Development Community (SADC).[8] On the basis of these recommendations, the final document adopted by the Heads of State details an elaborate structure for the planned force that consists of five regionally-managed standby brigades supported by civilian police and one continentally-managed permanent body responsible for final oversight, coordination and harmonization. Conceptually, the ASF is thus based on three levels, namely, the continental level (that is, the AU Commission), the regional level (that is, the Regional Economic Communities (RECs) or specifically dedicated coordinating mechanisms) and the national level (that is, the contributing countries).

At the continental level, the Policy Framework envisages the establishment of a permanent 15-person Planning Element (PLANELM) within the AU's Peace and Security Department to provide for a multi-dimensional, strategic-level management capability. The core function of this unit is to supervise the system of regional standby arrangements to ensure standardization, interoperability and currency of information. In addition, the AU PLANELM is in charge of (1) developing and, if necessary, updating key documents such as the ASF doctrine, standard operating procedures and training manuals, (2) coordinating the efforts to establish a logistical infrastructure consisting of a central and five regional depots,

---

5   *Ibid.*, para. 3.

6   *Ibid.*, para. 1.

7   See *Policy Framework for the Establishment of the African Standby Force and the Military Staff Committee* (AU Document EXP/ASF-MSC/2(I), 16 May 2003, Addis Ababa).

8   AU, *Policy Framework for the Establishment of the African Standby Force and the Military Staff Committee*, Part II, Annex.

(3) coordinating the efforts to mobilize, harmonize and focus external support activities, (4) developing and maintaining relationships with the UN Standby Arrangement System and other relevant organizations and (5) establishing and maintaining central standby arrangement systems including rosters for individual AU Headquarters (HQ) staff, up to 240 civilian police and 300–500 military observers.[9] In a mission situation, the continental PLANELM provides the basis for an AU Strategic HQ capable of planning, managing and conducting all necessary arrangements for the effective employment of the ASF.

At the regional level, each of the continent's five geographic regions has one REC or specifically dedicated coordinating mechanism in charge of setting up and administering a standby component for the ASF.[10] Each standby component is to be between 3,000 and 4,000 troops strong, (giving the ASF an overall strength of 15,000 to 20,000 troops) and provide a number of predefined military capabilities.[11] Regional PLANELMs, similar in form to the one at the continental level and ideally co-located with the regional brigade headquarters, are responsible for the planning, preparation and training, including the verification of the standby elements and the brigade headquarters. In addition, the regional PLANELMs coordinate with the AU headquarters and each other and administer designated regional training centers as well as the envisaged regional logistics infrastructure including the regional military depots.

At the national level, member states contributing contingents to the regional brigades are expected to train the individuals and units that form part of the standby brigades in basic military tasks as well as in the standardized doctrine and operating

---

9   *Ibid.*

10   It is important to note that the idea of the ASF is built on geographic regions rather than the RECs. Thus, a contingent of the ASF can be established by regional states in an independent arrangement that has little or no connection with any REC (this has been the case in Eastern Africa, see section on EASBRIG). If member states in a region are unable to come together to establish their branch of the ASF, the Policy Framework provides that 'encouragement be given to potential lead nations to form coalitions of the willing as a stop-gap arrangement, pending the establishment of a regional standby forces arrangements'. See AU, *Policy Framework for the Establishment of the African Standby Force and the Military Staff Committee*, 17.

11   AU, *The Roadmap for the Operationalization of the African Standby Force* (EXP/AU-RECs/ASF/4(I), 22–23 March 2005, Addis Ababa) specifies the following capabilities in its Annex A: A brigade HQ and support unit of up to 65 personnel and 16 vehicles; a HQ company and support unit of up to 120 personnel; four light infantry battalions, each composed of up to 750 personnel and 70 vehicles; an engineer unit of up to 135 personnel; a light signals unit of up to 135 personnel; a reconnaissance company of up to 150 personnel; a helicopter unit of up to 80 personnel, 10 vehicles and 4 helicopters; a military police unit of up to 48 personnel and 17 vehicles; a light multi-role logistical unit of up to 190 personnel and 40 vehicles; a level 2 medical unit of up to 35 personnel and 10 vehicles; a military observer group of up to 120 officers; a civilian support group consisting of logistical, administrative and budget components.

procedures developed by the AU.[12] Accordingly, all designated regional training centers as well as national military schools have to follow the guidelines set by the AU in consultation with the regional PLANELMs and coordinate their training cycles. Member states are also required to allow access to the units and personnel that form part of the ASF by the relevant authorities from the regional planning and management organs or the AU Commission for the purpose of periodic reviews including the verification of training standards and interoperability as well as the identification of possible shortfalls.

This three-level structure, according to the Policy Framework, allows the continent's decision-makers to employ the ASF effectively in all likely mission scenarios, reaching from simply providing military advice to a political mission to full-blown military peace enforcement operations to halt an ongoing genocide or grave violations against human rights (see Figure 11.1).

The Policy Framework has set very ambitious timelines for deployment in the above scenarios. It envisages that the ASF can deploy within 30 days for scenarios one to four, within 90 days for scenario five and within 14 days for scenario six, all beginning from the decision of the AU Assembly and the Peace and Security Council to carry out the operation.[13] Such tight deployment timelines necessitate highly-trained and interoperable units, an established and fully stocked logistics infrastructure as well as a sophisticated command and control system. Both the Policy Framework as well as the ASF Roadmap have called on expert working groups to discuss these requirements in more detail.

With respect to training, the relevant workshops conducted between 2004 and late 2007 reiterated the importance of ensuring universal adherence to AU and UN training standards. To this purpose, they recommended the use of approved regional training centres such as the Kofi Annan International Peacekeeping Training Centre in Accra (for West Africa), the Regional Peacekeeping Training Centre in Harare (for Southern Africa) and the Peace Support Training Centre

Scenario 1	AU/Regional military advice to a political mission
Scenario 2	AU/Regional observer mission co-deployed with UN mission
Scenario 3	Stand-alone AU/Regional observer mission
Scenario 4	AU/Regional peacekeeping force for Chapter VI missions
Scenario 5	AU peacekeeping force for multi-dimensional peacekeeping mission
Scenario 6	AU intervention and peace enforcement mission

Figure 11.1   Mission scenarios for the ASF

Source: AU, *Policy Framework for the Establishment of the African Standby Force and the Military Staff Committee*, 3

---

12   AU, *Policy Framework for the Establishment of the African Standby Force and the Military Staff Committee*, 23.

13   *Ibid.*, 6–7.

in Nairobi (for Eastern Africa) which had been established with the help of international donors in order to build regional capacities for UN peacekeeping. The workshops also decided that while training is to remain primarily a national responsibility, the joint nature of the ASF inevitably means that both the regional and the continental level have to stay closely involved in the training process. Besides the determination of the training curriculum and the harmonization of training cycles, this involvement should include a continuous evaluation and validation process informed by lessons learned from previous operations and best practices from other organizations and operations.[14]

With respect to logistics, the ASF Policy Framework provides that missions deployed for scenarios one to three should be self-sustainable for up to 30 days, while those deployed for scenarios four to six should be self-sustainable for up to 90 days, after which the AU takes responsibility for mission sustainment. Together with the ambitious deployment timelines mentioned above, these goals present enormous logistical challenges. A Logistics Working Group has developed an ASF Logistics Support Concept as well as a 177-page Logistics Manual to help overcome the challenges associated with the deployment and sustainment of the ASF.[15] Regarding deployment, these documents state the importance of pre-deploying equipment into regional logistics depots and negotiating standing arrangements with lead nations, international donors or commercial contractors regarding strategic sea and airlift to ensure the ability of the ASF to deploy within the set timelines. Regarding sustainment in theater, they draw attention to the UN system in which troop contributing countries must be prepared to sustain their units from national sources from the time of arrival in the mission area until the mandating authority's logistics and reimbursement systems have been established. In addition, they recommend that the ASF be given the ability to negotiate support agreements with host nations and commercial contractors.

In addition to standardized and continuously monitored training and elaborate logistics, an effective ASF also necessitates a clearly defined Command and Control (C^2) structure in which commands and instructions can flow from a higher level to all levels of the hierarchy and control can be executed through specified feedback. While the Policy Framework is relatively silent on this matter, subsequent workshops have developed detailed C^2 systems for force generation

14   See Report of the PSD Training and Evaluation ASF Pre-Workshop held in Addis Ababa from 31 January to 2 February 2006.

15   For an early discussion of logistical and capacity considerations surrounding the ASF see Tsepe Motumi, 'Logistical and Capacity Considerations Surrounding a Standby Force', in *Peace in Africa – Towards a Collaborative Security Regime*, ed. Shannon Field (Johannesburg: Institute for Global Dialogue, 2004). For an alternative view on ASF Logistics see Rick Thompson, 'Afloat Depots for the African Standby Force', *Canadian Military Journal* 8, no. 4 (2007): 37–44.

and force utilization.[16] During force generation, that is the process of setting up and administering the standby force, command and control lies with the national authorities of the contributing nations or with the regional authorities whenever the national contributions are preparing or exercising jointly. During force utilization, that is the use of ASF forces for military purposes by the AU or the RECs, C^2 lies with the mandating authority. With regard to the AU, the Policy Framework states that 'the PSC as the decision-making institution should, be the sole authority for mandating and terminating AU peace missions and operations' and that the 'political command and control of missions mandated by the PSC should be vested in the Chairperson, who should then submit periodic reports to the PSC on the progress of implementation of the relevant mandates'.[17] The Chairperson also appoints the Head of Mission, Force Commander, Police Commissioner and the Head of the Civilian Component while delegating the political direction and administrative control to the AU Commissioner for Peace and Security. The Peace Support Operations Division is thus responsible for the strategic planning of ASF operations. As such it conducts all the staff work related to any mission, be it the organizing of reconnaissance missions, the drafting of mandates, concepts of operations and rules of engagement or the preparation of reports. In the field, the Head of Mission establishes the relationship between the military, police and political elements of the operation, assigns areas of responsibility and establishes mechanisms to integrate the activities of all involved parties and organizations.[18]

If a mission is mandated by one of the RECs or coordinating mechanisms, this chain of command is replicated on the regional level, that is, the regional political authority appoints the Head of Mission, Force Commander, Police Commissioner and Head of the Civilian Component through its peace and security mechanism. The AU should be kept informed through close contact between the regional and the continental PLANELM, but does not have any political authority over the conduct of the mission.[19] The following section will discuss to what extent this elaborate concept has been operationalized thus far.

----

16   See Final Report of the PSD Expert Workshop on Command and Control held in Cairo, 5–12 April 2006.

17   AU, *Policy Framework for the Establishment of the African Standby Force and the Military Staff Committee*, 25.

18   In large and complex operations (scenarios five and six), involving major civilian elements, the Head of Mission is called Special Representative of the Chairperson of the AU Commission. See ASF Peace Support Operations Doctrine, Sect 8, para. 68.

19   AU Working Paper, *The African Standby Force Command and Control System*, Annexure B.

The Operationalization of the African Standby Force

When the 3rd Ordinary Session of the AU Assembly approved the Policy Framework for the Establishment of the African Standby Force it also requested the Chairperson of the AU Commission 'to take all steps required for the implementation of the Policy Framework document'.[20] In line with this request and the recommendation of the Policy Framework that the ASF should be established in two phases, the Commissioner for Peace and Security, Ambassador Said Djinnit, convened a meeting of experts in March 2005 that provided a roadmap for the operationalization of Phase I.[21] In this phase, which the Policy Framework originally intended to be achieved by the end of June 2005, the plan was to establish a strategic management capacity at the level of the AU for scenarios one and two while the regions would establish standby components ready for scenarios one to four. In the second phase which is intended to be completed by June 2010, the AU should then continue to develop its management capacity to be able to deal with all scenarios, up to five, while the regions should increasingly focus on their rapid deployment capability.[22]

Given the ambitious scale of the project, it is not surprising that this original timeline for the establishment of the ASF has not been adhered to. Phase I was only completed at the end of 2006 and some aspects of it will carry over to Phase II which is now going to end in early 2010 and will be followed by a third phase which is expected to end in late 2010 or early 2011.[23]

Even though the first phase has taken substantially longer than originally planned, its outputs have surpassed many expectations.[24] Not only have most of the regions made remarkable progress in establishing their standby brigades, but there have also been several promising developments at the continental level. First, the five central documents that will regulate the functioning of the ASF, that is, the ASF Doctrine, a Training Policy, an ASF Logistics Concept, a Command and Control Plan and the Standard Operating Procedures (SOPs) have been finalized through a painstaking series of workshops and seminars and subsequently approved by the African Chiefs of Defence Staff at their 5th meeting in March 2008.[25] These

---

20   See *Decision on the African Standby Force and the Military Staff Committee* (AU Document EX.CL/110(V), 6–8 July 2004, Addis Ababa).

21   See *Experts' Meeting on the Relationship between the AU and the Regional Mechanisms for Conflict Prevention, Management and Resolution* (AU Document Exp/AU-RECS/ASF/4(I), 22–23 March 2005 Addis Ababa).

22   *Policy Framework for the Establishment of the ASF and the MSC*, 40.

23   Figure based on AU, *Roadmap for the Operationalization of the African Standby Force Phase II*.

24   See *Report of the Chairperson of the Commission for the Period July to December 2006*, Executive Council, 10th Ordinary Session, 25–26 January 2007, Addis Ababa, 13.

25   Correspondence with Colonel Reinhard Linz, EU MIL LO AU, 25 November 2008.

documents along with the results of the workshops on financial and legal matters provide the basic tools for operationalizing the ASF.

Second, the Peace Support Operations Division of the AU has managed to foster a wide base of international support for the operationalization of the ASF. Besides many national donors such as the US, the UK, Canada or Germany which have helped to build up the necessary infrastructure in Addis Ababa and have organized and financed many of the aforementioned workshops and experts meetings, the Peace Support Operations Division can count on the support of several institutional donors. The UN's Department for Peacekeeping Operations, for example, has established a liaison team to the PSOD in order to offer expertise and tailored support to the operationalization of the ASF.[26] The EU has financed many aspects of the emerging force through its African Peace Facility (APF) and has taken over the French capacity building programme *Renforcement des capacités africaines au maintien de la paix* (RECAMP) and adapted it to suit the training needs of the ASF.[27] Both organizations are extremely keen to bolster the capacities of the AU in the area of peace and security and ensure a smooth and sustainable operationalization of the ASF.

Third, the AU has managed to develop the strategic management capacity to deal with scenarios one to three.[28] Together with the regions, the AU is thus already able to deploy observer missions throughout the continent and, with substantial help from international partners, might even be able to conduct limited scenario four operations. Even though the PSOD has still not reached the staff level mandated by the 2003 Maputo Summit and no replacement for the deceased Chief of ASF Staff, the late Major-General Ishaya Hassan, has yet been found, the AU has recruited a number of highly-qualified staff to guide and support the operationalization of the ASF following its temporary move into an office building outside the AU compound in Addis.[29] The number of personnel is to increase further once the new purpose-built PSOD building (financed by Germany) will be completed in late 2009.

---

26   Interview with Dr Abdel-Kader Haireche, Team Leader DPKO-AU Peace Support Team, 12 June 2007, Addis Ababa.

27   The APF is an EU-funded financing instrument created in 2003 in order to support African-led peace and security efforts. Following an initial budget of €250 million, another €300 million have been earmarked under the 10th European Development Fund for the period 2008–10. RECAMP was originally created as a French peacekeeping training programme for allied African nations. It was taken over by the EU in 2007. EURO-RECAMP will provide the basis for the ASF Command Post Exercise (CPX) in early 2010. Interviews with Dr Genoveva Hernandez-Uriz, Administrator for Civilian Crisis Management, Council of the European Union and Mr Sébastien Bergeon, Defense Expert, Council of the European Union, 5–7 September 2007, Addis Ababa.

28   Interview with Mr Bereng Mtimkulu, Head of the AU PSOD, 20 September 2007, Addis Ababa.

29   Interview with Mr Hartwig Bretenitz, Consultant to the AU PSOD, 29 September 2007, Addis Ababa.

Fourth, the AU has established itself as the unquestionable authority in the operationalization of the ASF. Not only have all contributing states signalled their intention to adhere to and train their troops according to the documents developed by the AU in conjunction with the regions and external experts, but they have also acknowledged the leadership role of the PSOD in other matters such as the development of a logistics concept and the development of a rapid deployment capability (that is, the entry forces of the first regional brigade to deploy). Article IV of the Memorandum of Understanding (MoU) between the AU and the RECs regarding security cooperation reconfirms the 'primary responsibility of the Union in the maintenance and promotion of peace, security and stability in Africa'.[30]

While these are all promising signs, much remains to be done at the continental level. Following the approval of the five central documents of Phase I, Phase II now focuses on the development of a policy guiding document that addresses the political and legal aspects of mandating and deploying the ASF and the development of a concept of operation, capability development and force generation.[31] Besides these conceptual issues, the workshops conducted in Phase I have identified six other areas in need of further development, namely, (1) the communications and information system, (2) a training directive and needs analysis, (3) a logistics supply system to facilitate rapid deployment and sustainability, (4) the civilian aspects of the ASF, (5) the validation of key ASF documents such as the doctrine or the SOPs through exercises and lessons learned, and (6) a sustainable finance mechanism.[32]

Once these issues have been dealt with, Phase III envisages a validation command post exercise (CPX) 'Joint Brigades' that will test the ASF structures. The CPX will be developed around the AU Peace and Security Architecture decision-making process and will be based on the EU's adapted RECAMP format which many African states are already familiar with.[33] It will validate legal and financial aspects and involve the deployment of one or more of the regional brigades to deliver trained and equipped individuals and units to meet a contingency requiring rapid reaction. This will allow validation of ASF command and control, force generation, mobilization and deployment, training, logistics,

---

30 See *Memorandum of Understanding on Cooperation in the Area of Peace and Security between the African Union, the Regional Economic Communities and the Coordinating Mechanisms of the Regional Standby Brigades of Eastern Africa and Northern Africa* (AU Document AU-RECs/EXP/2(II) Rev. 3, 2 September 2007, Kampala) Article IV, para. (ii).

31 Interview with Captain (SA Navy) John Potgieter, Military Expert, AU PSOD, 12 June 2007, Addis Ababa.

32 For a good though somewhat outdated discussion on the financing of the ASF see Roger Kibasomba, 'Financing a Credible Standby Force Via the AU's Peace Fund', in *Peace in Africa – Towards a Collaborative Security Regime*, ed. Shannon Field (Johannesburg: Institute for Global Dialogue, 2004).

33 The Peace Support Training Centre (PSTC) in Nairobi has volunteered to develop the scenario for the ASF CPX until the end of April 2008.

standard operating procedures and communication systems. It will also test the AU's ability to cooperate with the UN and other international partners in tackling a rapidly developing crisis.

However, before the ASF capabilities can be evaluated in such an exercise, the regions must follow the continental example and build up their capacities in accordance with the roadmap for Phase II. In order to gauge the extent of this challenge and to get an impression of the regional aspect of inter-African security cooperation, the following three sections will briefly assess the progress of the three RECs (SADC, ECOWAS and ECCAS) and two coordinating mechanisms (EASBRICOM and NARC) currently establishing component standby brigades at the regional level.

Eastern Africa's Regional Brigade

In February 2004, the Intergovernmental Authority of Development (IGAD) which had been nominated by the region's states as the REC responsible for the interim coordination of efforts towards the establishment of a standby brigade in the East African region convened a meeting of experts in Jinja (Uganda) in order to discuss the process of operationalizing such a brigade. This meeting was followed later in the year by the 1st Meeting of Eastern Africa Chiefs of Defense Staff on the Establishment of the Eastern Africa Standby Brigade (EASBRIG) which adopted a Draft Policy Framework for the Establishment of the Eastern Africa Standby Brigade.[34] This Policy Framework was subsequently approved by a Council of Ministers meeting held in Kigali in September 2004 and the 1st Assembly of EASBRIG Heads of State and Government held in Addis in April 2005. It reconfirmed IGAD's interim coordination role and committed the 13 EASBRIG member states (Comoros, Djibouti, Eritrea, Ethiopia, Kenya, Madagascar, Mauritius, Rwanda, Seychelles, Somalia, Sudan, Tanzania and Uganda) to the by then still two-phased approach to the operationalization of the ASF. In addition to the Policy Framework, the Assembly also adopted a Memorandum of Understanding on the Establishment of EASBRIG and approved the necessary budget.[35]

In July 2005, the Chiefs of Defense Staff met again and operationalized the regional planning element in Nairobi. Faced with the refusal of some member states such as Eritrea to pay for the establishment of EASBRIG as long as the question of coordination was not finally resolved, they also appointed a Technical Committee of Experts to study the issue of coordination and make appropriate

---

34   See Proceedings of the 1st Meeting of Eastern Africa Chiefs of Defense Staff on the Establishment of the Eastern African Standby Brigade (EASBRIG), 16–17 February 2004, Jinja, Uganda.

35   See *Decision of the 1st Assembly of Heads of State and Government on the Establishment of the Eastern Africa Standby Brigade* (EASBRIG Document AHG/1/05).

recommendations to resolve the matter once and for all. The committee reported to the 4th Meeting of the Chiefs of Defense Staff in August 2005 and recommended the creation of an independent coordination mechanism to account for the non-IGAD member states, such as Tanzania, involved in the establishment of EASBRIG. Other topics discussed by the Chiefs of Defense Staff included the hosting agreements for the PLANELM in Nairobi and the Brigade HQ in Addis as well as the operationalization of the regional logistics base.

The 3rd Council of Ministers met in September 2005 in Kigali and adopted the recommendations of the Chiefs of Defense Staff on the operationalization of the PLANELM, the skeleton Brigade HQ, the establishment of an independent coordination mechanism (EASBRICOM) and the deferment of the operationalization of the logistics base until the AU had finalized its logistics concept.[36] Following another meeting of the Council of Ministers in April 2006, the 1st Extraordinary Meeting of the Heads of State and Government of Eastern Africa approved the operationalization of the independent coordination mechanism in January 2007 and the 2nd Extraordinary Meeting[37] of the Council of Ministers held in Nairobi in March 2007 implemented this decision by mandating EASBRICOM to serve as the secretariat of EASBRIG. In addition, the Council of Ministers commissioned several studies to make recommendations on (1) the duplications in functions and inconsistencies in the EASBRIG structures, (2) the harmonization of the Policy Framework and the MoU on the establishment of EASBRIG, and (3) the development of policy documents for EASBRIG including a Procurement Manual, Financial Regulations and an Employment Policy.[38] In August 2007, the 5th Meeting of the Council of Ministers accepted the experts' recommendations and asked EASBRICOM to take all necessary actions. The meeting also approved the membership request of Burundi and agreed on the formation of a Friends of EASBRIG Committee in order to offer international partners a forum for support and consultation.

Since its inauguration in January 2007, the new EASBRIG structure has made substantial progress in achieving the milestones set by the AU's roadmap for the operationalization of the ASF. Both the PLANELM and the Brigade HQ are fully operational and the Logistics Depot is currently being built up in Addis Ababa.[39] Several of the member states, including Tanzania, Rwanda and Uganda, have

---

36 See Report of the 3rd Ordinary Meeting of the Council of Ministers of Defense and Security, September 2005, Kigali, Rwanda, http://www.easbrig.org/docs/com3kigalisep05.pdf.

37 http://www.easbrig.org/docs/com2exonairobimar07.pdf.

38 See Report of the 5th Ordinary Meeting of the Council of Ministers of Defense and Security, 17 August 2007, Nairobi, para. 2, http://www.easbrig.org/docs/com5nairobiaug07.pdf.

39 Interviews with Colonel Moustapha Handouleh, Deputy Chief of Staff, EASBRIG Planning Element, 28 August 2007, Addis Ababa and Mr Simon Mulongo, Director EASBRICOM, 29 August 2007, Addis Ababa.

begun to earmark and train units for EASBRIG and Kenya is currently in the process of establishing a rapid deployment capability for the standby brigade.[40]

In November 2007, EASBRICOM adopted a Strategic Development Plan for the period 2007 to 2015 which specifies eight objectives to help it achieve its vision of an initial operational capability by 2010 and full operational capability by 2015.[41] These objectives include the development of (1) cohesive political decision-making structures by 2010, (2) a command, control and communications (C^3) structure capable of preparing, planning for, and commanding the deployed forces by the end of 2009, (3) an initial operational capability of a trained force of brigade size on standby and maintained in member states to the required readiness level by the end of 2010, (4) a trained civilian police element on standby and maintained in member states to the required readiness level by the end of 2010, (5) a roster of trained civilian experts available for deployment by the end of 2010, (6) a logistics system capable of supporting the deployment and sustainment of EASBRIG by 2010, and (7) an integrated training system able to provide individual and collective training for regional forces by the end of 2010. In order to achieve these objectives EASBRICOM relies heavily on the continuing support of its international partners which have organized themselves into an EASBRIG Development Support Committee (EDSC) to coordinate their donor support.[42]

While Eastern Africa's progress in operationalizing its regional standby brigade is encouraging, several formidable challenges remain. First, the rise of violent conflict in the region, ranging from Ethiopia's invasion of Somalia to combat Islamic extremism and the resultant independence struggles in Somaliland and Puntland to the escalation of the situation in Darfur and the recent electoral crisis in Kenya, diverts vital attention and resources, both financial and military, away from the EASBRIG process. States like Burundi and Uganda, for example, are currently too preoccupied with their participation in the AU Mission in Somalia to earmark and prepare units for the regional standby force. Another example is the smoldering border conflict between Ethiopia and Eritrea which limits both states' ability (and willingness) to commit military capabilities to EASBRIG.

Second, this effect is further compounded by the fact that not all 14 EASBRIG member states are currently contributing to its operationalization. Given these and other problems such as the fact that several member states, including Ethiopia and Eritrea, increasingly drag their political tensions into the EASBRIG process,[43]

---

40   Interview with Colonel Reinhard Linz, EU MIL LO AU, 1 September 2007, Addis Ababa.

41   EASBRICOM, *Eastern Africa Standby Force Strategic Development Plan 2007–2015*, November 2007, Nairobi.

42   The EDSC has met five times since its inaugural meeting in June 2007. The author was present at the second meeting.

43   The struggle between Ethiopia and Kenya for regional hegemony, for example, has had a substantial impact on the location of EASBRIG elements, the appointment of EASBRICOM staff as well as the concept of a regional rapid deployment capability.

implementing the EASBRIG strategy and achieving its eight objectives will certainly be difficult.

However, the increasing institutionalization of EASBRICOM, the formulation of a detailed EASBRIG strategy and the inception of training cycles at the Regional Peace Support Training Centre (PSTC) in Nairobi are promising signs that the region's states will continue to overcome their inhibitions and cooperate on the establishment of their standby brigade. In addition, the high level of focused partner support, particularly from the United Kingdom, and the region's heartfelt ambition to prove its skeptics wrong are powerful assets for the operationalization of EASBRIG.[44]

West Africa's Regional Brigade

Several years before the AU decided on the establishment of the ASF, the ECOWAS Security Protocol of 1999 already called for the institutionalization of its Cease-Fire Monitoring Group (ECOMOG) in the form of a standby force of brigade-size consisting of specially-trained and equipped units of national armies ready for deployment at short notice.[45] This force was to be used in the case of (1) aggression or conflict within a member state, (2) a conflict between two or more member states, and (3) internal conflicts that threaten to trigger a humanitarian disaster, pose a serious threat to regional peace and security, result in serious and massive violations of human rights and/or follow the overthrow or attempted overthrow of a democratically elected government. Even though all 15 ECOWAS states pledged one battalion each to the proposed force, the implementation of the Protocol's provisions was delayed by the need for emergency responses to the armed conflicts in Liberia and Côte d'Ivoire and the political crisis in Togo.

By April 2004, all ECOMOG interventions had transitioned to UN operations and ECOWAS military planners were finally able to concentrate on developing the proposed standby force.[46] As the AU had agreed on the establishment of the ASF in the meantime, the 9th Meeting of the ECOWAS Defense and Security Commission (DSC) formulated a military strategy that provided some guidance to the establishment of the so-called ECOWAS Standby Force (ESF) as a regional component of the ASF. According to the strategy, the ESF was to consist of 6,500 troops divided into a Task Force of 1,500 troops (deployable within 30 days) and a Main Brigade of 5,000 troops (deployable within 90 days) all of whom were to be highly trained, equipped and prepared to deploy as directed in response to a crisis

---

44   For more information on the operationalization of EASBRIG see www.easbrig. org.

45   See ECOWAS, *Protocol Relating to the Mechanism for Conflict Prevention, Management, Resolution, Peacekeeping and Security*, 1999, Chapter III.

46   See Cilliers, Jakkie and Mark Malan, *Progress with the African Standby Force*, 5, http://www.iss.co.za/pubs/papers/98/Paper98.htm.

or threat to peace and security.[47] In order to coordinate the establishment of this force and adhere to the AU's call for the establishment of regional PLANELMs, ECOWAS (with Canadian support) set up a permanent Mission Planning and Management Cell (MPMC) in early 2005 to be responsible for strategic and operational planning.

In February 2005, the MPMC and a number of international military advisors formulated an operational framework which specified activity strands and benchmarks for the operationalization of the ESF. This framework was approved by the 12th Meeting of the DSC in April 2005. It contains the strategic and operational guidance to assist ECOWAS to sequence and coordinate its activities with the AU and its international partners. The operational framework bases the ESF force generation process on a tiered system in line with the AU Policy Framework for the Establishment of the ASF.

On the ESF readiness model Tier One represents the baseline capability of member states and incorporates their military forces and civilian police elements. For pledges from this pool to be acceptable to ECOWAS, they must be able to achieve an entry level of operational readiness in line with UN standards. Tier Two consists of a pool of 3,000 soldiers from which the Task Force of 1,500 troops (Tier Three) will be drawn on a case-by-case basis, depending on the specifics of the mission and the political situation at the time. Rotation from Tier One to Tier Two will be coordinated by the MPMC in consultation with the member states and is for a minimum period of two years which allows for extensive training. Tier Two units are under the direct authority of the ESF, but remain under the operational command of member states while held in readiness for ESF deployment.[48]

In July 2005, the 13th Meeting of the DSC endorsed the selection criteria for staff for the Task Force HQ as well as the site for the ECOWAS Peace Support Operations Logistics Depot at the Hastings Airfield in Freetown, Sierra Leone.[49] A second depot is to be established in Mali.

In November 2005, the 14th Meeting of the DSC approved a five-year training plan for the ESF in order to enable it to meet the challenges of peace support operations in the region.[50] Based on training modules consistent with UN standards, the endorsed program is categorized into individual, collective and specialized components and is to be executed at three regional training centres, the so-called Centres of Excellence. These centres are the Nigerian War College in Abuja (for strategic training), the Kofi Annan International Peacekeeping Training Centre

---

47   See Proceedings of the 9th Ordinary Session of the Defense and Security Committee, September 2004.

48   ECOWAS Secretariat, *ECOWAS Standby Force (ESF) Operational Framework*, 10 April 2005, para. 16.

49   See Proceedings of the 13th Meeting of the Defense and Security Committee, 10 July 2005, Yamoussoukro.

50   See Proceedings of the 14th Meeting of the Defense and Security Committee, 9 November 2005, Lome.

(KAIPTC) in Accra (for operational training) and the *Ecole Maintien de la Paix* in Bamako (for tactical training). In addition, the DSC urged all ECOWAS member states to participate in international exercises such as those provided by RECAMP or the US-led African Contingency Operations Training Assistance (ACOTA).

In June 2006, the Task Force HQ was operationalized and it is currently envisaged that the Task Force itself will become operational following its certification at the beginning of 2010 while the Main Brigade will follow the AU timetable for the operationalization of the ASF. The first joint exercise of the Task Force took place in Senegal in December 2007 and proved a great success for the participating countries.[51] While the ESF is thus certainly among the more advanced regional standby brigades, many challenges remain. As in Eastern Africa, the continuing presence of violent conflicts in Nigeria's River Delta, in Mali, Guinea, Niger and the Manu River Union as well as political tensions between many of the region's states endanger the progress achieved thus far. Despite the optimism spread by the publication of an ECOWAS Strategic Vision in June 2007 which envisions a borderless West Africa by 2020, not all historic suspicions between Anglophone and Francophone states and between the region's smaller states and the unquestionable hegemon Nigeria have yet been overcome so as to guarantee the smooth functioning of the ESF decision-making structures in times of crises.

Another problem relates to the financing of the ESF. Even though Article 16 of the ECOWAS Protocol Relating to the Mechanism for Conflict Prevention, Management and Resolution, Peacekeeping and Security provides for one percent of the annual levy of member states (0.5 per cent of GDP) to be used for an ECOWAS Peace Fund, financing the ESF remains a critical issue as not all member states pay their dues.

Despite these challenges, however, the operationalization of the ESF appears well on track.[52] Due to its extensive experience in force generation gained from the ECOMOG operations in Liberia and Sierra Leone as well as the substantial partner support from the US, the EU, France, Germany and the Scandinavian countries, ECOWAS has been able to earmark and train most of the necessary troops (6,200 out of 6,500) and has held several exercises throughout the region.[53] In addition, it has built a Task Force HQ in Abuja and has almost finalized its logistics concept. By all indications, ECOWAS has thus already come a long way in establishing its regional standby brigade.

---

51   Agence France-Press (AFP), *West African Troubleshooting Force starts Military Maneuvers*, 6 December 2007.

52   Official Report and Update by the German Military Advisor to ECOWAS, Colonel Klaus-Peter Koschny, 6 February 2008. Also, interview with Colonel Werner Rauber, Head of the Peacekeeping Study Section, Kofi Annan International Peacekeeping Training Centre, 2 February 2008.

53   See Report of the ECOWAS Workshop, *Lessons from ECOWAS Peacekeeping Operations: 1990–2004*, 11–12 February 2005, Accra.

Southern Africa's Regional Brigade

In the case of Southern Africa's regional standby brigade, the region's relatively long history of security cooperation and its institutional set-up within the framework of SADC simplified the initial stages of the establishment process considerably. Rather than having to go through the tedious process of conceiving, approving and implementing new structures for inter-state collaboration, the SADC members could use the forum provided by the Inter-State Defense and Security Committee (ISDSC) and its associated bodies to coordinate their activities and harmonize their policies. Following an ISDSC staff meeting in Lesotho in 2004, a Ministerial Defense Sub-Committee was mandated by the ISDSC to set up a technical team that would plan the establishment of a SADC Standby Force (SADCBRIG) as part of the ASF.

This team was able to build on previous attempts to set up a regional peacekeeping force in Southern Africa. As early as 1998, a SADC military delegation had visited the SHIRBRIG headquarters of the UN's Standby High-Readiness Brigade (SHIRBRIG) in Denmark in order to discuss ways to establish a SADC peacekeeping force. In March 1999, the ISDSC approved a roadmap for the establishment of such a force which was to consist of a mobile headquarters, three infantry battalions, one reconnaissance company, an engineer squadron, a logistical support company, a military police company, a civilian police component and an air and naval component.[54] The brigade was supposed to be established over a period of five years and include a standing brigade headquarters. Little, however, happened until the Strategic Indicative Plan of the Organ (SIPO) was eventually approved by SADC in August 2003. It provided for the development of a regional peace support operations capability based upon the standby arrangements of individual member states.[55]

With this background, the technical team quickly developed a roadmap for operationalization that was in line with the AU schedule for the ASF. By the end of 2005, SADC had established an interim PLANELM, approved a logistics support and financial management system and held its first combined military exercise.[56] In addition, member states had pledged over 6,000 troops to the proposed force and the Regional Peacekeeping Training Centre in Harare had developed training standards in line with the standards developed by the AU. Despite these successes, however, financial and logistical reasons forced the ISDSC during its meeting in Windhoek in July 2006 to postpone the official launch of SADCBRIG by one year. Consequently, SADCBRIG was officially launched by the SADC Summit on 17 August 2007 in Lusaka. At this summit the SADC Heads of States and

---

54   See Cilliers and Malan, *Progress with the African Standby Force*, 12.

55   SADC, *Strategic Indicative Plan for the Organ on Politics, Defense and Security*, August 2003, para. 8.3.1.

56   Statement by Brigadier-General Les Rudman to a Center for International Political Studies Seminar, 19 September 2005, Pretoria.

Government also signed a Memorandum of Understanding in order to establish and provide a legal basis for the operationalization of SADCBRIG.[57]

The MoU provides for a permanent and autonomous PLANELM headquartered at the SADC Secretariat in Gaberone (Article 6) as well as a Main Logistics Depot (MLD) also to be based in Botswana (Article 9). It also regulates member states' contributions to SADCBRIG (Article 7) as well as issues regarding command and control (Article 12), training and exercises (Article 13) and deployment, movement and transportation (Article 14). By April 2009, most of the provisions of the MoU had already been implemented.

However, despite the encouraging progress made so far, not all of the obstacles endangering the success of the project have yet been overcome. For example, at the moment the standby brigade is too dependent on the regional hegemon, South Africa (whose military forces are overstretched and eroded by a spiralling HIV crisis).[58] This dependence not only runs the risk of creating the impression that the force may become subservient to South Africa's national interest, but also detracts from what is supposed to be a collective effort and thus an expression of regional unity. It may also discourage increasingly constructive actors like Angola from further vital concessions.

Other potential problems include the political estrangement between SADC and its international donors over the role of Mugabe's Zimbabwe in the region, increasing tensions with the AU over the distribution of funds and competencies and a decline in the political will of member countries due to shifts in their cost-benefit considerations. The latter would have especially detrimental consequences for SADC's hopes of having its brigade ready for deployment by 2010, as political will is based less on the region's impressive-looking institutional arrangements and structures than on the collective commitment of its member states to the idea of permanent military cooperation.

Despite the many challenges outlined above, the prospects for effective military collaboration and integration in Southern Africa have never looked better. The region's states have made enormous progress toward creating a Southern African standby brigade by building on already-existing patterns of military cooperation and firmly anchoring the emerging entity within the stabilizing framework of SADC. Given that the region was characterized by deep divisions and rivalries until relatively recently, today's level of security cooperation in Southern Africa is a major achievement.

---

57 SADC, Memorandum of Understanding amongst the Southern African Development Community Member States on the Establishment of a Southern African Development Community Standby Brigade, 17 August 2007, Lusaka.

58 Studies have shown that over 40 per cent of South Africa's National Defence Forces are affected by the disease in one way or another. See Stephan Elbe, 'Strategic Implications of HIV/AIDS', *Adelphi Papers*, no. 357 (2003).

The Other Regional Brigades

While EASBRIG, the ESF and SADCBRIG are generally ahead of the ASF operationalization timeline, both the northern and central region are lagging behind. However, contrary to prevailing opinion, both regions have quietly begun to catch up.

As in Eastern Africa, the existence of overlapping regional organizations forced the states of Northern Africa to establish an independent coordination mechanism outside of existing RECs for the operationalization of their standby brigade. In November 2005, the Chiefs of Defense Staff of Algeria, Egypt, Libya, Mauritania, Western Sahara and Tunisia met in Tripoli in order to sign a Memorandum of Understanding on the Establishment of the North Africa Region Capability (NARC) in the African Standby Force.[59] The MoU not only provides for the establishment of a permanent PLANELM (Article 13), a logistics base (Article 14) and a Brigade HQ (Article 16), but Appendix 2 also already details some offers of contributions by member states. Libya, for example, offered a light infantry battalion, a signal company and 30 military observers. Egypt reiterated its previous offer of a supported infantry battalion, a reconnaissance unit, a signal unit, an engineering unit and up to 30 military observers. Algeria offered to participate with two light infantry battalions, a signal unit, a military police unit, a reconnaissance group and up to 40 military observers.[60]

Since the signing of the MoU in late 2005, the Northern African states have participated in the AU's central workshops, set up the Brigade HQ in Egypt and the PLANELM in Libya and have designated the Cairo Centre for Conflict Resolution and Peacekeeping as regional training centre. Even though the progress of establishing the standby brigade is definitely slower than in all other regions, the operationalization of NARC and the joint participation in continental ASF initiatives such as the African Peace Support Training Association (APSTA) are promising steps for the notoriously rivalrous states of North Africa.[61]

In Central Africa, the process of establishing a regional peacekeeping capability has been ongoing since the formation of the Council for Peace and Security in Central Africa (COPAX) in February 1999. The COPAX Protocol also provided for the establishment of a non-permanent *Force Multinational d'Afrique Central* (FOMAC) 'to accomplish missions of peace, security and humanitarian relief'.[62]

---

59   See NARC, *Memorandum of Understanding on the Establishment of the North Africa Region Capability in the African Standby Force*, 16 November 2005, Tripoli.

60   See NARC, *Memorandum of Understanding on the Establishment of the North Africa Region Capability in the African Standby Force*, 16 November 2005, Tripoli, Appendix 2.

61   Interview with Captain (SA Navy) John Potgieter, Military Consultant to the AU PSOD, 21 September 2007, Addis Ababa.

62   ECCAS, *Protocol Relating to the Council for Peace and Security in Central Africa (COPAX)*, 25–26 February 2007, Yaoundé, Articles 25 and 26.

In June 2002, the ECCAS Ministers of Defense and Security finally agreed on the Standing Orders for FOMAC.[63] These orders defined the force in more detail as 'composed of national inter-service, police and gendarmerie contingents from ECCAS member states of the Economic Community of Western African States' (Article 1). Annex A detailed the military composition of the force and put its total strength down as 3,171 troops. In October 2003, the ECCAS Chiefs of Defense Staff met in Brazzaville in order to discuss the incorporation of FOMAC into the ASF concept proposed by the AU. They agreed on the establishment of several working groups to work out the details of the force as well as on a joint peacekeeping training centre and the organization of joint military exercises every two years.

From July 2003 to December 2004, ECCAS held six meetings at the levels of experts, Chiefs of Defense Staff and Ministers of COPAX. At these meetings four issues were adopted, namely (1) the structure of the ECCAS PLANELM, (2) the structure and tables of equipment for the standby brigade as well as its revised strength of 2,177 troops, (3) an action plan for the establishment of the PLANELM and the standby brigade, and (4) the exercise paper for the multinational training exercise known as Bahl El Ghazel 2005.[64] In April 2005, the Chiefs of Defense Staff met again and in light of the volatile security situation in the region revised the strength of the brigade back up to 3,600 troops. Since then, ECCAS has made remarkable progress in establishing its standby force even though Rwanda had to withdraw from the community in order to reduce its integration engagements to fewer regional blocs. FOMAC not only participated in several peacekeeping missions in the Central African Republic (FOMUC I-III), but in November 2006 also led the fifth RECAMP cycle peacekeeping exercise in Cameroon and in 2007 finally operationalized a permanent Brigade HQ in Gabon. In January 2009, ECCAS held a three day seminar in Kinshasa to discuss possible ways to further speed up the operationalization of its brigade.

Remaining Challenges for the Operationalization of the ASF

The decentralized nature of the ASF means that there are two very different types of challenges remaining. At the continental level, the AU's lack of institutional capacity remains the most serious impediment to the effective operationalization of the force. A study for the European Parliament conducted in 2008 has shown that the AU Commission and its various departments continue to be severely understaffed and hampered by a high staff turnover rate, widespread lack of training, cumbersome recruitment procedures and an inefficient top-down

---

63   ECCAS, *Standing Orders for the Central African Multinational Force (FOMAC)*, 17 June 2002, Malabo.

64   Cilliers and Malan, 'Progress with the African Standby Force', 16.

management structure.[65] As a result, crucial parts of the African Union are simply not able to cope with their workload and the organization's absorption capacity for international support measures has declined accordingly.

Over the last few years, international actors like the EU have begun to address some of the AU's capacity constraints. Since its creation in 2004, the EU–AU military liaison office situated within the European Commission Delegation to Ethiopia has been at the forefront of these efforts. Led by Colonel Reinhard Linz, the office has assisted with the establishment of the AU's Peace Support Operations Department and *ad hoc* planning cells for the AU missions in Darfur and Somalia, organized the formulation and translation of key ASF documents on the basis of EU Battlegroup concepts and helped with the integration of liaison officers from various regional organizations into the AU structures. More recently, the European Commission has earmarked another €100 million for capacity-building and has established a separate delegation to the AU Headquarters in Addis Ababa in order to improve its ability to identify AU needs and coordinate EU support activities. However, far too much of the international support still goes straight to the AU Commission's Department for Peace and Security and its various subdivisions like the Peace Support Operations Department without helping to improve the institutional capacity of less glamorous but equally essential departments like finance and human resources.

The regional challenges are very different, mainly because the need for institutional capacity-building, though existent, is not as pronounced and urgent as it is at the continental level. For one, almost all of the regional organizations have been in existence for much longer than the AU and thus have already had some time to establish appropriate institutional structures and processes. But also, in the continent's envisaged multi-layered security architecture institutional capacity is more important for the AU in its role as legitimizing institution and coordinating body than for the regions which have to carry the brunt of the military burden. As a result, international support at the regional level should really focus on enabling the five regions to operationalize their ASF component brigades in line with the agreed schedule. Two political sensitivities, however, prevent partners from doing so effectively.

First, even though the lack of inter-operable military equipment remains the most serious impediment to the operationalization of the ASF at the regional level, the desire to adhere to the OECD's criteria for Official Development Assistance prevents many donors from providing such hardware. While a certain reservation about funding military equipment is perfectly understandable given the meagre human rights record of many African regimes, the outfitting of regionally-managed depots with armoured personnel carriers and transport helicopters, for example,

---

65   Vines, Alex and Roger Middleton (2008), *Options for the EU to Support the African Peace and Security Architecture*. Study for the European Parliament's Committee on Foreign Affairs. Brussels: European Parliament.

would already go a long way in addressing one of the most serious needs of the ASF without running the risk of (national) misuse of the provided material.

Second, the same political sensitivities that are responsible for the restrictions on the use of aid for military purposes have also led to an overemphasis on the provision of peacekeeping training. The fact that such training is easy-to-sell to domestic constituencies because of its perceived harmlessness has led many Western actors to focus their support on its provision regardless of the actual needs of the African states contributing to the ASF. Even though such initiatives are certainly useful in the long-run, peacekeeping training simply is not the requirement of the moment, especially so as the relevant experience of many African soldiers is often fresher and more substantial than that of their trainers (after all, African countries are among the most frequent troop contributors to UN peace operations). Instead of providing peacekeeping training years before the envisaged operationalization of the ASF, partners should focus their attention on material and military infrastructure support to those regions that lack behind in the creation of their component brigades.

Conclusion

However brief this discussion of the ASF and its regional components has been, it nonetheless allows for a number of tentative conclusions with respect to the extent and quality of contemporary inter-African security cooperation. First, the establishment of the regional brigades and their continental coordination mechanism necessitates an extraordinarily high level of inter-state cooperation including difficult decisions regarding political processes and military details. The list of tasks associated with the establishment of such a brigade is daunting. The *Guidelines for the Establishment of a Regional Peace Support Operations Standby Brigade* compiled by the AU's PSOD detail 84 specific tasks to be completed during the operationalization. They range from the creation of a funding mechanism and an early warning system (Tasks 6 and 7) to the establishment of a standby roster of at least 240 police officers (Task 72) and the development of a regional training policy (Task 78). In addition to these region-specific duties, each region also has to participate in collective (that is, continental) tasks, such as developing a joint command and control structure and synchronizing logistical infrastructure. These requirements place a heavy burden on the regions and the states within them. Even though some of them have a history of military cooperation and, in the case of ECOMOG, of military integration, the creation of a compatible standby brigade requires new levels of military interaction as well as considerable political will and financial commitment. In order to ensure that the various national contingents follow standardized operational procedures, for example, states not only have to raise the level of interaction between their military decision-makers and institutionalize some sort of working relationship, but also to collaborate in extremely sensitive areas such as Command, Control, Communication, Intelligence and Surveillance (C^3IS) systems.

Second, despite these difficulties and even though the five regional brigades are at widely varying stages of development, reaching from SADC's already fully operational force to Northern Africa's nascent capability, it appears as if most of the continent's states have overcome their inhibitions to cooperate with each other in military matters and have joined the collective effort. The basic factors responsible for the failures of pre-ASF initiatives as well as the reasons for the success of the current attempt are easy to discern. Whether one talks of a high command, a military standby system or any of the other known appellations referring to some joint African force, it seems that the underlying problem is the inevitable tension between states' perceived need to maintain full control over national capabilities in order to keep peace at home and project strength abroad and the necessity of relinquishing at least certain aspects of their national command authority to a supra-national body like the AU? inherent in the principle of a Pan-African force. Many of the previous attempts at establishing such a force failed because their institutional setup was not able to resolve this and similar tensions and was thus considered a threat by many states. Through its unique reliance on regional frameworks, the ASF's likelihood of failure in this area is significantly lower than that of its predecessors. The decentralized character of the ASF ensures that the states feel ownership in the process of establishing a continental peacekeeping capability and allows the AU to incorporate all states into a common framework without infringing on their national and regional authority or responsibilities. This almost symbiotic relationship not only reduces the risk of competition between the continental, regional and national levels of inter-African security cooperation, but also increases the stakes all actors have in the process, builds up helpful peer group pressure and thus reduces the chances of failure.[66]

Nonetheless, tensions continue to exist and are not likely to disappear any time soon. Consequently, the AU and its international supporters need to ensure that the bridges built over the past years are not torn down in a moment of crisis, but are instead continuously reinforced. In addition, the AU still has to find persuasive answers to many of the arguments raised against previous Pan-African security initiatives, namely, the difficulty of agreeing on a workable funding arrangement (in order to decrease and eventually erase the ASF's dependence on international financial aid) and ensuring the force's interoperability. However, given the level of cooperation achieved thus far, these objectives do not seem out of reach.

---

66   For a detailed discussion of the impact of competing regionalism(s) on Africa's emerging security architecture see Benedikt Franke, 'Competing Regionalisms in Africa and the Continent's Emerging Security Architecture', *African Studies Quarterly* 10, no. 1 (2007).

Chapter 12

A 'Public' Duty? Building Citizen Focused Accountability and Oversight Mechanisms in Global Peace and Security Governance

Michael Hammer[1]

At the heart of globalization runs a sometimes contradictory and all but linear process of increasing densification of exchanges in ideas, knowledge, goods, services, and people from all backgrounds and across all over the world. Globalization is thus a truly public process in which decisions by individuals or organizations, often taken in polycentric[2] rather than hierarchical ways, are of mutual relevance to everyone involved. Yet while the reality of globalization as a measurable process of integration and exchange is largely uncontested, there is less unity of thought about whether the in consequence emerging, and growingly contingent Global Public Sphere is in need of global principles and mechanisms along which the impact of globalization on people can be purposefully guided at a global level in ways that ensure respect for human rights and access to opportunity for all.

In addition to this, policy areas which are key for developments at the international level: national foreign policy and decision-making concerning the use of force outside the national boundaries, are to date largely excluded from the level of democratic accountability and oversight applied to other areas of policy. In

---

1   Michael Hammer is Executive Director of the One World Trust, an independent UK based think-tank conducting research into practical ways to make global governance more accountable. He may be reached via email: mhammer@oneworldtrust.org.

2   Whereas traditional hierarchical ways of decision making, mostly found within single organizations, involve clearly defined and linear systems of aggregating evidence, mostly upstream from bottom up to feed into top level decision making, polycentric models of production of knowledge and policy formation involve more fluid and non linear circulation of information and interaction between a broader range of stakeholders. Global governance is by its very nature a multi-stakeholder process in which many not necessarily connected parties contribute to the build up of understanding and eventually decisions. For a more detailed discussion of linear versus complex policy formation processes see Whitty, Brendan (2008): *Accountability Principles for Research Organizations* (London: One World Trust), pp. 15–16; and on the relationship between accountability and legitimacy in polycentric regulatory regimes see Balck, Julia (2008): *Constructing and Contesting Legitimacy and Accountability in Polycentric Regulatory Regimes*, in: Regulation and Governance, no. 2: 137–64.

many countries, independent of their form of government but importantly including democracies, the prerogative to decide on the use of force abroad resides with the executive. In the UK for instance, pending current proposals for constitutional reform,[3] the Prime Minister, empowered by the Royal Prerogative, is still under no formal obligation to consult Parliament prior to taking the country to war.[4] In fact the parliamentary debate and vote on taking action in Iraq in 2003 was the first time such a debate was held, and the vote was technically non-binding. In France, the leadership of the President on issues of policy, including defence and foreign affairs,[5] is combined with a lack of ability of parliament to hold the President to account, effectively removing these areas from regular democratic oversight.[6]

The controversy about the Responsibility to Protect (R2P), illustrated, for instance, in relation to the situation in Burma and Zimbabwe, demonstrates that the question of the use of force and the way decisions are made about it are amongst the most critical issues of our time. Having emerged from the broader human security debate of the 1990s, the R2P as a doctrine seeks to address in particular the question when a state fails or is unwilling to protect its citizens from widespread and systematic human rights abuses, who and in what form should and can take action to fulfil obligations for their protection under international law. While the International Commission on Intervention and State Sovereignty (ICISS)[7] focused the application of the R2P on the prevention of genocide, war crimes, crimes against humanity and ethnic cleansing (the latter not being a category defined under international criminal law), it did not pronounce itself on the question whether crimes against humanity considered under the R2P had to be limited to situations of, or to be connected to, armed conflict. In fact, the International Criminal Tribunal for Rwanda decision in the Akayesu case of 1998 clarified that crimes against humanity did not have to be connected to

---

3   For the consultation see the original government proposals at UK HMG (2007): War powers and treaties. Limiting executive powers, Consultation paper CP 26/07, 25 October 2007. A draft Constitutional Renewal Bill was put through pre legislative scrutiny in early 2008, and has come with revisions in July 2009 back on the legislative agenda. The current proposal is silent on the question of war powers (see Constitutional Reform and Governance Bill 142–08–09, http://www.publications.parliament.uk/pa/cm200809/cmbills/142/2009142.pdf).

4   See *A World of Difference* (2009), Parliamentary Oversight of British Foreign Policy (London: One World Trust), p. 7.

5   Nicolas Sarkozy: Une démocratie irréprochable, Speech on the French institutions, delivered at Epinal, 12 July 2007, http://www.elysee.fr/elysee/elysee.fr/francais/interventions/2007/juillet/allocution_a_epinal_sur_le_theme_de_la_democratie_irreprochable.79092.html.

6   Article 34 of the Constitution of 1958, as modified in June 2008 limits the oversight functions of the Assemblée Nationale to the government, excluding the President, http://www.assemblee-nationale.fr/connaissance/constitution.asp.

7   International Commission on Intervention and State Sovereignty (2001): The Responsibility to Protect, http://www.iciss.ca/pdf/Commission-Report.pdf.

armed conflict.[8] This opens up the possibility for further exploring the R2P in cases of gross violations of economic, social and cultural rights (ESC rights) for instance resulting from states neglecting their duty to fulfil citizens' rights under the International Covenant on Economic, Social and Cultural Rights, such as following the Cyclone Nargis in Burma in 2008 or years of misguided economic policies in Zimbabwe. However, the mainstream of the R2P debate has focused on human rights abuses committed in, and in connection with, armed conflict. This interpretation also underlies the unanimous commitment of all UN member states in the 2005 World Summit outcome document to the R2P doctrine.[9] Critics of the application of the doctrine, particularly if connected to ESC rights, are concerned about opening the possibility for political abuse of the doctrine especially by veto wielding UN Security Council members.[10] Importantly the R2P doctrine seeks to move from issues of intervention to responsibilities associated with sovereignty, and support that the international community can offer ahead of, during and after periods of widespread and systematic human rights abuses. The question of the use of force, while the most divisive, is framed very much as a means of last resort.

Different understandings of state sovereignty and the transformation of this concept are, in particular in conjunction with the debate about the justiciability of ESC rights, also shaped by the progressive adoption of the notion of standard of due diligence in the interpretation of international human rights standards. As more questions have to be asked about the proactive responsibilities of the state as primary duty bearer to respect, protect and fulfil rights under duties of care for the people living within its boundaries, more clarity is also needed about the mechanisms of public accountability that can be used to hold decision-makers who affect the public to account and the broader principles that underpin these.

Defining Accountability in the Context of Peace and Security Governance

For many accountability is a nebulous term, often applied only to specific and technical issues, such as finances, and regarded purely as an ex-post tool of evaluation or judicial review. However, in a political context, using a definition

---

8   Prosecutor v. Akayesu, Judgment, No. ICTR-96-4-T, 02 September 1998, para. 565.

9   'Each individual State has the responsibility to protect its populations from genocide, war crimes, ethnic cleansing and crimes against humanity. This responsibility entails the prevention of such crimes, including their incitement, through appropriate and necessary means. We accept that responsibility and will act in accordance with it ...', UN World Summit (2005), Outcome Document, para. 138.

10   Reflected for instance in the introductory statement to the debate on the R2P on 23 July 2009 by the President of the 63rd UN General Assembly Miguel d'Escoto Brockman', pp. 2–3, http://www.un.org/ga/president/63/interactive/protect/conceptnote.pdf.

by Mark Boven,[11] it can be better defined as an actor's obligation to explain and justify his/her conduct to a significant other, such as an independent accountability forum. In Boven's definition accountability is characterized by openness, and creates a social relationship between those exercising power and those affected by decisions. This is underpinned by frameworks of understanding accountability, such as proposed by the One World Trust,[12] which focus on stakeholders as those affected by decisions and identify different overlapping dimensions as contributing to fuller accountability, such as transparency, participation, evaluation, and complaint and response.[13]

Yet this is not static: research conducted on the basis of the above framework by the One World Trust assessing the accountability capabilities of powerful international institutions from all sectors demonstrates that many global organizations recognize accountability to be an ongoing process of balancing relationships. Using the One World Trust's definition of 'Accountability [as] the processes through which an organization makes a commitment to respond to and balance the needs of stakeholders in its decision making processes and activities, and delivers against that commitment',[14] the people who are most affected by actions and decisions are thus put by a growing number of actors, at least conceptually, if not always in practice, at the centre of the equation.[15] Critical to the promotion of accountability is, however, also the clarification of ownership of the issues at stake. Here, David Held asserts that one of the bigger challenges is the 'fundamental lack of ownership of global public problems at global level', leading to both competition of jurisdiction and lack of engagement as issues can fall between agencies.[16] A powerful illustration of his point is, for instance, situations of imbalance of influence between those excluded from access to basic public services and access to rights resulting from poverty and repressive

---

11   Boven, Mark (2005), *Public Accountability*, in Ferlie, Ewan; Lynn, Laurence E.; Pollitt, Christopher; eds (2005), *The Oxford Handbook of Public Management*, p. 185. Mark Boven is Professor of Public Administration and Research Director at the Utrecht School of Governance.

12   Founded in 1951 by UK parliamentarians the One World Trust is an independent think-tank focusing on research on accountability principles and their practical application for the reform of global organizations, the engagement of citizens, and international law and regulation.

13   Blagescu, Monica; de las Casas, Lucy; Lloyd, Robert (2005), *Pathways to Accountability. The Global Accountability Project Framework* (London: One World Trust).

14   Lloyd, Robert; Oatham, Jeff; Hammer, Michael (2007), The 2007 Global Accountability Report, One World Trust, London, p. 6.

15   Scholte, Jan Aart (2004), *Civil Society and Democratically Accountable Global Governance*, in: *Government and Opposition*, 2004, p. 215.

16   Held, David (2003), *Democratic Accountability and Political Effectiveness from a Cosmopolitan Perspective*, Paper for the Centre for the Study of Global Governance, p. 9 (also published in 2004 in Government and Opposition, pp. 364–91).

government, and those purporting to support them. By their own statements the purpose of many global organizations, including intergovernmental organizations and international NGOs is the delivery of global public goods. The World Bank says about itself, for instance, 'Our mission is to help developing countries and their people reach the goals by working with our partners to alleviate poverty'.[17] Oxfam International states that it is '… an international group of independent non-governmental organizations dedicated to fighting poverty and related injustice around the world'.[18] Yet both organizations, which are by no means alone in this situation, are largely funded by people and states where poverty and exclusion and repression are not primary issues, and both struggle to respond to this imbalance with truly effective accountability mechanisms that can resolve the legitimacy challenges that arise from their organizational structure and practice. In the context of the R2P the issues may even get more problematic. While since 2005 there has been a global commitment to the doctrine, neglect by an individual state actor of its duties to its citizens does not necessarily result in action being taken, and hence, such as in Darfur tens of thousands die because the lay of the land in terms of interests at global level that lead to inaction have nothing to do with people's needs.

The inherent accountability challenges associated with this situation mean not only that a real need of people may not get dealt with, but also that no institution can be effectively held to account for this by the people affected by the resulting neglect.

Clearly, as in many other cases regarding peace and security governance, the key stakeholders in such cases are the people living with and affected by conflict, defined on a broader rather than a narrower human security concept.[19] Investigations by the Uppsala Conflict Data Program (UCDP) into the changing nature of conflict provide evidence that while the number of conflicts[20] appears to have peaked in the early to mid 1990s, the proportion of internal conflicts in the total number of conflicts is growing, including 'one sided violence'.[21] However it is worth noting that the UCDP first does not record deaths when the perpetrator cannot be established, and second that because of the nature of one-sided violence many deaths will go unreported anyway. The Human Security Project concludes

---

17   World Bank (2009), About Us – Working for a World Free of Poverty, http://web.worldbank.org/WBSITE/EXTERNAL/EXTABOUTUS/0,,content MDK:20040565~menuPK:34563~pagePK:34542~piPK:36600~theSitePK:29708,00.html.

18   Oxfam International (2009), Mission Statement, http://www.oxfam.org/en/about/what/mission.

19   Human Security Centre (2005), *The Human Security Report. War and Peace in the 21st Century*, University of British Columbia, p. VIII.

20   Figures for internal, internationalized, interstate, and extra-systemic conflicts as defined by the UCDP taken together.

21   Harbom, Lotta; Wallensteen, Peter (2005), Armed Conflict and Its International Dimensions 1946–2004, in: 2005 *Journal of Peace Research*, vol. 42, no. 5, 2005: 623–35.

from this that there is a very high level of unknown civilian deaths resulting from such armed violence and conflicts.[22] It is therefore highly likely that the higher the proportion of internal conflicts in the number of conflicts overall, the higher the number of civilians affected is going to be as well. In addition, reports show that the abuse suffered by civilians in armed conflict extends beyond death or injury directly attributable to the use of force, and affecting in particular women and girls, reaches across the whole spectrum of civil and political, economic, social and cultural rights, such as obvious in the conflict in the Democratic Republic of Congo, or Darfur, where the number of civilian deaths resulting from lack of access to health care exceeds those dying of actual physical violence against a person in conflict.[23]

When developing effective public accountability, including in peace and security governance, key questions that need to be addressed include therefore not just who knows what, who decides, and who has the mandate to decide and to review, but also who is accountable to whom for what actions (or inaction) and their consequences. Built on the four dimensions of transparency, participation, evaluation, and complaints and response, accountability is thus more than merely creating a reporting relationship. It has to go beyond ad hoc arrangements and should follow a set of good practice principles which inform the individual accountability framework developed to suit the specific peacekeeping or protection mission context and its long-term objectives. At the end, the aim of accountability in peace and security governance is to enable progress on the substantive issues at stake: ending conflict, establishing justice, achieving durable peace and rebuilding societies. Making sure that it works for and serves the people most affected is not up for negotiation.

Accountability in the Operationalization of the Responsibility to Protect

The Responsibility to Protect doctrine places an extended set of duties onto the international community: to prevent conflict, to react in response to war crimes, crimes against humanity, genocide and ethnic cleansing, and to rebuild societies after such acts. The doctrine proposes that these responsibilities kick in when an individual national state, through the government, fails to discharge its obligations under international human rights standards and international humanitarian law. This includes obligations resulting from standards of due diligence: to respect, protect and fulfil human rights of its citizens, also when under threat from non-state actors. As the outgoing UN High Commissioner for Human Rights Louise Arbour argues, neglect of duties of care have to be conceptualized as human rights abuses

22   Mack, Andrew; et al. (2007), *Human Security Brief 2007*, Simon Fraser University, Vancouver, p. 42.
23   See for instance Human Rights Watch (2002), *The War within the War. Sexual Violence Against Women and Girls in Eastern Congo*, New York, p. 17ff.

when their impact is widespread and systematic, and become an international concern: 'Whether we call it responsibility to protect or anything else, States do have a responsibility ... to extent (sic) protection [to the people on their territory] equally against genocide as against famine, disease, ignorance, deprivation of the basic necessities of life, discrimination and lack of freedom. To suggest otherwise would be a very regressive and legally untenable position.'[24]

The doctrine thus defines a relationship of public accountability between citizens and duty bearers which have power over them. The prime duty bearer is the state but eventually also the international community, embodied by the United Nations, who may act either directly, under Chapter VI and VII of the Charter, or under Chapter VIII task relevant regional organizations to act on its behalf, while retaining overall authority under sections 52 and 53 of the Charter, which empower the UN to seek the collaboration of regional organizations to discharge its duty to maintain regional peace and stability.

The role of regional and sub-regional actors in prevention and response to conflict has thus been promoted for several reasons in particular since the 1990s: their perceived advantages in detecting early warning signs, existing communication lines with neighbouring governments and armed groups, and shared political and cultural understandings of interaction. It is also true that neighbouring countries have a major interest in regional stability, since its absence will affect their own. The 2005 World Summit Outcome Document therefore gives, in the context of country specific peacebuilding, special responsibility to 'relevant regional organizations' in mobilizing appropriate action when national authorities fail.[25] In extension of this approach, for instance, the European Union has set up its support for the African Union in form of the African Peace Facility, which received in its first seven year phase from 2000–2007 EUR 440 million, and in its current two year phase from 2008–2010 is planned to receive EUR 300 million. The vast majority of this funding has been used to support R2P akin African Peace Support Operations in different African countries, mostly under a combined AU and UN mandate.[26]

Mandates Give Formal Authority, but Who is in Charge?

While the UN Charter is very clear that the locus of responsibility to authorize missions to guarantee regional and global peace and security rests firmly with the UN, the question of who may be best placed, equipped and prepared to implement

---

24   Arbour, Louise (2008), The Responsibility to Protect as a Duty of Care in International Law and Practice, in: *Review of International Studies* 34/2008: 458.

25   United Nations (2005), 2005 World Summit Outcome Document, A/RES/60/1, art. 71, 93, 100 (referring to country-specific peacebuilding commissions).

26   Pirozzi, Nicoletta (2009), EU Support to African Security Architecture – Funding and Training Components, European Institute for Security Studies, Occasional Paper No. 76, p. 10 (re R2P), and p. 26 (re funding).

and sustain peace and security missions in individual situations or regional contexts is a different matter. In many cases individual nations, or groups of concerned nations, are mandated to serve as agents on behalf of the UN. At times, and often problematically, this occurs only ex-post. The perceptions of legitimacy of such missions span wide territory: in the case of the 2003 French-led EU mission to the Democratic Republic of Congo (Artemis) in Ituri, the northeastern part of the country, both the DRC government and most international observers welcomed the intervention. The mission was requested by the UN Secretary General Kofi Annan to stabilize the security situation in and around the district capital Bunia, authorized in UN SC Resolution 1484. Conflict had erupted between ethnic militias after visible weaknesses in mandate, troop strength, and equipment of the existing UN peacekeeping force MONUC, inability of the government of the DRC to intervene and the withdrawal of the Ugandan army from the area. Large-scale killings and displacement ensued. The mission was limited in time, focus and participation and led to an overall positive feedback. In the case of Iraq, the equipment of the US/UK led coalition with a mandate by the UN following the invasion was regarded by some as inevitable. Yet the ex-post legitimacy conferred on the presence of the coalition was in a way farcical for a UN Security Council which previously could not agree on the use of force that brought them into the country in the first place. In Darfur, even the AU/UN hybrid mission (UNAMID) faces the challenge of a government in Khartoum which is de facto hostile to their presence. The national government hence seeks to undermine the mission and confound the forming of joined up international opinion. So far their tactic has had some success as the views on international involvement in Africa are split amongst leaders. The AU request for suspending the ICC prosecutor's charges against President Omar Hassan Al Bashir over systematic and widespread human rights abuses confirms this.[27] Formally indicted for war crimes and crimes against humanity by the ICC in March 2009, Sudanese President Al Bashir has effectively been given by the African Union countries a safe haven as the organization declared in early July 2009 that it would not implement the arrest warrant, despite the majority of African states being bound by the ICC Statutes to do so.[28]

However, amongst regional organizations outside the European context, the African Union is certainly currently the most advanced in terms of the formal powers and instruments it has equipped itself with, especially since the creation of its Peace and Security Council in 2003.[29] It builds very much on experiences

---

27   Communiqué of the 142nd Meeting of the African Union Peace and Security Council, 142nd Meeting 21 July 2008 Addis Ababa, Psc/Min/Comm(CXLII).

28   African Union Decision On The Meeting Of African States Parties To The Rome Statute Of The International Criminal Court (ICC), Doc. Assembly/AU/13(XIII), Assembly/AU/Dec.245(XIII).

29   African Union (2002): Constitutive Act, Art 4(h) states 'the right of the Union to intervene in a Member State pursuant to a decision of the Assembly in respect of grave circumstances, namely: war crimes, genocide and crimes against humanity'; and African

gathered in particular by the Economic Community Of West African States (ECOWAS), which doted itself with a detailed peace and security mechanism already in 1999.[30] Other regional or similar organizations such as the Association of South East Asian Nations (ASEAN),[31] the Commonwealth Association, the Francophonie,[32] the Southern Africa Development Community (SADC),[33] or the Arab League, are catching up and increasingly committing themselves to playing a role in conflict prevention amongst their member states.

Despite these mostly general mandates and commitments in most cases the question of how a regional body's work in the area of conflict prevention or even active military or policing missions to guarantee peace and security in another country is accountable to the overarching authority of the UN, however, remains unclear. While the SADC for instance clearly states this high authority of the UN, the AU, acknowledging in UN-level discourse the importance of cooperation with the UN, claims a broader right to determine regional responses including the use of force on its own, echoed by the ASEAN, giving clear preference to regional settlement. Yet, as Louise Arbour points out, while geographical proximity strengthens the practical pressures to respond, international law does not absolve the wider international community beyond the immediate sub-region from its responsibility to engage as well.[34] This situation of tension between what is legally binding and a politically preferred process therefore results in practice and policy in frequently ad hoc engagement with crises, with the international community and regional organizations negotiating often late roles and responsibilities, without clear lines of accountability if action fails or does not live up to principles of international law. Over-reliance on the role of regional organizations in the operationalization of the Responsibility to Protect and peacekeeping therefore

Union (2002): Protocol relating to the establishment of the Peace and Security Council of the African Union, Durban, 9 July 2002.

30   ECOWAS (1999): Protocol relating to the mechanism for conflict prevention, management, resolution, peace-keeping and security, Lomé 10 December 1999.

31   Association of South East Asian Nations (1976): Treaty of Amity and Cooperation in South-East Asia, Bali/Indonesia 24/02/1976, Chapter 1 (Purpose and Principles), Article 2, and the July 2007 decision of the ASEAN Forum to create a quick reaction group, http://www.aseanregionalforum.org/News/tabid/59/newsid399/48/Default.aspx, accessed 25 July 2008.

32   Déclaration de Saint-Boniface (Canada) of the Francophonie, adopted 14 May 2006.

33   See Preamble of the Southern Africa Development Community (2001): Protocol on Politics, Defence and Security Co-operation, and Article 4 of the Southern Africa Development Community (2001), Consolidated Text of The Treaty of the Southern African Development Community, as amended in Blantyre.

34   Arbour, Louise (2008), The Responsibility to Protect as a Duty of Care in International Law and Practice, in: *Review of International Studies* 34/2008, p. 454, referring to the 26 February 2007 Judgement of the International Court of Justice in the case of Bosnia and Herzegovina v. Serbia and Montenegro, General List no. 91.

bears some risks that could be addressed by more strongly focusing on the accountability of the governance arrangements they interact with global bodies.[35]

Who Holds Whom to Account?

While one could argue that with increasing practice these relationships between different organizations and levels of international authority are bound to gradually clarify themselves, they suffer, however, from an additional systemic weakness which at least challenges, if not undermines the principle of stakeholder accountability. To date, in none of the treaties and protocols is there specific mention of the role of people in peace and security governance, for instance through parliaments or civil society engagement. Determining the use of force, as is clear for instance from the way responsibilities are allocated to no other institution but executive governments and their agents in the ECOWAS peace and security mechanism, remains problematically exclusively within the remit of executive power with no mention of citizens' participation in the oversight of such policy development and decision-making. This is particularly worth noting as experienced peace negotiators and peacebuilders such as Marack Goulding point out the value of civil society involvement while respecting the need to conduct some of the earlier stages in the process under strict confidentiality.[36]

The formal recognition of initially eight sub-regional organizations in Africa by the AU which is currently in course would establish for the first time a formal framework to govern the relationship between the regional and sub-regional level and assert the AU's role as a continental umbrella group to which the sub-regional organizations stand in a relation of subsidiaries. This is an important step in the right direction, although still fraught with numerous practical and political problems.[37] Yet it still only addresses the relationships of different multilateral bodies within the region. The development of UNAMID as a hybrid AU/UN mission in Darfur, including the lack of clarity of command and control structures and reporting lines, demonstrates the continuing absence of a systematic and principle based approach to building accountability frameworks in peace and security governance that regulate the relationship between the regional and the global level, despite a commitment to '… the development of a stronger and more structured relationship between the UN Security Council (SC) and the AU Peace and Security Council (PSC), inter alia on conflict prevention, management and resolution, peacekeeping

35   See also Bateman, Maeve; Hammer, Michael (2007), Don't Call Me, I'll Call You? Challenges and Opportunities to Realising the Responsibility to Protect in Regional Peacekeeping, One World Trust Briefing no. 107, London.

36   Goulding, Marack (2002), Public Participation and International Peacemaking, in: Barnes, Catherine; ed. (2002), *Owning the Process. Public Participation in Peacemaking*, Accord Issue 13, London, Conciliation Resources, pp. 86–9.

37   Ajayi, Titilope (2008), The UN, AU and ECOWAS – a Triangle for Peace in West Africa?, FES Briefing paper 11, November 2008, p. 8.

and peacebuilding, including Post Conflict Reconstruction and Development, as well as sharing of information on conflict situations on the agendas of the two bodies'.[38] Indeed, formal and public reporting of the AU (including through its PSC) to the UN on its work remains sparse and is often limited to communiqués on process and intent. In addition, neither the current practice of public information sharing with the UN SC or the public, nor the new MoU between the AU and sub-regional organizations resolves the exclusion of parliamentary or civil society organizations from the accountability framework.

This exclusion is problematic not only in terms of democracy as formally mandated (elected bodies cannot play the oversight role they owe to citizens), but it also disempowers civil society as it blocks an important conduit of information from the executive sphere into the public domain. At the same time civil society is frequently called upon to engage more with peace and security issues at sub-regional, regional and global levels.

Whether towards parliament or civil society organizations, the effective, meaningful and regular flow of relevant information to the appropriate accountability forum is a cornerstone of public accountability. Yet, as said earlier, much of peace and security governance takes place near to exclusively in the executive domain, effectively limiting transparency and scrutiny. How can civil society and parliaments fulfil their function if they are systematically excluded from information they need to play their role?

Continuing Weakness of Parliamentary Oversight of Peace and Security Governance

Research on parliamentary oversight of foreign policy, security and responses to conflict conducted by the One World Trust, in particular over the past years, has shown that in many countries in and outside Africa, the grasp of parliaments of both the broad sweep of strategy and the detail of policy in these areas is often very weak and ad hoc. An interesting research finding in this area is that that these weaknesses can be found both in countries with a more limited exposure to democracy, and more mature systems. Research however shows that the reasons for the situation may be different. Capacity issues are certainly one reason, which is also underpinned by findings of other work conducted for instance by the Overseas Development Institute together with the One World Trust in the area of parliamentary strengthening,[39] but in both weaker and stronger parliamentary systems one of the major issues is a culture of tacit acceptance of government

---

38   United Nations Security Council and African Union Peace and Security Council (2007), Joint communiqué agreed on 16 June 2007.

39   Hudson, Alan; Wren, Claire (2007), *Parliamentary Strengthening in Developing Countries*, Final report for DFID (London: ODI / One World Trust), http://www.odi.org.uk/resources/download/103.pdf.

prerogative on foreign policy. Parliaments frequently fail to request relevant reporting from government and mostly do not generate themselves the public information basis that could empower civil society to engage with these issues as well. In this, they fail to claim their ground of oversight of government in a crucial policy area in which public accountability is central to delivering the public good of peace and security to citizens.[40]

Further, ongoing review for instance of information available about the work, or even the composition of relevant select or standing committees of parliaments in Nigeria, Ghana and Senegal yields disappointingly little.[41] Beyond records of debates in the Chamber documented for the English speaking countries in various Hansard-type documentation systems[42] it is virtually impossible for the ordinary citizen to find out what parliaments and in particular their committees do, who sits on them, and how in consequence they discharge their duty of oversight and public scrutiny in key areas of policy that affect us all. The South African Parliament is virtually the only parliament in the African context which bucks the trend a little by being clearer about the work the relevant committees are engaged in, but even here, no detailed information about peace and security policy and government reporting, experiences with bilateral support for missions, etc., as dealt with in the committees, is easily available to the general public.[43] In addition many foreign policy processes and decisions are dealt with at the level of the Presidency, breaking the link between departmental scrutiny mechanisms such as the foreign affairs committee, and the locus of action. These weaknesses are also recognized by the South African Parliament, which asked in its review of the President's 2007 State of the Nation address whether 'in this context, the time is perhaps more opportune now to raise questions as to whether Parliament has been able to conduct effective oversight of South Africa's foreign policy'.[44] Key to improving the situation would be in a first step to strengthen reporting and documentation capacity at committee level, as the Parliamentary Monitoring Group in South

---

40   See for instance Hammer, Michael; Boutillier, Clément; Upadhyay, Anuya (2008), *Ready for the Global Pitch? Making the Foreign Policy Process in Emerging Powers such as South Africa and India Democratically Sustainable*, One World Trust Briefing Paper (London: One World Trust), no. 110.

41   Hammer, Michael; Boutillier, Clément; Gordon, Laura (2009, forthcoming), 'Time to Embrace the World' for the 'Crippled Giant'? Global policy engagement and accountability of the foreign policy process in Africa's forgotten leadership contender, One World Trust Briefing Paper (London: One World Trust).

42   Westminster model inspired verbatim records of parliamentary debates.

43   Currently it is largely only by way of a civil society research initiative such as the Parliamentary Monitoring Group that committee records and related government reports are accessible to users beyond those who have the opportunity of constant and direct access to parliament.

44   Parliament of the Republic of South Africa (2007), *A Foreign Affairs Perspective on the 2007 State of the Nation Address*, Cape Town, http://www.parliament.gov.za/content/10_Chapter%209.pdf, p. 105, accessed 10 August 2008.

Africa puts it 'the engine room of parliament'[45] by parliament itself. The support provided for external observers such as by the civil society initiative Parliamentary Monitoring Group in South Africa is useful, but eventually it is problematic if the public is informed about what is going on in parliament by a third party, and not by parliament itself. In a second step, dependencies of parliamentary careers on party loyalty requirements may need to be reviewed, as these can be a constraint to the development of a culture of critical oversight. This is especially true in countries where large majorities dominate and the link to local constituencies through full proportional representational systems, in which it is the parties which agree to the list of candidates, is weak.[46]

Also, newly established accountability fora such as the Pan African Parliament (set up in 2004 as one of the nine formal organs of the AU, and based in South Africa), while detailing their advisory mandate on peace and security governance, provide only very limited information that would allow citizens to understand not only what the AU is doing in this policy field, but also how scrutiny of its work is carried out in practice.[47] Admittedly this last institution, and the ECOWAS Parliament (established in 2002 under the ECOWAS revised Treaty), are still in their infancy and of yet have no legislative mandate and scrutiny powers, but it will be important to make progress on public accountability early. Currently the externally accessible documentation base on activities and actual records of work remains weak, which for engagement of civil society with public policy formation is a major drawback. It will be important to strengthen these capacities commensurate to the general development of activities and scope of work to ensure that no precedent is set for continued exclusion of these policy fields from scrutiny.

These findings are interestingly true not only for parliaments which could be assumed to be structurally weak, strapped for resources, or in the early stages of development, such as in many African countries. A One World Trust study of the UK parliament, rightly or wrongly often considered to be 'the mother of all parliaments' and mandated to oversee the workings of a government that is amongst the globally most active in the peace and security arena (including from a permanent seat on the UN Security Council to engagement in Sierra Leone, Iraq, Afghanistan, to a wide range of advisory and command support functions in UN missions), has shown that the problem is at the root the same.

---

45   http://www.pmg.org.za/about.

46   Hammer, Michael; Boutillier, Clément; Uphadyay, Anuya (2008), *Ready for the Global Pitch? Making the Foreign Policy Process in Emerging Powers such as South Africa and India Democratically Sustainable*, One World Trust Briefing paper 110 (London: One World Trust), p. 4.

47   The Pan African Parliament Website has displayed since mid 2008 an increasing range of documents in relation to peace and security issues, yet these are primarily news items and AU documents rather than records of actual scrutiny carried out by parliament.

The UK parliament does not engage anywhere near as closely in oversight of foreign, global conflict and security policy, as it does on domestic issues, largely accepting a tradition of pre-democratic executive prerogative on these issues. In addition the narrowly departmentally focused remit of the different committees does not mirror the increasingly cross departmental ways of working of government on cross cutting strategic issues such as conflict, and there are no dedicated and joined reporting tools in place that would enable a strategic review and effective public accountability. In the case of the UK this is all the more alarming as the government itself has recently set a cross-departmental target (Foreign and Commonwealth Office, Department for International Development, and Ministry of Defence) to implement the Responsibility to Protect.[48]

Research on country specific case studies such as Zimbabwe, Sudan and Chad revealed that parliamentary oversight of the UK government's policies in conflicts around the world is generally superficial and sporadic at best, and virtually non-existent in less visible cases. The reason for this is that much oversight is carried on through ad hoc querying by individual MPs or peers acting on their own or with colleagues on informal all-party groups to raise country specific issues. The strategic review of policies in response to conflict is further hampered by the absence of regular and systematic, rather than just country specific, reporting or engagement, including by parliamentarians only at the time of crisis, often driven by media attention and NGO concern more than in depth understanding of the situation or long-term government response. There is thus little political incentive for government to take them too seriously in terms of policy and process and in result gaps of years in scrutiny, even of the most high-profile crises, are common.

In conclusion, like many other parliaments, the parliament in the UK lacks the institutional framework for continuous strategic analysis of foreign policy issues. While, therefore, some policy initiatives such as on the Responsibility to Protect have to be welcomed as they signal a willingness to take international obligations towards people at risk more seriously, with no systematic scrutiny, neither the British public nor other people in the world affected by these policy commitments will be able to gauge decisions taken in their pursuit and hold the government to account over them.[49]

---

48   HM Treasury (2007), PSA Delivery Agreement 30/2007, Reduce the Impact of Conflict through Enhanced UK and International Efforts, in particular paragraph 3.38, http://www.hm-treasury.gov.uk/d/pbr_csr07_psa30.pdf, last accessed 8 December 2009.

49   A World of Difference (2007), Parliamentary Oversight of British Foreign Policy, One World Trust, Democratic Audit, Federal Trust (London: One World Trust), pp. 42f.

Conclusion

Currently peace and security governance fails to live up to democratic standards. This is essentially the case at all levels: global, regional and national. Not only is the level of engagement and clarity of commitment fragmented with regional organizations still in the process of tooling up, also there are no clear accountability arrangements in place between them and the United Nations, which remains the only body universally mandated to ensure global peace and security. In addition, national parliaments that are in many cases directly mandated to ensure policy oversight lack the institutional framework and culture of oversight for a continuous strategic analysis of these areas. This leads to a continuing virtual exclusion of people from peace and security governance and a low level and quality of policy scrutiny of the foreign and security policies pursued by important global and regional actors.

Yet, peace and security governance and foreign policy more widely are substantively and by expression of people amongst the most critical to address in today's world.

Public accountability is key to ensure that the decisions taken in this field by national and multilateral actors are effective and serve the people they are meant to help, those living with conflict, in the best possible way.

Based on our research into the systemic and practical weaknesses of public accountability in this area, a number of avenues offer themselves to be pursued for reform:

1. Regional and global organizations, in particular the AU and the UN need to establish sustainable protocols that fix the principles of accountability between them applicable to the mandating process, reporting and lines of authority concerning peace and security missions that involve multiple actors operating under the UN Charter and Chapter VIII in particular.
2. Governments and multilateral organizations involved in governance and implementation of peace and security missions at regional and global levels should strengthen their own organizational public accountability policies and systems, including the establishment of regular and meaningful reporting instruments directed at parliaments and civil society to establish greater transparency and facilitate their active engagement in policy oversight and scrutiny of relevant developments.
3. Parliaments and civil society organizations need to take steps themselves, and be supported in efforts to strengthen their capacity for engagement and scrutiny of peace and security governance, and to hold governments and multilateral institutions to account over their policies and decisions with respect to all dimensions of the Responsibility to Protect doctrine, including the responsibility to prevent conflict, protect civilians affected by armed conflict, and rebuild societies after war.

4. Governments and multilateral institutions involved in peace and security operations and their governance should work to strengthen and broaden awareness of the full concept of the Responsibility to Protect amongst their own officials, parliamentarians and civil society organizations.

Index

THE INTERNATIONAL POLITICAL ECONOMY OF NEW REGIONALISMS SERIES

Other titles in the series